CW00670642

# EARLY SCOTTISH GARDENERS
# AND THEIR PLANTS

*This book is dedicated to my wife*

# EARLY SCOTTISH GARDENERS

## AND THEIR PLANTS

### *1650 – 1750*

Forbes W. Robertson

TUCKWELL PRESS

First published in Great Britain in 2000 by
Tuckwell Press
The Mill House
Phantassie
East Linton
East Lothian EH40 3DG
Scotland

ISBN: 1 86232 085 3

Thanks go to the following for their support of this publication:
Scotland Inheritance Fund
Stanley Smith (UK) Horticultural Trust
Incorporation of Gardeners of Glasgow
Commonweal Fund Committee, Glasgow
JTH Charitable Trust
Russell Trust

*British Library Cataloguing in Publication Data*

A catalogue record for this book is available
on request from the British Library

Design: Janet Jamieson

Printed and bound in Spain
by Bookprint, S.L., Barcelona

# Contents

# *Preface*

This book grew out of curiosity about what was growing in Scottish gardens of the seventeenth and eighteenth centuries. Searching through primary sources of information, it became difficult to avoid the conclusion that the gardener's skills in orchard, kitchen and flower garden flourished in the gardens of the gentry earlier and more often than has been commonly supposed. The medieval European tradition, introduced and sustained to no small extent by the numerous monastic institutions, had left its mark. The evidence from contracts between laird and gardener and from the long-established Gardeners' Fraternities, especially of Glasgow, East Lothian and Aberdeen, and the frequent reference in their records to competition with 'outen men' from the surrounding country, implied the existence of a substantial number of craftsmen throughout Lowland Scotland. They provided the basis for the conspicuously successful emigration of Scottish gardeners to positions of responsibility on English estates or as nurserymen in London during the eighteenth century.

Historical investigation of this kind is never completed. It is hard to know when to pause and summarise the evidence, although awareness of diminishing returns for effort expended acts as a stimulus. An additional and important inducement is the hope that publication will bring to light further evidence, such as some early gardener's diary or inventory of plants in his garden, which will extend our understanding of what was grown in the period concerned or shed light on the working life of the gardener and his duties in seventeenth- and eighteenth-century rural Scotland.

A study of this sort relies to a great extent on the co-operation and help of the staff in charge of libraries and archives. I should particularly wish to thank the photographic Department of the Royal Botanic Garden, Edinburgh for preparing the slides of plant illustrations. I wish to express my appreciation of the advice provided by the staff of the National Register of Archives (Scotland), especially Susan Corrigall, who has been unfailingly helpful, and also the staff of the National Library of Scotland, the Royal Commission on the Ancient and Historical Monuments of Scotland and Historic Scotland. I wish also to thank Mrs Jean Pirie of the Department of Special Collections and Archives, the University of Aberdeen. I wish to express my gratitude to the private holders of archives (mostly NRAS) who have kindly granted permission to quote or comment on relevant items in their possession. They include Lady Seton, the Duke of Hamilton, the Duke of Roxburghe, the Earl of Dalhousie, the Earl of Mansfield, the Earl of Moray, the Earl of Morton and the Marquess of Linlithgow. I am indebted to both Neil Hynd and John Donald, Publishers, for permission to quote the former's significant account of early evidence for Scottish gardens. On a personal note I should like to thank Dr Niall Green for comment on Parkinson's 'Scottish pea', Mr Denholm Reid for information about catalogues and Mr S.A.J. Oldham for references in *The Gardeners' Chronicle* and other observations.

# Illustrations

*Sources of illustrations*
Most of the illustrations of flowers and shrubs, other
than roses, are from late eighteeenth or very early
nineteenth century issues of *The Botanical Magazine*.
Some are also from *Familiar Garden Flowers* by
E.Edward Hulme and Shirley Hibberd n.d. The roses
are almost entirely from *Roses, a Mongraph of the
Genus Rosa* by H.C Andrews 1805–29. The fruits
are from *Pomologia Britannica* by J. Lindley 1841
and *The Fruit Grower's Guide* by J. Wright, n.d.
The remainder of the plant illustrations are from
the Royal Botanic Garden Edinburgh collection of
reproductions. Sources of other figures are indicated
in the legends.

Cullen
Banff
Kilravock
Gordon Castle
Rothiemay

Monymusk
Paradise

Brechin

Taymouth

Panmure
Rossie
Methven Scone
Abercairney
Kinloss
Lochgelly

Inveraray

Blair Drummond
Airth

Kinneil
Saltoun
Hopetoun
Hamilton
Houston Canongate
Coltness Dalkeith
Ravelston Arniston
Brunstane
Culzean
Whim

Castle Kennedy

FIGURE 1
Location of the principal seventeenth- and eighteenth-century estates from which
information has been obtained.

# Introduction

The content of early Scottish gardens has received little detailed attention. It has been assumed that the horticultural scene was too lacking in interest and variety to merit much notice. It is true that if we ask the question: 'What kinds of flowering plants, shrubs, vegetables and fruit trees were grown in Scotland before the mid-eighteenth century?', the answer does not come easily, since the evidence is scattered through the records of many estates lodged in different institutions. But there are several historical observations which suggest that a search for an answer to our question will be neither fruitless nor unable to shed a little shaft of light on a particular aspect of Scottish life and times.

We learn from Hume Brown's (1891) account of early travellers in Scotland how, in 1600, the French traveller Henri Duc de Rohan noted that there were more than a hundred country seats within a two-league radius of Edinburgh. A Cambridge graduate, Fynes Moryson, visiting Scotland about the same time, made a similar comment about the number of country houses about Edinburgh. He remarked on the well populated district of Fife which was well endowed with dwellings of the gentry, conspicuous in a treeless landscape by the little groves of trees which sheltered them. It is likely that most, if not all, of these seats had a kitchen garden, with a few apple, pear and plum trees, together with a gardener to look after them. When he came to East Lothian he was impressed by the fair orchard and garden of Seton Palace. In 1618, another English traveller, Taylor the Water Poet, commented on the fine gardens and orchards about the ruins of Dunfermline Abbey. In 1661, another Frenchman, Jorevin de Rocheford, was impressed by the spacious, walled garden at Paisley and the large garden filled with fruit trees in the vicinity of Glasgow University. In or about 1662 the English botanist John Ray remarked on the beautiful garden at Heriot's Hospital in Edinburgh. In Linlithgow he met a Mr. Stewart, who 'hath nourished in his garden divers exotick plants, more than one would hope to find in so northerly and cold a country'. Some of the plants he had not seen before included species of *Archangelica, Fumaria, Carduus, Verbascum, Anchusa* and *Alcea*. In 1669 the English parson, James Brome, was delighted with the orchards and gardens of Glasgow. Such tantalising glimpses of early Scottish gardens whet the appetite for more substantial information.

Apart from royal gardens, the religious institutions in Scotland were chiefly responsible for introducing and sustaining the European tradition of gardening. The monks frequently tilled their own gardens or joined in a communal effort. The wealthy abbeys and priories, especially those of the Cistercians, employed lay gardeners and helped to lay the foundations of the subsequent Scottish distinction in gardening. But, in spite of centuries of monastic horticulture, and as evidence of the elusiveness of the information we seek, contemporary records of exactly what was grown in the monastic gardens of Scotland or, indeed, in Europe, are virtually non-existent. The one notable exception is the *Capitulare de Villis* in Charlemagne's time *c.*800 AD, which comprised a substantial list of recommended vegetables, culinary and medicinal herbs, fruit trees etc. largely of southern European origin. This list helped to standardise what was grown in many parts of Europe.

Later, when horticultural skills and knowledge had become a purely secular craft, the tradition of instruction by oral precept and example continued from generation to generation. Very often the gardener followed in his father's and his grandfather's footsteps, inheriting and practising what was an ancient wisdom. In Scotland, it was not until 1683 that the first book about gardening methods appeared. That was John Reid's *The Scots Gard'ner*, which held the field until James Justice's *Scots Gardener's Director* appeared in 1754. The gardeners were employed on estates, large and small, as part of the traditional complement of servants, which included the butler, the housekeeper, the blacksmith, the groom, the herd etc. Therefore it is to the gardens of the gentry we must look for evidence of the continuity of the gardening tradition. The gardens of ordinary folk were either non-existent in the Highlands or very simple affairs in the rural Lowlands, with the emphasis on kitchen garden fare such as cabbage, kale, turnip, peas and beans.

In the present study the information about what different plants were grown is derived almost exclusively from primary sources. These refer to estate accounts of seeds, plants or fruit trees purchased, gardeners' notes and inventories, correspondence, apothecaries' accounts for medicines and family recipes for herbal cures of various diseases, in short, any kind of first-hand information about the species which were grown or used. The period covered is roughly from the mid-seventeenth to the mid-eighteenth century, i.e. approximately a couple of generations both before and after the Act of Union of 1707, and not later than 1760 for ornamental plants. Evidence from earlier times is not ignored when it turns up nor is later evidence, but only if it serves to complement the information about gardeners' pay, status or achievements during the main period of interest.

This period was chosen for several reasons. Firstly, as already noted, the Scottish garden scene of that time has been largely neglected, apart from Stuart and Sutherland's (1992) pioneering study. Secondly, it marks a transition from an old-established garden flora to the beginning of an era of dramatic change, most evident in the new shrubs which were coming in from eastern North America in the early eighteenth century. It was distinguished also by the beginning of the English-inspired period of landscape gardening. Finally, the commonly held view, promoted by Cox in his *History of Scottish Gardening* (1935), that Scottish gardening expertise and performance were conspicuously absent in the seventeenth century appeared unduly pessimistic. Instead, we find evidence of unbroken continuity of the European tradition of gardening.

Nurserymen's catalogues, which were first produced in Scotland in the latter part of the seventeenth century, have been examined but have not been used in drawing up the lists of plants which were grown on estates. Such catalogues provide little indication of which species were the really popular ones and which were only occasionally grown. Also, the catalogue contents were often inflated beyond what could be provided and could be misleading as a consequence. If anyone should doubt that, consider what a respectable Edinburgh nurseryman, William Boutcher, had to say in 1775 about some of his contemporaries: 'They have published pompous catalogues of they know not what, collected I know not where, and strangely jumbled together nobody knows how, of half the plants in creation, and some I believe never were in it; but they have forgot to provide specimens of many of these wonderful productions, and when you go to purchase them, you have the mortification to find they were sold the preceding week or day'. So catalogues have to be handled with caution and not taken at face value. The apparent garden flora could be increased by referring to them but we have preferred not to do so in favour of the greater reliability of the primary sources.

Curiosity about the plants which were formerly grown, the starting point of this study, leads naturally to an interest in the men who looked after them, their status in society, their wages, terms of contract and their fraternities in areas where these flourished. During the eighteenth century there was apparently a remarkable increase in the numbers of Scottish gardeners, a great many of whom migrated to England to become Head Gardeners on English estates or set up successful businesses as seedsmen and nurserymen in London. The genesis of this period of outstanding Scottish achievement in practical gardening and horticulture has exercised the ingenuity of earlier commentators. It has been re-examined in its historical context and broadened to take notice of the most distinguished practitioners, many of whom were also proficient botanists.

Information is uneven as to what species were present in the gardens of the period we are concerned with. For vegetables we have a great number of accounts from the early seventeenth century onwards, from many estates, so we can follow the introduction of new varieties into more general use. The records for culinary herbs are quite good, since these items were generally included in vegetable seed accounts. In spite of the undoubted widespread use of medicinal herbs there is a dearth of information about which species were regularly grown, although the situation improves for the early eighteenth century. For inferences about the likely occupants of the physic garden we have to rely largely on apothecaries' accounts and family recipes.

For ornamental plants the early evidence is patchy and often frustrating. Thus, for annuals we often meet with an entry at the bottom of a seventeenth-century vegetable account: '20 sorts of flower seeds'. Towards the middle of the eighteenth century the number rises to 30 or 40 but, more often than not, there is no mention of what sorts of flowers were included. Fortunately there were exceptions, where the species were listed, to provide sufficiently reliable information about what the 'different sorts' were. The vegetables were taken seriously while the annual flowers were the preserve of the ladies and regarded as less important. Sometimes the account would even refer to 'Seeds for my lady'.

Before the era of foreign introductions the variety of herbaceous plants commonly grown was quite modest and there was great emphasis on bulbous and tuberous species, so the records for them are quite good. Early records of shrubs are not easy to find and it is only toward the latter part of the seventeenth century that the accounts become more rewarding. For fruit trees, with their long history of cultivation in Scotland, we have excellent records of the names of apples, pears, plums, cherries, apricots, peaches and nectarines and even detailed orchard inventories.

Because of the nature of the evidence, buried in estate papers, family documents and the like, statements about the garden flora of the period concerned must be partly provisional. The search for further data is never over. At any time, a new source of information in, say, a gardener's inventory or an old diary may turn up unexpectedly in some collection of family papers to add to our knowledge of what was grown in those days. Indeed, it is the hope of the author that the publication of this study will bring to light such potentially valuable new evidence, which readers may know about, so that we can arrive at a more fully documented picture of the early gardening scene.

An attempt has been made to distinguish between the most popular species and those which were grown less frequently or only occasionally. The former can be regarded as the kinds of plants to be met with in most gardens of the gentry for the period concerned. This last qualification is important. As time passed, fashions changed, a greater variety of plants were grown, some species declined and others rose in gardeners' esteem so that the composition of the garden flora was not static. Any classification into commonly and less commonly grown species applies only to a particular timespan.

Occasionally, the idiosyncratic seventeenth-century spelling and script, as well as the use of old names, poses problems of identifying what plant was meant. The gardeners most often spoke braid Scots and, occasionally, a name turns up which even the dictionaries do not include. But these are inherent problems which add flavour, interest and occasional despair to the study of old documents.

It should be clear by now that this book is not concerned with the more general aspects of gardening history. It does not deal with the design of gardens or landscapes, which belongs rather to architecture and aesthetics than horticulture. It focuses on the plants which were grown and on the men who looked after them. Plants and people are our themes.

# 1

# *Vegetables and Culinary Herbs*

## *Vegetables*

There are good reasons why we should introduce our survey with the vegetables. The evidence for what was grown is more complete than for ornamental plants, especially in the earlier part of our period. Accounts from many estates tell us exactly what the seedsmen supplied to the gentry. Comparison of early and later accounts shows how the variety of vegetables on offer increased as time passed or fashions changed.

Cultivation of most of our familiar vegetables has a long history, often predating classical times and, sometimes, in the case of the beans and peas, going back to the earliest days of agriculture. It is unlikely that the basic vegetables grown in medieval Scotland differed a great deal from what was grown in northern Europe generally. A key medieval landmark was the *Capitulare de Villis* of Charlemagne's time. This catalogue of plants to be grown throughout the Carolingian domains was a very practical list which included the principal vegetables and herbs, both culinary and medicinal. As Harvey has observed, it has particular historical significance since it was a fresh compilation, almost certainly by an ecclesiastic, based on practical experience rather than a repetitive culling from classical authors, so often the case in those early days. It seems very likley that this list encouraged widespread similarity in what was grown in many European gardens. The Norman Conquest and the establishment of the network of monastic institutions in Britain perpetuated the Carolingian tradition which strongly influenced medieval gardening in Scotland, where close links with French monastic institutions were so numerous. To give some historical perspective, those species which appeared in the *Capitulare de Villis* are marked with an asterisk in the lists that follow. Not surprisingly, there are instances where there is doubt about just what was meant by some of the old names. However, this is not too great a problem and, when in doubt, we have adopted Harvey's (1981) interpretation as the most likely.

A notable feature of the accounts for vegetable seeds is the appearance of new named varieties during the eighteenth century. Up to the latter part of the seventeenth century it was sufficient to order, say, carrots, cabbages or lettuces, but quite soon thereafter the 'ordinar' types of vegetable gave way to or were supplemented by named varieties. Very often the status of these varieties cannot be defined in contemporary botanical terms. Individual nurserymen either propagated from a novel plant or plants, which were sufficiently different to attract notice, or they may have selected, more or less unconsciously, for perhaps size or earliness, to establish a variety distinct enough to warrant a name. Introductions from different countries played a part. Geographical separation between the sources of seed could also contribute to differences in appearance or yield, since the plants would be grown under different climatic and soil conditions, so there would be scope for differences in natural selection. Very often, however, the same variety was labelled according to country or district where the seed happened to be sold. It is also likely that some of the differences between putative varieties were more apparent than real, illustrating the age-old nurseryman's habit of giving new names to present a spurious appearance of novelty. Nevertheless, the increasing appearance of named varieties in the lists as the eighteenth century progressed certainly reflects the great increase in the numbers of nurserymen and seedsmen and the expansion of the horticultural trade generally. So, even if we remain uncertain in what way the varieties may have differed from their predecessors and from one another, they are certainly worth noting for the historical record. Also, further work may yet shed light on the origins of some of the different named varieties and how they differed.

The evidence is presented in a way which provides both a guide to the relative frequency with which particular named varieties appeared in the seed accounts and also a ranking, which identifies the earliest named sorts from those which appeared later. The lists of vegetables are set out in three columns. The column on the left includes the names which occurred most frequently in the lists, while the middle and right-hand columns include the varieties which appear respectively less and least frequently for the period concerned. In the later eighteenth century, of course, the distribution of names changed and many old varieties dropped out. In addition, within each column, the varieties which appeared in the earliest accounts are at the top and those which were introduced later are ranked below them. This rough classification is in part provisional since fresh information may alter the apparent popularity of a given variety, or show that it was available earlier than currently supposed, or add a new name. But, at least, this procedure highlights the earliest and most commonly grown vegetables and indicates the new ones which appeared as time passed. That is sufficient for our purpose. With these qualifications in mind we can now consider the evidence. Where there was no qualification as to variety the term 'ordinary' has been inserted.

**Onions** (*Allium cepa*)*

| Ordinary | Spanish Red | Blood Red |
| --- | --- | --- |
| Strasburgh | Portugal (white) | |
| Flanders | English | |
| Dutch | | |
| Silver-skinned | | |
| Sybows | | |

The widely grown, hardy and strong-flavoured Strasburgh onion appeared in early seventeenth-century accounts. It is uncertain whether the Flanders or Dutch onions were really Strasburgh onions sold by Flemish or Dutch seedsmen or were sufficiently distinct to merit their varietal names. English onions were probably quite similar to them. Spanish Red and Portugal onions were similar in mildness and had flat bulbs. The Blood Red onion, hardy and strong-flavoured, was later widely grown in Scotland and Wales according to Loudon. The silver-skinned onion, with flattened, more elegant bulbs, ripened earlier and was often used for pickling.

The term sybow or variants such as 'sybo', 'sybae', etc., appeared in accounts in the latter part of the seventeenth century but became much less frequent in the early eighteenth century, although Justice (1754) referred to it. There is some confusion as to what exactly was meant by these names. It is generally accepted that 'sybow' is derived from the French 'ciboule', which stems from the Latin 'cepula' – a little onion. But this name properly belongs to a different species, *Allium fistulosum*, the Welsh onion. The latter has an ancient history in China and Japan and was never common in the West. It does not form bulbs and is endowed with abundant leaves. By some authors it is called the Spring onion. The dictionary definition of sybow is French onion or scallion. More usually the term 'French onion' refers to the variety of salad onion which is gathered before the bulb develops or the shape may be always more or less cylindrical, as in modern varieties of Spring onion. It seems most likely therefore that sybow was the name for this sort of onion and not the Welsh onion, in spite of its linguistic origin. Somewhere along the line the original name was switched from one species to the other. But there is no doubt the sybow was a distinct variety. For example in 1683 the seedsman Walter Christy supplied the Earl of Cassilis with '8 unc onyons' and '8 unc sybos'. In 1688 Sir John Foulis of Ravelston bought from 'Harie fergusone', the Edinburgh seedsman, seed of 'Leiks, onions, sybaes …' There is at least one complaint in the records that onions which should have been left till the autumn were being gathered early and passed off as sybows. The term 'scallion' appears to have been used rather loosely, to refer not only to sybows but also to the green shoots growing from an onion bulb of the previous year.

### Welsh Onion (*Allium fistulosum*)

This is rather a misnomer since there is nothing Welsh about it. The name is derived from the German 'welsch' meaning foreign. It has been grown so long in the East that its wild progenitor is uncertain. Although not regularly included in vegetable seed accounts, it was not uncommon in vegetable orders in the eighteenth century.

### Shallot*

Although formerly regarded as a distinct species with the specific name 'ascalonicum' and perhaps one of the plants mentioned in the *Capitulare*, and thereby meriting an asterisk, today it is regarded as a type of onion. Anyway, in Scotland in our period it was only moderately popular.

### Leek (*Allium porrum*)*

| Ordinary | Miller's | Scots |
| French | | English |
| London | | |

The leek is a long-established vegetable, widely grown in Europe in the Middle Ages and, according to Loudon, introduced to Britain in the mid-sixteenth century, although one suspects it may have arrived before then. 'Miller's' refers to a leek offered by William Miller of Holyrood but it was probably a French or London leek. Our ancestors were great consumers of leeks and onions. It is recorded that one fourteenth-century gardener had his wages stopped one year because he had failed to supply sufficient onions to the royal household.

### Garlic (*Allium sativum*)*

This species was not commonly grown although it turned up sporadically in eighteenth-century accounts between 1733 and 1779.

### Rocambole (*Allium scorodoprasum*)

Rocambole, or, more recently, the Sand Leek is a native species which occurs locally in sandy grassland from the English Midlands nearly to Aberdeen. Familiar to Gerard (1596), mentioned by Sutherland in his *Hortus Medicus Edinburgensis* (1683) and also by Justice (1754), and not uncommon in seventeenth-century accounts, it had largely dropped out of use by the early eighteenth century. It is another member of the onion tribe with small garlic-like cloves on the roots and also a cluster of bulblets at the tip of the stem (Figure 2). The name 'Rocambole' has sometimes been applied to a particular variety of garlic, but the occasional reference to exuberant growth identifies it as the true Rocambole. It has recently been reported growing in a suburb of Edinburgh, doubtless descended from former garden plants.

FIGURE 2
Rocambole (*Allium scorodoprasum*) left; Scorzonera (*Scorzonera hispanica*) right. Rocambole is a native species of onion, found locally on sandy grassland, with garlic-like cloves on the roots. It dropped out of culinary use by the early eighteenth century. Scorzonera, a member of the dandelion family, was introduced from central and southern Europe. The root, when boiled, served as a vegetable and the leaves as a salad. It was sometimes known as Viper's grass.

**Turnip** (*Brassica napus/campestris*)*

| | | |
|---|---|---|
| Ordinary | White | Early Yellow |
| Yellow | Round | Early White |
| Early | Orange | Early Dutch |
| Hanover | | |

Turnips were distinguished as early, maincrop or maturing late in the season. It is likely there were more names than truly distinct varieties. The 'ordinary' turnip was probably a round, white maincrop. White turnips could be round or flattened, and were later selected for early maturity, hence the reference to Early White which may have been the same as the flat-topped Early Dutch. The Yellow and the closely related Orange were hardy late, purple-top varieties with yellow flesh. It is uncertain to what

Hanover referred. Justice mentions several others, i.e. Red Topped, Green, Muscovy and French, but these names do not appear in the seed lists and could not have been regularly stocked by the seedsmen who supplied the Scottish estates.

**Carrot** (*Daucus carota*)*

| | | |
|---|---|---|
| Ordinary | Horn | Yellow |
| Orange | Early Horn | Red |

Before and during the sixteenth century carrots were either purple or yellow in colour. As time passed, the yellow colour was preferred, probably because the anthocyanin pigment of the purple carrot gave an unappetising brown colour to soups and stews and conferred a bitter taste on the uncooked carrot. From the early seventeenth century selection by carrot breeders in Holland led to the development of the long-rooted orange carrot, from which, by further selection and crossing, the stump-rooted Horn carrot was derived which, in turn, became further differentiated into earlier or later maturing types. The Red carrot included in the list probably referred to an early form of what later was known as the Large Red carrot, often grown as a field crop and attaining large size. In 1691 the Edinburgh seedsman Ferguson was offering seed of both the old Yellow and the more recently available Orange varieties. The references merely to Carrots in orders dated 1716, 1727 and 1742 would almost certainly have referred to the Orange variety.

**Parsnip** (*Pastinaca sativa*)*

| | | |
|---|---|---|
| Ordinary | Smooth | Dutch Swelling |
| | Dutch | |
| | English | |

The parsnip is another long-cultivated species, devloped originally in Central Asia. Both Loudon (1826) and Neill (1813) agree in referring simply to 'parsnip', which would refer to the improved long-rooted type. Except for the Dutch Swelling parsnip, it is safe to assume that all the others would have been of this form. The Dutch Swelling parsnip of Justice's list no doubt refers to the round top parsnip, derived by selection from the long-rooted form. So far, reference to parsnip has turned up only from the mid-eighteenth century onward and it was not popular in the period we are dealing with.

**Beetroot** (*Beta vulgaris*)*

| | | |
|---|---|---|
| Red | Betterave | White Green |
| | | The Beet Chard |

The red beetroot, or betterave as it was generally called, has been grown from the earliest times. It was included in almost all seed orders. The White beet was a larger, white-fleshed variety, later classed as a sort of mangold. The Green beet, mentioned by Justice, but rarely supplied, was probably the same as the Green-Topped beet which Loudon reports as widely grown in Scotland in the nineteenth century. The Beet Chard, derived from the same wild species as the others, was grown for its edible leaves. Although included in Ferguson's 1691 catalogue, it has turned up only occasionally in the seed accounts.

## Radish (*Raphanus sativus*)*

| | | |
|---|---|---|
| Ordinary | Black Spanish | White Spanish |
| London | Turnip | Dutch Striped |
| | Sandwich | |
| | Early Salmon | |

The Radish has been in cultivation for a very long time. According to Herodotus, radishes, accompanied by garlic and leeks, were supplied to the builders of the Pyramids. By the eighteenth century they had been selected to offer a choice of varieties which differed in having either a long, tapered or a short, turnip-shaped root. The external colour varied although the flesh was white. 'Ordinary' radishes had tapered roots and this was probably also true of the Early Salmon variety. It is unclear what the Dutch Striped referred to. The two Spanish radishes, White and Black, were winter varieties with white flesh and large roots. Radishes and turnips are very closely related and it is just possible the Black Radish may have been a variety of turnip.

## The Cabbage tribe (*Brassica oleracea*)* includes cabbage, cauliflower, broccoli, borecole, kail and the coleworts.

## Cabbage

| | | |
|---|---|---|
| Battersea | Dutch | Early White |
| Red/Dutch Red | Sugarloaf | Russia |
| Savoy | Alnwick | Flat-sided |
| Green Savoy | Early York | Scottish |
| Yellow Savoy | May/Early May | Large English |
| Dutch Savoy | | Large American |

Among the cabbages there is a great variety of names but they can be grouped into three main categories comprising the white, round-headed, the red and the savoy cabbages. The various white cabbages differed in the size and shape of their heads, for example Sugarloaf, and/or the time of the year when they were best harvested. Battersea was mentioned most often. It is likely that the list includes synonyms; Alnwick and Scottish may be the same and the differences between some of the the named varieties may not have been very great. The reference to the Large American cabbage in 1751 is worth noting. The Savoys were generally either Green, Yellow or without a prefix. The Red cabbage was in moderate demand compared with Battersea or the Savoys. The old Scots name for cabbage was 'bowcaill', a name which dropped out of general use after the early seventeenth century.

### Cauliflower

Ordinary                 English

Cauliflower regularly appeared in the seed lists throughout the period, while young plants were often bought as well. It was not distinguished by variety until about the middle of the eighteenth century. Although it does not appear in the lists for our period, Justice referred to Italian cauliflower. One account from 1736 refers to 'wild cauliflower', posing a problem.

### Broccoli

Purple                  Common  
                         White  
                         Long Irish  
                         Beet Broccoli  
                         Turnip Broccoli  
                         Cauliflowered

### Borecole/Kail

Ordinary                Curled                  German Greens  
Kilmaur's Kail

### Coleworts (see below)

The Coleworts, Borecoles, Kail and Broccoli are best considered together. They are all descended from the wild cabbage and, when crossed, produce an almost continuous array of intermediate types. 'Colewort' is the general name for an open-headed cabbage, and its use goes back to antiquity. Young cabbages before they headed were often gathered early as 'coleworts'. Borecole or kail was grown for its open heads of tasty leaves. The Curled was generally preferred to the flat-leaved variety which was probably more often fed to cattle. Notoriously hardy, kale was a regular feature of the Scottish cottager's garden, but neither the ordinary Scottish kind nor a named variety was often included in the seed accounts. Perhaps the gentry thought it too plebeian. According to Loudon and Neill, the term 'German Greens' was equivalent to Borecole and hence a kind of kail. Broccoli is more closely related to cauliflower with terminal shoots whose differences in size, arrangement and colour determine the varietal differences. Broccoli was not in demand before the middle of the eighteenth century, and then only to a minor degree.

**Pea** (*Pisum sativa*)\*

Hasting/Hasten
Crown or Rose
Hotspur – Ordinary
    "    Charleton
Green Rouncival
Sugar – ordinary
    "  Large
    "  Dwarf

White Rouncival
Marrowfat
Spanish Moratto
Crooked Sugar
Barn's Hotspur

Egg
Sandwich
Gray Rouncival
Blue Rouncival
Lisbon
Russel
White Russel
Green Russel
Reading Hotspur
Leedman's Hotspur
Hanoverian Hotspur
Dwarf Marrowfat
Flanders
Harlem
Forty Day

At first glance the varieties of pea appear legion but they can be classed into three main categoreis: early, maincrop and sugar. Sometimes a given variety appears in both tall and dwarf forms, due to a simple genetic difference. The old names to indicate earliness were Hasting or Hastenis in Scots and, later, Hotspur. The commonly grown peas listed on the left had mostly been around for a long time. Parkinson (1629) lists Hasting, Rouncival, Scottish or Crown and Sugar peas. The origin of the name 'Scottish' is intriguing. There is a genetic trait, widespread among north European pea populations, in which the flowers and hence the pods are confined to the top of the shoot, hence the name 'Rose' or 'Crown'. But whether or not this trait is expressed depends on the day-length. In short day-length conditions plants with this genetic potential do not show it whereas in long day-length they do. So the appearance of this very distinct form is correlated with latitude, hence the term 'Scottish'.

In the period we are concerned with, Hastenis, ordinary Hotspur and later, Charleton Hotspur accounted for most of the seed orders for early peas. Among the maincrops Marrowfat, Crown or Rose, and especially the Green Rouncival, were the preferred options. The others listed on the right appeared only occasionally. Seeds supplied by William Miller the second included Russel and also White and Green Russel. Whether 'Russel' was a corruption of 'Rouncival' is open to question. 'Sugar pease', almost always included in the seed order, referred to the tall variety and/or the Crooked Sugar peas. It is worth noting that peas practise self-fertilisation; they are inbreeders, so novelties arising by mutation are easily fixed and propagated. This biological fact helps to explain why so many varieties turn up in this species, although we can only surmise how distinct many of them really were.

**Broad Bean** (*Vicia faba*)*

| | | |
|---|---|---|
| Turkey | Hotspur | Nonpareil |
| Windsor | Toker | Early |
| | | Geneva |
| | | Black Spanish |

The variety mentioned most often in the seed accounts was the Turkey Bean, followed by Windsor and then Toker or Hotspur. Justice, as usual, produces a few others, namely Early Lisbon and Sandwich. The Black Spanish probably referred to a variety with black seeds but of no particular merit.

**Kidney Bean** (*Phaseolus vulgaris*)

| | | |
|---|---|---|
| Ordinary | White | French |
| Barbary | Black | Scarlet |
| Lisbon | | Dwarf |
| | | Battersea |

More often than not this introduced South American species is referred to simply as 'Kidney Bean'. It is very variable in flower colour and also the colour, size and shape of the seeds. Such variation was responsible for the several varieties listed here and also by Justice, who referred to Black Spanish, Oriental, Battersea and Speckled varieties.

**Lettuce** (*Lactuca sativa*)*

| | | |
|---|---|---|
| Cabbage | Brown Dutch | Rose |
| Roman | Capuchin | Domburgh |
| Imperial | | Prince |
| Silesian | | White Cos |
| Ice | | Early Dutch |
| | | Hammersmith |
| | | Closter |

Lettuce is another vegetable well known in classical times and long cultivated. In Scotland it was highly esteemed, at least by the gentry, and almost invariably three or four varieties were included in the seed orders of the eighteenth century and these appear in the list on the left. They were all of the cabbage headed form. Brown Dutch and Capuchin were occasionally included and the others only rarely. The Cos lettuce did not appear in the accounts until about the mid-eighteenth century, probably related, historically, to the development of narrow-leaved, upright lettuces in the Mediterranean area, while the cabbage-headed types arose in northern Europe. The spelling of the name 'Silesian', which referred to a moderately hardy, winter variety, clearly taxed the gardening fraternity, and some of the versions are very odd.

**Scorzonera** (*Scorzonera hispanica*)
This member of the dandelion family (Figure 2), native to Central and Southern Europe, with a white-fleshed tap root, has been grown in Britain since the late sixteenth century. The root was boiled as a vegetable and the leaves were eaten as a salad. It was sometimes called Viper's Grass because the tapering root appeared snake-like – at least to the imaginative. It was frequently included in seventeenth- and eighteenth-century orders but the latest mention so far encountered was in 1751, so it had dropped out of favour by the middle of the century, although Justice included it.

FIGURE 3
Skirret (*Sium sisarum*)
A hardy, umbelliferous plant native to China and esteemed as a root vegetable since mediaeval times. It was displaced by the potato about the mid-eighteenth century. The old Scots name for it was crummock.

**Skirret** (*Sium sisarum*)*
This hardy, tuberous-rooted, umbelliferous plant has been grown in Europe since medieval times and was probably, but not certainly, included in the Capitulare. It was frequently grown in Scotland during the seventeenth and first third of the eighteenth century and even appeared in an order dated 1779, although by that time it was only rarely mentioned. This might seem a little surprising since, for Justice, it was 'one of the best roots we have for the garden', while John Reid (1683) advised: 'When skirrets are boyled and peeled, Roll them in floure, and fry with butter'. However, the rise in popularity of the potato sealed its culinary fate.

**Asparagus** (*Asparagus officinalis*)
This crop, known to the ancient Greeks, was moderately popular in the Scotland of our period. A Dutch variety was very occasionally mentioned. In the early seventeenth century it often appeared as 'Sparrowgrass'.

**Celery** (*Apium graveolens*)*
Ordinary                    Broad Leaved
Italian

'Sellery' was generally included in the seed orders either without qualification or as 'Italian Sellery'.

**Spinach** (*Spinacia oleracea*)
The spinach is native to south-western Asia. It is a more recent addition to the kitchen garden since it was not known to the Greeks and Romans. Varieties differ in having either the original prickly or round seeds and these distinctions were often specified in the accounts. The later seed accounts sometimes referred to Hardy Winter Spinach, which was an improved type derived from the original, wild form. Spinach increased in popularity during the eighteenth century.

**Cucumber** (*Cucumis sativus*)*
Ordinary                    Early Prickly                    Early
Long Green
Short Green

The cucumber is believed to have originated in India although it has not been traced to a wild species. Long grown in Europe, it was a regular feature of Scottish seed orders. Very often both the long and short varieties were grown.

**Melons** (*Cucumis melo*)*
Great store was set by melons which were grown on hot beds. The Musk melon was a favourite. Melons were almost always included in seed accounts along with the vegetables, so they are included here.

**Pumpkin** or **Pompion** (*Cucurbita pepo*)
This vegetable was moderately popular. The name is apparently derived from the Dutch or Flemish 'pompoen', later, according to Loudon, corrupted to 'pumpkin'. There was also occasional reference to 'Mekin' which was certainly a kind of gourd and may have been one of the many forms included in this variable species. Very occasionally a seed list includes pumpkin, mekin and gourd as separate items. In 1737 Robert McClellan junior, seedsman, supplied Mr Hugh Murray of Kynnynmound with seed of 'crown shap'd mekin'. Since this name was sandwiched in the seed list between Brompton stocks and red balsams, it was surely for ornamental rather than edible use.

**Artichoke** (*Cynara scolymus*)

This turned up fairly regularly from the late seventeenth century as well as the Cardoon, which belongs to the same species but is distinguished from the artichoke by the development of the leafy stem rather than the flower head.

**Jerusalem Artichoke** (*Helianthus tuberosus*)

According to Loudon, this species was introduced from Brazil in 1617. It was being grown at Brechin less than forty years later, although it never became popular.

**Potato** (*Solanum tuberosum*)

The early history of the potato in Scotland is rather confused. There appears to have been regional variation in its early use. Neil, writing in 1813, stated that the cultivation of the potato was little understood in Scotland until after 1740 and that it was not planted in fields until about 1760. Somerville (1741–1814), writing of his younger days, claimed that potatoes were part of the diet of the common people, but were considered a luxury, grown only in gardens and more costly than meal. He did not recollect any examples of potatoes grown in fields before 1760. But, on the other hand, John Reid, in *The Scots Gardner* (1683), includes potatoes, without special comment, among the roots for the kitchen and recommends cutting them in pieces, each with an eye, and planting them in rows. In an estimate of the value of 'Garden Stuff' at Rothiemay in 1703 there was reference to 'a Quantity of pottatos to be measured over when taken out of the ground'. In 1739 Robert Dickson of Hassendeanburn was selling potatoes regularly. A typical entry in his account book makes the point:

|  | £ | s | d |
|---|---|---|---|
| to Isobel Thompson of Denholm one bed of onions | 00 | 07 | 00 |
| 2 peck of purtatoes | 1 | 00 | 00 |

Certainly, from 1740 onwards, he was selling potatoes by the peck, the capfull and the halfull. A 'capfull' and a 'halfull or halffou' were old Scots measures of volume, equivalent respectively to a quarter of a peck and approximately half a bushel. In the Saltoun records there is a letter from the gardener (probably of 1748) asking for six men to lift potatoes in six days. Somewhat earlier Sir Archibald Grant was growing potatoes, together with a great many more kinds of vegetables, at Monymusk. It seems, therefore, that potatoes were grown quite early in the eighteenth century on some estates, but it was not until nearer the end of the century that they became generally available. That conclusion is consistent with the widespread occurrence of scurvy and pre-scorbutic conditions, especially at the end of winter. In the previous century no class in society was immune, and only when the potato became a regular part of the diet was the 'bane and scourge' of scurvy banished.

There is an interesting practical description from mid-eighteenth century of how potatoes were grown in England. A sandy soil was preferred, to be covered with horse litter or long muck, which was to be dug in in February before planting in March. A special iron-shod instrument for making the holes consisted of three spikes or dibbers, six inches long by four and a half wide and five inches apart. The seed potatoes were cut in pieces, each with an eye. Rows were to be nine inches apart to make it easier to hoe and weed.

It is to be noted that of the 26 species of vegetable listed above, four are of American origin, several are of minor significance, like Rocambole, Scorzonera and Welsh onion, and that the majority of the rest appeared in the *Capitulare*. The seventeenth-century Scottish kitchen garden of the gentry had a great deal in common with its medieval, European forerunner. We can also conclude that the Scottish gentry of our period enjoyed a very varied diet of vegetables. Indeed many of the eighteenth-century seed accounts make our own vegetable gardens look rather sparse. This was in sharp contrast to what ordinary folk ate. Those with a garden had to make do with cabbage, kale and perhaps beans and peas, although most towns-people would have had less variety than this.

The increase in the choice of vegetables by the early eighteenth century can be nicely illustrated by comparing a couple of seed accounts rendered to the incumbent Earl of Cassillis by different seedsmen in, respectively, 1689 and in 1739. Preserving the original spelling, they are as follows:

| Walter Christey, Feb. 26, 1689 | James McClellan, Feb. 5 & 24, 1739 |
| --- | --- |
| 8 unc onyons | 1 lib Stras. Onion |
|  | 2 ou bloody Do |
|  | 1 ou Silver Onion |
| 8 unc sybos |  |
| 12 unc leiks | 6 ou London Leek |
| 12 unc carrots | 2 ou Horn Carrot |
|  | 6 ou Orange Carrot |
| 1 lb turnip | 4 ou Early Turnip |
|  | 8 ou Red Turnip |
|  | 2 ou Yellow Turnip |
| 2 lb spinage | 4 lib Spinage |
|  | 1 lib Hardy winter Spinage |
| 1 lb rid cabage | 2 ou red Dutch Cabbage |
|  | 1 ou battersy Do. |
|  | 8 ou Dutch Cabbage |
|  | 2 ou green Do |
|  | 2 ou Dutch Savoy |
|  | 1 ou early May Cabbage |

| | |
|---|---|
| 8 unc rid beates | 3 ou beetraw |
| | 8 ou green beet |
| 4 unc pasnip | 1 ou parsneep |
| 4 unc purpie | 4 dr purpie |
| 4 unc latice | 1 ou Cabbage Lettuce |
| | 6 dr Ice Lettuce |
| | 4 dr brown Dutch Lettuce |
| | 2 dr Selesia Lettuce |
| | 2 dr Coss Lettuces |
| | 2 dr Closter Lettuce |
| 2 lb kidney beans | 2 lib Battersy kidnys |
| | 1/2 Barberry Do |
| 2 lb Turky beans | 1 peck windsor beans |
| | 1 peck Nopareil Do |
| | 1 forpit black Spanish beans |
| 1 unc colliflour | 8 dr Colyflower, 100 plants |
| 1 lb shugar pease | 1 lib Suggar pease |
| | 1 forpit fine dwarf pease |
| | 5 forpit Comon pease |
| | 1/2 peck hotspur pea |
| | 2 lb marrowfat Do |
| | 4 lib green Runcivel pea |
| | 1 lib Hanoverian hotspur Do |
| | 1 lib 40 day pea |
| 4 drap Indian cress | 4 dr Indian Cress |
| 2 unc curled cress | 1/2 lib Comon Cress |
| | 4 ou broad Do |
| 1 unc cucumbers | 1/2 ou Cucumber |
| 1 unc pumkins | |
| 1 unc marjorham | 4 dr Sweet marjoram |
| | 8 ou Lond: radish |
| | 2 ou turneep radish |
| | 2 ou black Spanish radish |
| | 1 ou Skirret |
| | 1 ou Scorzonera |
| | 1 ou Sellery |
| | 4 ou persel |
| | 2 ou Dutch persel |

8 dr Curled Endive
4 dr Surrell
1 ou brocoli
1/2 lib Garlick
1/2 lib Shallot
4 ou Asparagus
3 dr Savory
4 dr Summer Savory
3 dr Thyme
2 dr pot marjoram
1/2 ou dill

A 'forpit' or 'forpet' was a dry measure equivalent to about 2.3 litres. A 'drop' or 'drap' was 1/16 ounce. The 1689 list omits a few items commonly included in orders of that time such as 'carvi' (caraway), 'persel' (parsley), thyme, radish, endive, and peas in addition to sugar peas. Nevertheless the increase in variety in the later list is impressive.

FIGURE 4
Purslane (*Portulacaa oleracea*) Introduced from India to southern Europe where it became a weed. Purslane was almost always included in vegetable seed accounts for use as a salad. The old Scots name for it was 'purpie', from the French 'pourpier' There is a variety with almost yellow leaves, formerly known as 'gilded purpie'.

## Culinary Herbs

A number of both culinary and medicinal herbs were almost always included in the vegetable seed accounts. Others appeared sporadically and were evidently less used. An occasional gardener's inventory fills in the picture of what was available. In Tables 1 and 2 the categories 'Frequent' and 'Less Frequent' roughly indicate relative popularity. The Tables include both the common and Latin names as well as the general region of origin. Hardly any of the culinary herbs are native to Britain and only about 18% of the species in the Tables are certainly native. Many of these herbs have been in cultivation for so long that they have escaped their confines, become naturalised and are often taken for native. More recent comparative study of plant distribution has shown this not to be so. Most of the species are from southern Europe. Stace's 'New Flora of the British Isles' is the authority for species origins. As in the case of the vegetables, an asterisk indicates mention in the Capitulare and hence of ancient use in the kitchen garden.

**TABLE 1. Culinary herbs of frequent use**

| NAME | LATIN NAME | ORIGIN |
|---|---|---|
| Basil | *Ocimum basilicum* | India |
| * Carvi/Caraway | *Carum carvi* | Europe |
| * Chervil | *Anthriscus cerefolium* | Europe |
| * Coriander | *Coriandrum sativum* | Europe |
| * Cress | *Lepidium sativum* | Asia |
|     Common | – | – |
|     Curled | – | – |
|     Broad-leaved | – | – |
| Indian Cress | *Tropaeolum minus* | Peru |
| * Dill | *Anethum graveolens* | Asia |
| * Endive | *Cichorium endiva* | Asia |
| Marjoram, Sweet | *Origanum majorana* | Africa/Asia |
| * Mint | | |
|     Common | *Mentha spicata* | Europe |
|     Peppermint | " X *piperita* | Native |
| * Mustard, white | *Sinapis alba* | Europe |
| * Parsley | *Petroselinum crispum* | Europe |
|     Common | – | – |
|     Curled | – | – |
| Purslane/purpie | *Portulaca oleracea* | |
|     Green | *sativa* | Europe |
|     Gold/Gilded | – | – |
|     Rape | *Brassica napus* | Europe |
| * Sage | *Salvia officinalis* | Europe |

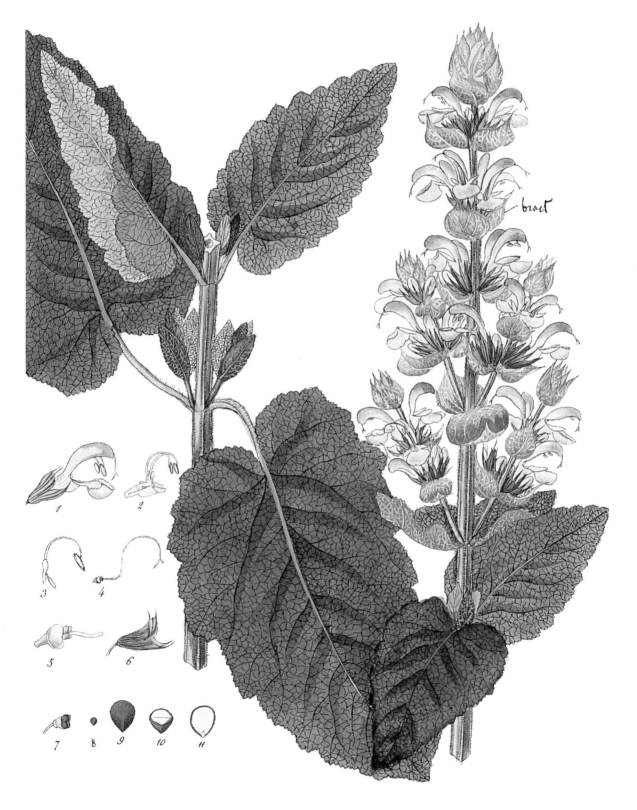

bract

*1*  *2*

*3*  *4*

*5*  *6*

*7*  *8*  *9*  *10*  *11*

FIGURE 6
Sweet Basil (*Ocymum basilicum*) This aromatic, annual herb of Indian origin required hot-bed treatment. It was a popular pot herb.

FIGURE 7
Blessed Thistle (*Cnicus benedictus,* formerly *Carduus benedictus*). This was almost invariably included in vegetable seed accounts during the seventeenth and eighteenth centuries. A handsome, south European annual, it was used medicinally. Preparations of the whole plant or leaves were believed to cure all manner of diseases including the plague, but by the early nineteenth century it was regarded as of no medical value.

OPPOSITE: FIGURE 5
Clary (*Salvia sclarea*) This aromatic herb from southern Europe was popular with the gentry in seventeenth- and eighteenth-century Scotland. Although perennial it was treated as an annual or biennial.

| | | |
|---|---|---|
| * Savory, Summer | *Satureja hortensis* | Europe |
| Savory, Winter | *Satureja montana* | Europe |
| Sorrel | *Rumex acetosa* | Native |
| Spinach | *Spinacia oleracea* | Asia |
| Thyme | *Thymus vulgaris* | Native |

## TABLE 2. Culinary herbs of less frequent use

| NAME | LATIN NAME | ORIGIN |
|---|---|---|
| * Alexanders | *Smyrnium olustratum* | Europe |
| Angelica | *Angelica archangelica* | Europe |
| * Anise | *Pimpinella anisum* | Europe/Asia |
| Borage | *Borago officinalis* | Europe |
| Chick Pea | *Cicer arietinum* | Europe |
| * Chives | *Allium schoenoprasum* | Native |
| * Fennel | *Foeniculum vulgare* | Native |
| Glasswort | *Salicornia herbacea* | Native |
| Horse-radish | *Armoracia rusticana* | Asia |
| Lamb's lettuce | *Valerianella locusta* | Native |
| Lentil | *Ervum lens* | Europe |
| Marjoram, Pot | *Origanum onites* | Europe |
| Oak of Jerusalem | *Chenopodium botrys* | Europe/Asia |
| * Orach/Mountain Spinach | *Atriplex hortensis* – | Asia – |
| Patience | *Rumex patienta* | Europe |
| Salsify | *Tragopogon porrifolius* | Europe |
| Spignel | *Meum athanaticum* | Native |
| Tansy | *Tanacetum vulgare* | Native |

'Purpie' was the old Scots name for Purslane. It appeared regularly in accounts in the seventeenth and early eighteenth century, interchangeably with 'purslane' but later fell out of use, although the old name occasionally turned up as late as 1779. This herb was generally included in seed orders. It came in two forms, green and golden or gilded. The name is derived from the French 'pourpier'. Cox's (1935) identification of purpie as a sort of purple kale is incorrect. Cresses were very popular. Usually several sorts were ordered, including the Indian cress or nasturtium (*Tropaeolum minus*), which was introduced before 1600. The terms 'salleting' or 'sallareen' often appear, sometimes dignfied by the prefix 'Italian'. They comprised a mixture of seeds, probably including lettuce, cresses, coleworts, radish, rape, mustard etc. which were gathered young. Nearly half of the herbs listed in the Tables also appeared in the *Capitulare de Villis*.

# 2

# *Ornamental Plants*

We deal next with the ornamental species which appear in the records from approximately the mid-seventeenth to the mid-eighteenth century and no later than 1760, the year from which we have a detailed inventory of the perennial plants and shrubs in the garden of Cullen House. During this period there was a modest increase in the number of species grown, especially of shrubs. By the mid-eighteenth century the number of sorts of annual flower seeds included in vegetable seed orders had increased to 30 or 40. To indicate how long species had been in Britain, the date of introduction is noted, derived from Loudon's *Encyclopedia of Plants* (1826), with the qualification that a particular year is quoted only for plants first recorded after 1600. For plants introduced before 1600 Gerard's *Herbal* (1597) is often the first record and so that date appears in the literature. However, these plants may have been growing in English and Scottish gardens before that date. To avoid a misleading appearance of precision such species have been listed as introduced B(efore) 1600. After that year Parkinson's *A Garden of Pleasant Flowers* (1629) provides the most reliable early record and from then on we can be more confident about the date of introduction.

The area where the plants originated is noted in very general fashion, without indicating regions. The species have been grouped into those which appear most often in the records and those which appear less frequently. This very pragmatic distinction has to be provisional. Further research is bound to turn up additional species so far not encountered and probabaly show that others were more widely grown than is presently supposed. The ornamental plants are considered in the order: Annuals and Biennials, Herbaceous Perennials, species with bulbs or corms, Shrubs and ornamental Trees and finally, Roses.

## *Annuals and Biennials*

About three quarters of the commonly grown annuals and biennials were introduced to Britain before 1600 and most of them were being grown a good deal earlier. The majority were from southern Europe ( Table 3). The only certain natives in the list of frequently grown species are the Blewbottle or *Centaurea cyanus*, the common Poppy, the Vetch, *Vicia sativa* and Venus' Looking Glass (Figure 21). Many of the annuals, including the south European species are colonists of disturbed land, field margins and roadsides. Such species include the Blewbottle, Candytuft, the two Chrysanthemum species, the two Larkspurs (Figures 11 and 12), Marygold, Poppy, Pheasant Eye (Figure 18), Nigella, Xeranthemum or the Pink Everlasting (Figure 22) and the small *Convolvulus tricolor* (Figure 9), which was so often depicted in seventeenth- and eighteenth-century Dutch and Flemish flower paintings. Such species are pre-adapted for growing in gardens. Long cultivated, they usually escaped and extended their distribution so successfully as to be often taken for native. In recent years changed agricultural practice has reduced their numbers. For example, *Centaurea cyanus* is now scarce in Britain although at one time it clothed cornfields in a blue haze. The attractive Common and Forking Larkspurs, as well as the native Venus' Looking Glass have all declined in frequency.

Introductions from Mexico and/or South America contributed a surprisingly large number of species to the annual border in early times. Some, like the Tomato or Love Apple and the Scarlet or Runner Bean, were grown at first for the decorative value of their fruit or flowers and only later did they find culinary favour. The bright red flowers of the Scarlet Bean made a pretty hedge. The Capsicum may also have been grown for the shape and colour of its fruits although early culinary use cannot be excluded. The annual Sunflower and the large climbing *Ipomoea purpurea* arrived from South America about the same time in the seventeenth century. The Marvel of Peru, *Mirabilis jalapa* (Figure 17), was a particular favourite. Although a tender perennial it was treated as a half-hardy annual or biennial and brought to flowering with the aid of a hot bed. It is a handsome plant, now rarely seen, with tubular fragrant flowers of different colour. They open late in the afternoon, hence its alternative name of Four o'clock Plant, and remain open during the night to allow pollination by moths. The Tree Primrose, *Oenothera biennis* from Virginia, has similar habits. Its flowers open at dusk and shut again in the early morning.

OPPOSITE: FIGURE 8
Balsam (*Impatiens balsamina*). This tender plant from tropical Asia was popular with gardeners of our period. They were expert in the management of hot-beds and would spare no effort in the care of such species.

## TABLE 3. Annuals and Biennials (B)

| POPULAR NAME | LATIN NAME | ORIGIN | DATE |
|---|---|---|---|
| *Most frequent* | | | |
| Balsam | *Impatiens balsamina* | Trop. Asia | B 1600 |
| Bottle, in colours | *Centaurea cyanus* | Native | '' '' |
| Campion, Rose | *Lychnis coronaria* | Europe | '' '' |
| Capsicum | *Capsicum frutescens* | S. America | '' '' |
| Candytuft, colours | *Iberis umbellata* | Europe | '' '' |
| China Aster | *Callistephus sinensis* | China | 1728 |
| Chrysanthemum | *Chrysanthemum coronarium* | Europe | 1629 |
| '' | *Chrysanthemum segetum* | Europe | B 1600 |
| Cock's Comb | *Celosia argentea cristata* | Asia | '' '' |
| Convolvulus | *Convolvulus tricolor* | Europe | 1629 |
| Convolvulus Major | *Ipomoea purpurea* | Mexico | B 1600 |
| Foxglove, | | | |
| Common, white | *Digitalis purpurea* | Native | B 1600 |
| Iron coloured | *Digitalis ferruginea* | Europe | '' '' |
| French Honeysuckle | *Hedysarum coronarium* | Europe | '' '' |
| Honesty | *Lunaria rediva* | Europe | '' '' |
| Hollyhock, colours | *Althaea rosea* | ? China | '' '' |
| Larkspur, Larksheel | *Consolida ajacis* | Europe | '' '' |
| ''      Forking | *Consolida regalis* | Europe | '' '' |
| Lavatera | *Lavatera trimestris* | Europe | 1633 |
| Lobel's Catchfly | *Silene armeria* | Europe | B 1600 |
| Love Lies Bleeding | *Amaranthuis caudatus* | Trop. Asia | '' '' |
| Lupin, Small Blue | *Lupinus varius* | Europe | '' '' |
| ''      Great Blue | *Lupinus hirsutis* | Europe | 1629 |
| ''      White | *Lupinus albus* | Europe | B 1600 |
| ''      Yellow | *Lupinus luteus* | Europe | '' '' |
|      Scarlet | ? *Vicia sativa var. fulgens* | Native | ? |
| Marigold, garden | *Calendula officinalis* | Europe | '' '' |
| ''      French | *Tagetes patula* | Mexico | '' '' |
| ''      African | *Tagetes erecta* | Mexico | '' '' |
| Mignonette | *Reseda odorata* | N. Africa | 1752 |
| Marvel of Peru | *Mirabilis jalapa* | WIndies | B 1600 |
| Pheasant's Eye | *Adonis annua* | Europe | '' '' |
| Poppy, corn | *Papaver rhaeas* | Native | B 1600 |
| ''      carnation | *Papaver somniferuhm* | Asia | '' '' |
| Prince's Feather | *Amaranthus hypochondriacus* | Trop Asia | 1684 |
| Red Hawkweed | *Crepis rubra* | Europe | 1632 |

| POPULAR NAME | LATIN NAME | ORIGIN | | DATE |
|---|---|---|---|---|
| Scabious | *Scabiosa atropurpurea* | Europe | | 1629 |
| Sunflower, annual | *Helianthus annuus* | N. America | B | 1600 |
| Sweet scented Pea, | *Lathyrus odoratus* | Europe | | 1699 |
| Painted Lady Pea | *Lathyrus odoratus* | Europe | | 1730 |
| Stock, Gillyflower | *Matthiola incana* | ? Native | B | 1600 |
| "      Ten week | " "          annual | – | | – |
|        Brompton | " "          biennial | – | | – |
| Sweet Sultan | *Centaurea moschata* | Iran | | 1629 |
| Sweet William | *Dianthus barbatus* | Europe | B | 1600 |
| Tricolor | *Amaranthus tricolor* | Asia | | " " |
| Venus Looking Glass | *Legousia hybrida* | Native | | " " |
| Wallflower | *Erysimum cheiri* | Europe | | " " |
| White Wallflower | ? *Matthiola incana alba* | ? Native | | " " |
| Xeranthemum | *Xeranthemum annuum* | Europe | | " " |

*Less frequent*

| | | | | |
|---|---|---|---|---|
| Balsam Apple | *Momordica balsamina* | India | B | 1600 |
| Beans, Scarlet | *Phaseolus coccineus* | S. America | | 1633 |
| Belvidere, | | | | |
|     Summer Cypress | *Bassia scoparia* | Asia | | 1629 |
| Coventry Bells | *Campanula medium* | Europe | B | 1600 |
| Diamond Ficoides | *Mesembryanthemum* | | | |
| | *crystallina* | Europe | | 1727 |
| Indian Mallow | *Sida abutilon* | India | B | 1600 |
| Globe Amaranth | *Gomphrena globosa* | India | | 1714 |
| Humble Plant | *Mimosa pudica* | S. America | | 1638 |
| Hedgehog | *Medicago intertexta* | Europe | | 1629 |
| Ketmia | *Hibiscus trionum* | Europe | B | 1600 |
| Love Apple | *Lycopersicon esculentum* | Mexico | B | 1600 |
| Nigella | *Nigella damascena* | Europe | | " " |
| Primrose Tree | *Oenothera biennis* | N. America | | 1629 |
| Sensitive Plant | *Mimosa sensitiva* | S. America | | 1648 |
| Snapdragon | *Antirrhinum majus* | Europe | B | 1600 |
| Tangier Pea | *Lathyrus tingitanus* | Europe | | 1680 |
| Virginia Stock | *Malcolmia maritima* | Europe | | 1713 |

FIGURE 9
Convolvulus Minor (*Convolvulus tricolor*). A Mediterranean species, which colonises disturbed ground and hence of easy culture. It was a popular annual often depicted in the Dutch and Flemish flower paintings of the period.

TOP LEFT: FIGURE 10
French Honeysuckle (*Hedysarum coronarium*).
A handsome, south European fodder legume,
growing to a metre or more in height and
formerly higly esteemed as a border biennial.

TOP RIGHT: FIGURE 11
Larkspur, Larksheel (*Consolida ajacis*, formerly
*Delphinium ajacis*). Introduced from the
Mediterranean where it occurs in cornfields.

LEFT: FIGURE 12
Forking Larkspur (*Consolida regalis*). This
introduced, European annual was formerly used
medicinally. The name 'consolida' derives from
its supposed ability to 'consolidate' wounds.

FIGURE 13
Lavatera (*Lavatera trimestris*). Also known as Tree Mallow. Another colonist of disturbed land in north west Africa and Greece, the flowers are pale rose or white in colour.

FIGURE 14
Lobel's Catchfly (*Silene armeria*). An introduced annual coloniser of disturbed ground, this was routinely planted in the seventeenth and eighteenth centuries. Matthias de L'Obel (Lobelius) (1538-1616) was a French botanist and physician who practised in both the Netherlands and England where he eventually settled to become botanist to James 1.

FIGURE 15. Love Lies Bleeding (*Amaranthus caudatus*). First known as the Great Purple Flower Gentle, this native of tropical Asia was used medicinally as well as for border decoration.

FIGURE 16
African Marigold (*Tagetes erecta*) left; French Marygold (*Tagetes patula*) right.
Both species are natives of Mexico. The former was introduced to Spain in the
sixteenth century and later spread to the north African coast from whence it was
re-introduced as Flos Africanus. In the eighteenth century there was a sweet scented
variety which was subsequently lost. The French Marygold probably had a similar
history. It is generally believed it was brought to Britain by the Huguenots in the
sixteenth century. Both species quickly established themselves as indispensable
flowers for the parterre.

TOP LEFT: FIGURE 17
Marvel of Peru (*Mirabilis jalapa*). Introduced to Britain from Peru in the sixteenth century, it was treated as a half hardy annual, although the roots could be over-wintered in a frost free place. It is also known as the Four O'Clock Plant because the handsome flowers open in late afternoon and remain so during the night for pollination by moths.

TOP RIGHT: FIGURE 18
Pheasant's Eye (*Adonis annua*) Introduced from Europe where it is widely distributed, extending to Asia and North Africa. It used to occur in southern English cornfields.

FIGURE 19
Sweet Scented Pea (*Lathyrus odoratus*). The illustration shows the wild form, found in southern Italy and introduced to England in 1699. A white form turned up in 1718, followed, about a decade later, by a pink flowered type called Painted Lady which became very popular. For a long time it was erroneously reported to have come from Ceylon, due, according to Coats (1968), to inclusion of a dried specimen of the pink variety in herbarium specimens from that country.

TOP LEFT: FIGURE 20
Stock, Gillyflower (*Matthiola incana*). This species
may be native on the sea cliffs of southern England,
but occurs sporadically elsewhere on old walls as
a garden escape. On the sea cliffs it behaves as a
perennial but both an annual (Ten Week Stock) and
a biennial strain (Brompton) Stock have been derived
from it. There is also a sterile double form in which
both stamens and carpels develop into petals.

TOP RIGHT: FIGURE 21
Venus' Looking Glass (*Legousia speculum-veneris*).
A colonist of arable and cultivated ground in western
areas of mainland Europe. The plant owes its name
to the polished surface of the seeds which are revealed
when the ripe capsule opens. There is also a related
native species with smaller flowers.

FIGURE 22
Xeranthemum, Everlasting or Immortelle
(*Xeranthemum annuum*). This hardy annual occurs
on dry, stony ground in the Mediterranean and south
east Europe. Recorded in England in 1570 it was
another popular species during the seventeenth and
eighteenth centuries.

FIGURE 23
Coventry Bells (*Campanula medium*). We now
know this species as Canterbury Bells although
that name, starting with Gerard, was long used for
the perennial *Campanula trachelium*, which is
shown in FIGURE 34. The biennial *C. medium* is
from southern Europe.

BOTTOM LEFT: FIGURE 24
Indian Pink (*Dianthus sinenis*). If sown early this
species from China behaves as an annual, if sown
later as a biennial, while in a mild climate it is
semi-perennial. It was a later addition to the
border, not arriving in Britain until 1715.

BOTTOM RIGHT: FIGURE 25
Globe Ameranth (*Gomphrena globosa*). First
reported in Britain in 1714, this tender annual
of Indian origin was given hot-bed treatment.

In spite of their names, the French and African Marygolds (Figure 16) are native to Mexico. Both were brought first to Spain in the sixteenth century and were grown in gardens there and elsewhere in southern Europe. *Tagetes erecta* got carried to the North African coast where it spread and from where it was introduced to Britain as `Flos Africanus'. *Tagetes patula* is believed to have come to Britain with the Huguenot refugees in 1573. Both species quickly established themselves as indispensable members of the annual flower border. By the mid-eighteenth century several colour forms were being marketed in both species. James Justice (1754) reported great success growing them in pots, disbudding and cosseting the African Marygold to a height of five feet so that it resembled a shrub rather than a border annual. He grew these pot plants for indoor decoration and used a long lost scented variety for that purpose.

Another couple of South Americans, the Sensitive (Figure 26) and Humble Plants, with repectively pink and white flowers, were grown for their curiosity value. Their sensitive leaflets droop when touched and then slowly recover. They also were treated as annuals or biennials. Only a few seeds, generally three or four in number, were sold at a time.

An interesting group of plants included five species which were at first grouped in the genus Amaranthus but are now split between several genera. Some have become so widespread in tropical countries as to make their origin rather uncertain. The Prince's Feather was introduced from Virginia comparatively late in the seventeenth century. Now known as *Amaranthus hybrida* it used to sound more impressive as *A. hypochondriacus*. *Amaranthus tricolor*, from tropical Asia, has red, white, yellow and green variegated leaves, hence its popular name of Joseph's Cloak. The Cock's Comb, also Asian, owes its name to the remarkable inflorescence which varies in colour, including brilliant scarlet. *Amaranthus caudatus*, Love Lies Bleeding (Figure 15), from tropical America, was an early favourite, best known in its deep purple colour. Both this species and the Cock's Comb make a brave display when planted as a group. Finally there is *Gomphrena* (Figure 25), which, in spite of its Indian origin, has been recognised by some as the Amaranth of Classical Greece.

Other plants of Asian origin included the handsome *Impatiens balsamina* (Figure 8), which came in a great variety of different colours. It is tender and needed hot-bed treatment. The Balsam Apple, introduced from India in 1568, is a climber with brightly coloured fruits which forcibly disperse their seeds when ripe. The China Aster arrived about 1730 via Philip Miller who got seeds from France. By the middle of the century double flowers had appeared. James Justice (1754) raised several sorts including 'extraordinary beautiful varieties of pink, deep carnation, blue and white', which he over-wintered in a cold frame. The Hollyhock came probably from China. Originally with single flowers it soon developed doubles in a wide range of colours, reigning as a major feature of the flower border until stricken by a rust fungus.

OPPOSITE: FIGURE 26
Sensitive Plant (*Mimosa sensitiva*) and the closely related Humble Plant (*Mimosa pudica*), both from South America, were grown for their sensitive leaves which collapsed when touched and then slowly recovered. The seeds were expensive and generally only three or four were sold at a time.

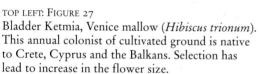

TOP LEFT: FIGURE 27
Bladder Ketmia, Venice mallow (*Hibiscus trionum*).
This annual colonist of cultivated ground is native
to Crete, Cyprus and the Balkans. Selection has
lead to increase in the flower size.

TOP RIGHT: FIGURE 28
Tangier Pea (*Lathyrus tingitanus*). An annual from
the Iberian Peninsula and North West Africa, this
was a relatively late introduction.

FIGURE 29
Pink, Gilloflower (*Dianthus plumarius*). Native to
limestone mountains from the Italian Alps eastwards to the Tartra, the wild forms are white or
pink, occasionally with a darker coloured patch.
Twelve varieties were known to Gerard, all single
flowered and clove scented. It became a florist's
flower and this led to the production of an
immense number of named varieties. The laced
pinks of Paisley have often been described.

Several of the regularly grown lupins were south European fodder plants such as *Lupinus albus* and *L. luteus*, esteemed for its fine scent. Another legume, *Medicago intertexta*, was grown for its curious spiny fruits, hence the name 'Hedgehog'. French Honeysuckle (Figure 10) was a south European fodder plant with handsome red flowers and a clover scent. Honesty was another long established plant, still with us and still esteemed for its use for winter decoration about the house. Two of the most handsome, popular annuals were the Bladder Ketmia, *Hibiscus trionum* (Figure 27) and *Lavatera trimestris* (Figure 13). The latter is a native of the European Mediterranean. The former, sometimes called Venice Mallow, extends from the Balkans eastwards. One of the most popular species was the Rose Campion, which varied in colour, and also had a double form which was greatly preferred. James Justice mentioned a variety called Painted Lady, with 'the prettiest flower of all the Campions', seed of which could be obtained from the Edinburgh seedsman Patrick Drummond. The Sweet Pea (Figure 19) was introduced to Britain in 1699. During the next 50 years or so a few colour forms appeared, including white and, most notably, the popular pink and white variety, called Painted Lady, which lost none of the delightful perfume of the original wild plant. For some rather obscure reason it was, for many years, erroneously reported as having arisen in what was then called Ceylon. Two relatives of the Rose Campion were also popular, the Sweet William and Lobel's Catchfly (Figure 14). L'Obel (latinised Lobelius) was a French botanist (1538–1616) who collected widely in Europe and eventually became botanist to James 1 of England. Latterly 'Lobel's Catchfly' became converted rather inappropriately to 'Sweet William Lychnis' and a little echo of botanical history was thereby extinguished. The Wallflower, like the Snapdragon, was introduced so long ago that it was generally regarded as native. It may have come over with the Normans and successfully colonised its favourite habitat of old walls, reaching as far north as Neidpath Castle on the Tweed by the fourteenth century. The favourite variety in the seventeenth century, especially at Hamilton Palace, was known as the Bloody Wallflower which may have been what was elsewhere known as the dark red Double Bloody Wallflower. The Stock, *Matthiola incana* (Figure 20), is typically perennial but has both annual and biennial strains. The annual form gave rise to the summer flowering Ten Week Stock and the biennial to the spring flowering Brompton Stock, both of which were developed in the early eighteenth century.

## Herbaceous Perennials

The origins of the perennial plants listed in Table 4 present a contrast with the annuals: being all hardy species there are none from South America in the list and only a few from North America. Unlike the annuals there is quite a high proportion of native species while the many species introduced from Europe are not so predominantly southern in their native distribution. Among the most popular was the Clove Gillyflower or Carnation (Figure 30). According to Harvey (1978) it was developed in the Ottoman Empire in the late Middle Ages and probably brought to Europe in the fourteenth century. The names 'Gillyflower' and 'July Flower' often cause confusion since they have been used rather indiscriminately for several different Crucifers as well as species of Dianthus. Thus we have Stock Gillyflower, Wall Gillyflower, and Queen's Gillyflower for repectively Stock, Wallflower and Dame's Violet or Sweet Rocket, all Crucifers, as well as Clove Gillyflower and July Flower for the Carnation and Pink. In other languages the two distinct groups of species are separately named. Thus the French *giroflee* applies only to the scented Crucifers.

As usual there are a few problems of identification. Bachelor's Buttons were either white or red but the name has been used for several different species. Originally the name referred to the double form of the Meadow Buttercup (Figure 33) but, as time passed, other plants with double flowers came to be called Bachelor's Buttons. White ones probably referred most often to the double form of *Ranunculus aconitifolius*, or possibly double *Silene latifolia*, while the double red Campion could also have been called Bachelor's Buttons. There were many others with double flowers, to which the name might refer, such as Sneezewort, Ragged Robin, the Cuckoo Flower (*Cardamine pratensis*), Scarlet Lychnis and the Meadow Saxifrage (*S. granulata*).

There is often confusion about the identity of Canterbury Bells. Latterly, this popular name has been applied to the biennial European species *Campanula medium* (Figure 23). But in the seventeenth and probably early eighteenth centuries, starting with Gerard, Canterbury Bell referred to the native, perennial *Campanula trachelium* (Figure 34), otherwise known as the Nettle Leaved Bellflower while *C. medium* was called Coventry Bells. To add to the confusion there was also *Trachelium caeruleum*, the Throatwort. The identity of the plant known as White Wallflower is obscure and there is more than one candidate. One possibilty is the rather woody, wild perennial form of *Matthiola incana* var *alba*. Another plant which comes to mind is the south European, annual Wallflower-leaved Stock, *Matthiola graeca*. Harvey (1972) has suggested the Garden *Arabis* which has escaped and colonised old walls. There were three species with Spiderwort in their names. The Virginian Spiderwort, *Tradescantia*, was erroneously believed to cure the bite of a particular spider. The Savoy Spiderwort, *Paradisea liliastrum*, got its name from the shape of the roots, while the identity of the Faery Spiderwort is uncertain but may be the related *Anthericum liliago*.

## TABLE 4. Herbaceous perennials

| POPULAR NAME | LATIN NAME | ORIGIN | | DATE |
|---|---|---|---|---|
| *Most frequent* | | | | |
| Bear's Ears | *Primula auricula* | Europe | B | 1600 |
| Clove July Flower | *Dianthus caryophyllus* | Europe | | " " |
| Columbine | *Aquilegia vulgaris* | Native | | " " |
| Daisy | *Bellis perennis* | Native | | " " |
| Gentianella | *Gentiana acaulis* | Europe | | " " |
| Pink, Pheasant Eyed, | *Dianthus plumarius* | Europe | | " " |
| "    Matted | *Dianthus gratianopolitanus* | Europe | | " " |
| Poppy, Great | *Papaver orientale* | Asia | | 1714 |
| Primrose | *Primula vulgaris* | Native | B | 1600 |
| Polyanthus | *Primula X polyantha* | Native | ? | 1660 |
| Queen's Gillyflower, Rocket, single, double } | *Hesperis matronalis* | Europe | B | 1600 |
| Scarlet Lychnis | *Lychnis chalcedonica* | Russia | | " " |
| Tobacco | *Nicotiana tabacum* | N. America | | " " |
| *Less frequent* | | | | |
| Acanthus | *Acanthus mollis* | Europe | B | 1600 |
| Adiantum | *Adiantum capillus veneris* | Native | | " " |
| Alyssum | *Alyssum saxatile* | Europe | | 1710 |
| Anthora Monkshood | *Aconitum anthora* | Europe | B | 1600 |
| Asarum | *Asarum europaeum* | Europe | | " " |
| Asphodel | *Asphodelus alba* | Europe | | " " |
| Assirian Balm | ? | – | | – |
| Aster | *Aster novae-belgii* | N. America | | 1710 |
| Bachelor's Buttons | Several species | – | | – |
| Betony | *Stachys officinalis* | Native | B | 1600 |
| Bloodwort | *Sanguinaria canadensis* | N. America | | 1680 |
| Bramble, double flowering | *Rubus fruticosus* | Native | ? | |
| Campanula | *Campanula pericifolia* | Europe | B | 1600 |
| "    pyramid | *Campanula pyramidalis* | Europe | | " " |
| Cardinal Flower | *Lobelia cardinalis* | N. America | | 1629 |
| Catchfly | *Lychnis viscaria* | Native | B | 1600 |
| Celandine | *Chelidonium majus* | ? Native | | " " |
| China Pink | *Dianthus chinensis* | China | | 1713 |
| Cowslip | *Primula veris* | Native | B | 1600 |
| Cuckoo Flower, Double | *Cardamine pratensis* | Native | ? | |
| Darius Woundwort | *Stachys sp.?* | – | | – |

| Popular Name | Latin Name | Origin | | Date |
|---|---|---|---|---|
| Esula | *Euphorbia esula* | Europe | | " " |
| Everlasting | *Anaphalis margaritacea* | N. America | | " " |
| | or *Helichrysum orientale* | Africa | | 1629 |
| Everlasting Pea | *Lathyrus latifolium* | Europe | B | 1600 |
| Feathered Columbine | *Thalictrum aquilegifolium* | Europe | | " " |
| Fraxinella | *Dictamnus fraxinella* | Europe | | " " |
| French Willow | *Chamerion angustifolium* | Native | | " " |
| Fumitory, | | | | |
| " Bulbous rooted | *Corydalis solida* | Europe | | " " |
| " White | *Pseudo-fumaria alba* | Europe | | " " |
| " Yellow | *Pseudo-fumaria lutea* | Europe | | " " |
| Gentian, Great Blue | *Gentiana asclepiadea* | Europe | | " " |
| Geranium | | | | |
| Knob rooted | *Geranium tuberosum* | Europe | | " " |
| Germander | *Teucrium chamaedrys* | Native | | " " |
| Globe Thistle | *Echinops sphaerocephalus* | Europe | | " " |
| Goat's Rue | *Galega officinalis* | Europe | | " " |
| Goldenrod | *Solidago canadensis* | America | | 1648 |
| Gold Knob | – | – | | – |
| Greek Valerian | *Polemonium coeruleum* | Native | B | 1600 |
| Gum Cistus | *Cistus ladaniferus* | Europe | | 1629 |
| Hawkweed | *Hieracium pilosella* | Native | B | 1600 |
| Hellebore, | *Hellleborus viridis* | ? Native | | " " |
| " Christmas Flower | *Helleborus niger* | Europe | | " " |
| " White | *Veratrum album* | Europe | | " " |
| Hepatica | *Hepatica triloba* | Europe | | " " |
| Hercules Allheal | *Prunella grandiflora* | Europe | | " " |
| Lavender Cotton | *Santolina chamaecyparis* | Europe | | " " |
| Leopard's Bane | *Doronicum pardalianches* | Europe | | " " |
| Lion's Foot, Canada | ? *Prenanthes alba* | N. America | ? | |
| Lisimachia | *Lysimachia vulgaris* | Native | | " " |
| Lychnidea | *Phlox paniculata* | N. America | | 1732 |
| Mallow Tree | *Lavatera arborea* | Native | B | 1600 |
| Mallow, Vervain | *Malva alcea* | Europe | | " " |
| Monkshood | *Aconitum napellus* | Native | B | 1600 |
| Marum | *Teucrium marum* | Europe | | 1640 |
| Mountain Crowfoot | *Ranunculus aconitifolius* | Europe | B | 1600 |
| Mountain Sage | *Teucrium scorodonia* | Native | | " " |
| Mule Pink | *Dianthus species hybrid* | Native | | 1717 |
| Navelwort | *Umbilicus rupestris* | Native | B | 1600 |
| None So Pretty | *Saxifraga umbrosa* | Europe | ? | |
| Orpine | *Sedum Telephium* | Native | B | 1600 |

| Popular Name | Latin Name | Origin | | Date |
|---|---|---|---|---|
| Pansie | *Viola tricolor* | Native | B | 1600 |
| Pellitory of Spain | *Anacyclus pyrethrum* | Europe | | " " |
| Periwinkle | *Vinca minor* | Native | | " " |
| Paeony | *Paeonia officinalis* | Europe | | " " |
| Pasque Flower | *Pulsatilla vulgaris* | Native | B | 1600 |
| Ragged Robin, Double | *Lychnis flos-cuculi* | Native | | ? |
| Reseda | *Reseda odorata* | Europe | | 1752 |
| Rock Rose | *Cistus ? laurifolius* | Europe | | 1731 |
| Roman Flowering Sage | *? Phlomis fruticosa* | Europe | B | 1600 |
| Sanicle | *Sanicula europaea* | Native | | " " |
| Savoy Spiderwort | *Paradisea liliastrum* | Europe | | 1629 |
| Saxifrage, double | *Saxifraga granulata flore pleno* | Native | | ? |
| Silver Rod | *Asphodelus racemosus* | Europe | B | 1600 |
| Sneezewort, double | *Achillea ptarmica* | Native | | ? |
| Spiderwort | *Tradescantia virginiana* | N. America | | 1629 |
| " ", Faery | *?Anthericum liliago* | Europe | B | 1600 |
| Starwort | *Aster amellus* | Europe | | " " |
| Sunflower, Perennial | *Helianthus X multiflorus* | America | | " " |
| Swallowwort | *Asclepias tuberosa* | America | | 1690 |
| | */syriaca* | America | | 1629 |
| Sweet Maudlin | *Achillea ageratum* | Native | B | 1600 |
| Teasel | *Dipsacus sylvestris* | Native | | " " |
| Thrift | *Armeria maritima* | Native | | " " |
| Throatwort | *Trachelium caeruleum* | Europe | | 1640 |
| Toadflax | *Linaria purpurea* | Europe | | 1648 |
| Toothwort | *Cardamine heptaphylla* | Europe | | 1683 |
| Valerian | *Centranthus ruber* | Europe | B | 1600 |
| Veronica | *Veronica ? longifolia* | Europe | | 1731 |
| Violet, double etc | *Viola odorata* | Native | B | 1600 |
| Winter Cherry | *Physalis alkekengi* | Europe | | " " |
| Wolf's Bane | *Aconitum lycoctonum* | Europe | | " " |

Most of the perennials were introduced to cultivation before 1600 and only a few in our list are recorded as eighteenth-century introductions. They include Alyssum, Phlox, the Mule Pink – Fairchild's famous hybrid between Sweet William and Carnation – Rock Rose, a species of *Cistus*, probably *laurifolius* which grows well enough in Scotland, the hardy Aster, probably *novae-belgii*, and the equally hardy Goldenrod, both from North America, the Chinese Pink, the European *Veronica longifolia*, which has hybridised with V. *spicata* and, from Armenia, *Papaver orientale* with the vermilion flowers and robust constitution. Early American introductions

TOP LEFT: FIGURE 30
Clove July Flower, Carnation (*Dianthus caryophyllus*). According to Harvey (1978) the garden plant was developed in the Ottoman Empire in the Middle Ages and brought to Europe in the fourteenth century. Widely cultivated it became naturalised in southern Europe, especially in stony, calcareous places. Perhaps no other plant exceeded the Clove July Flower in popular esteem during the seventeenth and eighteenth centuries. Even the most meagre collection of garden plants would include this one. It was a source of perfume. It became a florist's flower, especially in Germany and Italy. By the beginning of the eighteenth century there were some four hundred different, named varieties.

TOP RIGHT: FIGURE 31
Winged Pea (*Tetragonolobus purpureus*). A semi-prostrate European annual grown for its square shaped, winged and edible pods, hence the alternative name of Asparagus Pea. The plant may be grown in the same way as French beans. The seed has been used as a substitute for coffee. In Scotland it seems to have been grown for its flowers and curious pods.

OPPOSITE: FIGURE 32
Scarlet Lychnis (*Lychnis chalcedonica*). This species was also known by other names, such as Flower or Campion of Constantinople, Flower of Bristol, Nonsuch and Cross of Jerusalem. A double form was described by Parkinson. A native of Turkey and southern Russia, it is generally believed to have been introduced to England at the time of the Crusades.

TOP LEFT: FIGURE 33
Bachelor's Buttons (*Ranunculus acris, flore pleno*).
It is accepted that the double form of the Meadow
Buttercup was the first plant to be called Bachelor's
Buttons but the name has been used for the double
forms of several different species, including
*Ranunculus aconitifolius* or Fair Maids of France,
more than one species of Campion, Sneezewort etc.
The double condition is due to conversion of the
stamens or carpels, usually the former, into petals.
Unless vegetative reproduction is possible the
consequent sterility prevents spread.

TOP RIGHT: FIGURE 34
Canterbury Bells (*Campanula trachelium*). This
native perennial was first given the name which was
later applied to *Campanula medium*. It is now known
as the Nettle Leaved Bellflower and is quite widely
naturalised beyond its original native localities.

FIGURE 35
Mountain Knapweed (*Centaurea montana*). This
was one of the several 'Bottles', which included the
Cornflower and other Centaureas. Known to Gerard,
it is another of the species which has escaped from
gardens to become widely established on roadsides
and waste places.

included the Sunflower, (*Helianthus multiflorus*) (Figure 37), which came in before 1600, the everlasting *Anaphalis*, the Bloodroot with the red sap and the occasional, unfamiliar species like Lion's Foot from Canada, also known at home as White Lettuce or Rattlesnake Root. Apart from the Oriental Poppy the only other eastern European and Asian species were the Day Lilies, *Hemerocallis flava* (Figure 39), with scented, yellow flowers and *H. fulva* with scentless, orange flowers.

Several of the plants in the list like Auricula, the Pink and Polyanthus were to become Florists' Flowers with many different named varieties. In the period 1731–9 the Edinburgh nurseryman Robert McClellan was importing Auriculas from England and Holland and supplying customers with up to twenty different kinds. James Justice was reputed to have one of the finest collections in the country. Auriculas, together with Thrift, Gentianella, None so Pretty, species of Corydalis and Fumitory, Pinks, Polyanthus and, to some extent, Lavender Cotton, were used to edge borders. The long cultivated Scarlet Lychnis (Figure 32) is generally believed to have been in Britain since the Crusades.

The perennials grown in Scotland in our period were mostly long-familiar species. They included a number of native species like the Primrose, Cowslip, Cranesbills, Campion, Lychnis, Campanulas and Dianthus species. Since they were not purchased, but simply transferred to the garden from the wild, they tended to go unrecorded in the accounts of what was grown.

FIGURE 36
Perennial Poppy
(*Papaver orientale*).
Introduced from
Armenia in 1714 it
soon became an essential,
hardy border plant.

## Bulbs, Corms etc.

The plants in Table 5, the bulbs, corms and tubers, are all monocotyledons except for Ranunculus and Anemone, which are included here simply for traditional reasons. With few exceptions the list includes familiar species which were introduced to Britain before 1600, generally from Turkey, Iran and neighbouring regions. Many, like the Turban Ranunculus and the Crown Imperial had been cultivated for centuries before they reached Europe, often becoming naturalised and, sometimes,like the Tulip, difficult to trace back confidently to a wild ancestor. Hybridisation and selection in the Ranunculus, Tulip and Hyacinth gave rise to an immense number of different varieties. When first introduced to Europe there were only four different colours in the Hyacinth but by 1725 the number of named varieties had soared almost incredibly to some two thousand. Although many of the differences were trivial yet the vast increase in diversity of colour and form was remarkable. The Turban Ranunculus (Figure 45) was derived from *R. asiaticus* which occurs wild in red, white, yellow and orange forms whose relative frequency differs between regions. In this genus double flowers, due to conversion of stamens into petals, are not uncommon in nature and, like the original Bachelor's Buttons, would have been selected for cultivation, although in the Meadow Buttercup there was no further development. By 1629 Parkinson knew eight varieties of Turban Ranunculus; by 1777 the number had increased to some eleven hundred. However the interest in these florist's flowers eventually faded so that most of the varieties became extinct, although they could be recreated if there was sufficient interest in doing so.

In the early seventeenth century there were dozens of varieties of Narcissus, many of them hybrids of natural origin. However, the accounts almost invariably refer simply to Narcissus so, although we suspect several varieties were grown, we have little choice but to refer to *Narcissus pseudonarcissus*, the Trumpet Daffodil, which is widespread in Europe, posing familiar doubts as to whether particular populations are native or descendants of once cultivated plants. Jonquils (Figure 43), including doubles, were particularly popular and often used for edging parterres.

Anemones, especially *A. coronaria* (Figure 38), were favourites in the seventeenth and eighteenth century Scottish garden. They came in a range of colours, red, white, blue, purple and many intermediates but never developed into florists' flowers. The hardy, rhizomatous *Iris germanica* (Figure 40) has been in cultivation longer than any other Iris. It arose in the Mediterranean region and is probably of hybrid origin. The white Florentine Iris (Figure 41), a single clone, can be regarded as one of the many forms of *germanica*. It was grown commercially in Italy for its orris root used in the perfumery trade. The so-called English Iris, (*Iris latifolia*, formerly *xiphioides* (Figure 42) with bulbous roots, is a native of the Pyrenees, while the Spanish Iris, (*I. xiphium*) occurs throughout Spain and North Africa. The Chalcedonian Iris of the accounts referred to *I. susiana*.

OPPOSITE: FIGURE 37 Perennial Sunflower (*Helianthus X multiflorus*). This North American species, familiar to Gerard, was probably introduced from Virginia. Its hardy nature and showy flowers on metre high stems ensured its place in the border.

## TABLE 5 Bulbs, Corms, Tubers

| POPULAR NAME | LATIN NAME | ORIGIN | | DATE |
|---|---|---|---|---|
| Anemone | *Anemone coronaria* | Europe | B | 1600 |
| Autumn Narcissus | *Narcissus serotinus* | Europe | | 1629 |
| Colchicum | *Colchicum autumnale* | Native | B | 1600 |
| " Indian | *Colchicum byzantinum* | Asia | | 1629 |
| Corn Flag | *Gladiolus communis* | Europe | B | 1600 |
| Crocus | *Crocus vernus* etc | Europe | B | 1600 |
| Crown Imperial | *Fritillaria imperialis* | Asia | B | 1600 |
| Cyclamen | *Cyclamen hederifolium* | Europe | | " " |
| | *Cyclamen coum* | Europe | | " " |
| Day Lily | *Hemerocallis flava/fulva* | Asia | | " " |
| Dog's Tooth Violet | *Erythronium dens canis* | Europe | | " " |
| Fritillary | *Fritillaria meleagris* | Native | | " " |
| Hyacinth | *Hyacinthus orientalis* | E. Med | | " " |
| Iris, Chalcedonian | *Iris susiana* | N. Africa | | " " |
| " Bearded Flag | *Iris germanica* | Europe | | " " |
| " Florentine | *Iris florentina* | Europe | | " " |
| " Great Bulbous | *Iris latifolia* | Europe | | " " |
| " Spanish | *Iris xiphium,* | Europe | | " " |
| " Striped Flag | *Iris pallida variegata* | Mid East | | " " |
| Jacinths, Blue | *Scilla spp* | Europe | | " " |
| Jonquils | *Narcissus jonquilla* | Europe | | " " |
| Lily, Orange | *Lilium bulbiferum* | Europe | | " " |
| White | *Lilium candidum* | Europe | | " " |
| Martagon | *Lilium martagon* | Europe | | " " |
| Lily of the Valley | *Convallaria majus* | Native | | " " |
| Moly | *Allium moly* | Europe | | 1604 |
| Muscari | *Muscari botryoides* | Europe | B | 1600 |
| " | *Muscari comosum* | Europe | | " " |
| Narcissus | *Narcissus pseudo-narcissus* | Native | | " " |
| Ranunculus | *Ranunculus asiaticus* | Europe | | " " |
| Snowdrop | *Galanthus nivalis* | Native | | " " |
| Star of Bethlehem, | | | | |
| Great | *Ornithogalum umbellatum* | Europe | | " " |
| Dwarf | *Ornithogalum comosum* | Europe | | " " |
| Tuberose | *Polianthes tuberosa* | Mexico | | 1629 |
| Tulip | *Tulipa gesneriana* | Asia | B | 1600 |
| " Dwarf | " " | – | | – |
| Winter Aconite | *Eranthis hyemalis* | Europe | B | 1600 |

TOP LEFT: FIGURE 38
Anemone (*Anemone coronaria*). This species,
with red, white, blue or pink flowers, flourishes on
cultivated ground in the Mediterranean region. The
'coronaria' of its name derives from the use of its
flowers to make floral crowns in classical times.

TOP RIGHT: FIGURE 39
Day Lily (*Hemerocallis flava*). This asiatic species
with scented flowers, was established early in
gardens. The closely related, scentless *H. fulva*,
with orange flowers, has an immense distribution
as far east as China. According to Gorer (1970) a
clone of *H. fulva*, with three in place of the normal
two sets of chromosomes, known as 'Europa', has
persisted since at least 1576 to the present day.

FIGURE 40
Iris (*Iris germanica*). This iris which is a native of
the Mediterranean region, has been in cultivation
longer than any others of the genus. It is of hybrid
origin. Formerly juice extracted from the roots
was used in the treatment of dropsy and also as a
cosmetic.

TOP LEFT: FIGURE 41
Florentine Iris (*Iris florentina*). Also known as
Flower de Luce or Flower de Luce of Florence, it
is best regarded as a form of *I. germanica*. It was
grown on a large scale in Italy for its orris root
which was used in perfumery.

TOP RIGHT: FIGURE 42
Great Bulbous Iris (*Iris latifolia*, formerly
*xiphioides*). A native of the Pyrenees, by the
second half of the sixteenth century it had become
abundant in Bristol gardens, via importations from
Spain, hence its other name of English Iris. Even
in Parkinson's time several colour forms were
known and these had increased in number by the
early eighteenth century.

FIGURE 43
Jonquil (*Narcissus jonquilla*). Native to central and
southern Spain, Portugal and North Africa it has
become naturalised in southern Europe. It has
been established in Britain since the sixteenth
century; Parkinson referred to a double form.
Famous for its sweet scent, a volatile oil has been
extracted for use in perfumery.

FIGURE 44
Orange Lily (*Lilium bulbiferum*). The orange lily
is found in hill pastures and rocky places in
Central Europe. It was known to Gerard.
Once established in a garden its future is assured.

LEFT: FIGURE 45
Ranunculus (*Ranunculus asiaticus*). The Turban
Ranunculus developed as a garden flower in
Turkey and was probably introduced to Britain in
the sixteenth century. The wild plants have several
colour forms, including yellow, red and white,
which differ in occurrence or frquency in different
parts of its Mediterranean distribution. It was
taken up as a florist's flower and a vast number
of named varieties were produced. According to
Duthie (1988) some eleven hundred sorts were
known in 1777, but, in due course, it fell from
favour and almost all of them disappeared.

## Shrubs, Climbers and Ornamental Trees

The plants in this category are listed in Table 6. The most widely grown shrubs include many which had been grown in Britain since before 1600 and these were mostly European in origin. The less frequently grown species included a number introduced from North America. They were often labelled as Virginian, indicating their immediate origin, although invariably they had a wide distribution in eastern America. A few of the popular names have led to confusion, none more so than 'Syringa', which was the name for the Mock Orange, *Philadelphus coronarius*, but was also applied to the lilac, *Syringa vulgaris*. These two shrubs were introduced about the same time in the sixteenth century from Turkey and soon became indispensable small trees. They were also known as Pipe Trees, Blue (lilac) and White (Philadelphus), from their hollow stems which were used in their native country for making pan pipes. There was also the Persian lilac (Figure 52), a hardy and attractive shrub of hybrid origin, which had been known in India and Iran for many centuries.

The Laurels can also confuse. *Laurus nobilis*, which may grow to twenty to forty feet, is a native of the Mediterranean and grown in Britain since the sixteenth century. It is the laurel of the ancients who crowned their heroes with its leaves. The term 'bachelor', used for the recipient of a first degree, appears to be derived from 'baccalaureus' i.e. laurel bearing which, according to *O.E.D.*, was a pun on 'baccalarius'. Two other laurels are both members of the rose family, *Prunus laurocerasus*, the Cherry Laurel, and *P. lusitanica* the Portugal Laurel. Both have been prized as evergreens, especially the hardier and more attractive Portugal Laurel. Lastly there is the Alexandrian Laurel, *Danae racemosa*, a small dense shrub with occasional red berries, belonging to the lily family and native to Iran and Asia Minor. It was introduced to Britain in 1713.

The name 'Elder' was also used for more than one spcies. The Elder proper is the Bour Tree, *Sambucus nigra*, a native which was grown in several varieties e.g. with light green in place of the usual dark purple fruits or with finely divided, laciniate leaves. But there was also the Rose, Water or Marsh Elder, alternative names for the Guelder Rose, *Viburnum opulus*, which is not a member of the rose family. There was also the Dwarf Elder, *Sambucus ebulus* (Figure 49), a herbaceous shrub, spreading by aggressive rhizomes, and the American Box Elder, *Acer negundo*, introduced to Britain in 1688, where it proved hardy and successful. It occurs from eastern and central Canada to Texas and was one of the sources of maple syrup, well known to the native Indians.

The Common Barberry (Figure 47) and the Cornelian Cherry, *Cornus mas* (Figure 60) were once valued especially for their fruit. The former is a native, deciduous shrub with a wide distribution through Europe and temperate Asia. It grows to a fair size and produces red, egg shaped fruits about half an inch long. These are very acid in taste but were once esteemed for garnishing meat and were also used in salads. The Cornelian Cherry, quite unrelated to true cherries, is a small tree of European origin whose fruits were used to make preserves or candied. Its culinary use lapsed but it was retained in the garden for its winter display of yellow flowers on bare twigs as well as the handsome appearance of its scarlet fruits.

Honeysuckles were very popular, none more so than the native species, which gave rise to a number of garden varieties e.g. Late Blowing Honeysuckle. *L. alpigena* from central and southern Europe, with long stalked flowers and paired, scarlet fruits, was recorded in Britain as early as 1596. However it did not prove garden worthy and eventually dropped out. *L. caprifolium*, which can climb to twenty feet, was introduced from Europe, doing well enough to become naturalised in south-east England. It is very fragrant. *L. caerulea*, a small species from upland Europe, although quite widely grown after its introduction, can be added to the long list of introduced species which failed to establish themselves as garden plants. *L. sempervirens* (Figure 50), the Trumpet Honeysuckle, introduced in 1656, is an evergreen species from eastern and southern North America of less hardy disposition than the others. *L. X americana* is a hybrid between *L. caprifolium* and the European *L. etrusca*. The hybrid more closely resembles *caprifolium* and is of unknown, but early and probably garden origin. The 'American' in its original name was inappropriate and has been replaced by *X etrusca*. It was in cultivation in Britain about 1730. It has become very common as a garden honeysuckle and has escaped successfully. Finally there is the Fly Honeysuckle which may be native to southern England but is now widespread in Britain.

There were several Jasmines. *Jasminum officinale* was introduced before 1600. It has an immense distribution from northern Iran to China, where its cultivation goes back beyond the records. There was also a larger flowered, rather tender species *J. grandiflorum* (Figure 51). Of the other two commonly grown species *J. fruticans*, introduced before 1600 is a native of southern Europe and Asia Minor. It grows to two or three feet but considerably higher if given the protection of a wall, which was very often the case. *J. humile* (Figure 52), often called the Italian Yellow Jasmine, arrived about half a century later. Originally of Asian origin it was often grafted on *J. fruticans*.

Early in the eighteenth century there were not many evergreens and those at hand were greatly prized. We have already considered the laurels. Other evergreens included the Common Privet, especially the form known as *sempervirens, Pyracantha*, the Mediterranean *Phyllerias*, of which there were several species, although the most commonly grown in Scotland were probably *angustifolia* and *latifolia*, with respectively narrow and broad leaves, Alaternus, (*Rhamnus alaternus*) and Laurustinus, (*Viburnum tinus*) (Figure 53) and, of course, Yew. They were generally hardy species, some of which like Privet, Pyracantha, Phyllerea and Yew could be clipped to shape. An additional evergreen which turned up in seed accounts in the early eighteenth century desrves a mention for its curiosity value. This was the South Sea Tea Tree, (*Ilex vomitoria*), which, in spite of its romantic name, was an American holly which acquired its specific name from the practice of certain North American tribes, who gathered periodically for several days to drink infusions of the leaves, which induced vomiting and may have served as a cure for worms.

## TABLE 6. Shrubs, Climbers, Trees

| POPULAR NAME | LATIN NAME | ORIGIN | | DATE |
|---|---|---|---|---|
| *Most frequent* | | | | |
| Alaternus | *Rhamnus alaternus* | Europe | | 1629 |
| Aller, Alder | *Alnus glutinosa* | Native | B | 1600 |
| Althaea frutex | *Hibiscus syriacus* | India/China | | " " |
| Arbor vitae | *Thuja occidentalis* | N. America | | " " |
| Balm of Gilead Fir | *Abies balsamea* | N. America | | 1629 |
| Berberis | *Berberis vulgaris* | Europe | B | 1600 |
| Bitter Sweet, white | *Solanum dulcamara* | Native | | ? |
| Bladder Senna | *Colutea arborescens* | Europe | B | 1600 |
| Box, Dwarf | *Buxus sempervirens* var. *suffruticosa* | Native | | " " |
| Cytisus | *Cytisus sessiliflorus* | Europe | | 1629 |
| Dwarf Almond | *Prunus nana* | Russia | | 1683 |
| Elder | *Sambucus nigra* | Native | B | 1600 |
| Dwarf Elder | *Sambucus ebulus* | ? Native | | " " |
| Filbert | *Corylus avellana, vars.* | Native | | " " |
| Guelder Rose | *Viburnum opulus* | Native | | " " |
| Holly, various | *Ilex aquifolium* | Native | | " " |
| Honeysuckle, Common | *Lonicera periclymenum* | Native | | " " |
| " Early | *Lonicera caprifolium* | Europe | | ? |
| " Trumpet | *Lonicera sempervirens* | N. America | | 1656 |
| " Upright red berried | *Lonicera alpigena* | Europe | B | 1600 |
| " Upright blue berried | *Lonicera coerulea* | Europe | | 1629 |
| " Fly | *Lonicera xylostemum* | ? Native | B | 1600 |
| " Evergreen | *Lonicera sempervirens* | Europe | | 1656 |
| Ivy, various | *Hedera helix* | Native | B | 1600 |
| Jasmine, Jessamine | *Jasminum officinale* | Asia | | " " |
| " Spanish | *Jasminum grandiflorum* | Asia | | 1629 |
| Yellow Jasmine | *Jasminum humile* | Europe | | 1656 |
| | *Jasminum fruticans* | Europe | B | 1600 |
| Juniper, Common | *Juniperus communis* | Native | | " " |
| Swedish | var *suecica* | Europe | | ? |

| POPULAR NAME | LATIN NAME | ORIGIN | | DATE |
|---|---|---|---|---|
| Laurel, Sweet Bay | *Laurus nobilis* | Europe | B | 1600 |
| ''      Common | *Prunus laurocerasus* | Europe | | 1629 |
| ''      Portugal | *Prunus lusitanica* | Europe | | 1648 |
| Laurustinus | *Viburnum tinus* | Europe | B | 1600 |
| Lavender, Common | *Lavendula X intermedia* | Europe | | '' '' |
| ''      French | *Lavendula stoechas* | Europe | | '' '' |
| Lilac, Lilyoak | *Syringa vulgaris* | Asia | | '' '' |
| ''      Persian | *Syringa persica* | Asia | | 1640 |
| Mezerion | *Daphne mezerion* | Native | B | 1600 |
| Mock Willow | *Spiraea salicifolia* | Europe | | 1640 |
| New England Pine | *Pinus strobus* | N. America | | 1705 |
| Norway Spruce | *Picea abies* | Europe | B | 1600 |
| Perrywinkle | *Vinca major* | Europe | | '' '' |
| Phillyrea | *Phillyrea angustifolia* | Europe | | '' '' |
| | " *latifolia* | Europe | | '' '' |
| Pinaster | *Pinus pinaster* | Europe | | '' '' |
| Privet | *Ligustrum vulgare* | Native | | '' '' |
| ''      Evergreen | var. *sempervirens* | Native | | ? |
| Pyracantha | *Pyracantha coccinea* | Europe | | 1629 |
| Saugh, various | *Salix* spp. | Native | | ? |
| Savin | *Juniperus sabina* | Europe | B | 1600 |
| Scorpion Senna | *Coronilla emerus* | Europe | | '' '' |
| Shrub Cinquefoil | *Potentilla fruticosa* | Native | | '' '' |
| Spanish Broom | *Spartina junceum* | Europe | | '' '' |
| St John's Wort | *Hypericum hircinum* | Europe | | 1640 |
| Sumach | *Rhus typhina* | N. America | B | 1600 |
| Syringa | *Philadelphus coronarius* | Europe/Asia | | '' '' |
| Thorn, Hawthorn | *Crataegus monogyna* | Native | | '' '' |
| ''      Double | var. *pleno* | Native | | ? |
| ''      Cock's Spur | *Crataegus crus-galli* | N. America | | 1691 |
| Traveller's Joy | *Clematis vitalba* | Native | B | 1600 |
| Tree Mallow | *Malva arborea* | Native | | '' '' |
| Tutsan | *Hypericum androsaemum* | Native | | '' '' |
| Virgin's Bower | *Clematis viticella* | Europe | | '' '' |
| Walnut | *Juglans regia* | Europe, Asia | | '' '' |
| Yew | *Taxus baccata* | Native | | '' '' |

*Less frequent*

| | | | | |
|---|---|---|---|---|
| Acacia | *Robinia pseudacacia* | N. America | | 1640 |
| Alexandrian Laurel | *Danaë racemosa* | Iran area | | 1713 |
| Almond, single | *Prunus dulcis* | Asia | B | 1600 |
| Angelica Tree | *Aralia spinosa* | N America | | 1688 |

| POPULAR NAME | LATIN NAME | ORIGIN | | DATE |
|---|---|---|---|---|
| Arbutus | *Arbutus unedo* | Native | B | 1600 |
| Ash leaved Maple | *Acer negundo* | N. America | | 1688 |
| Bird Cherry, | | | | |
|     Virginian | *Prunus virginiana* | N. America | | 1729 |
| Bladder Nut, | *Staphylea pinnata* | Europe | B | 1600 |
| "   Three leaved | *Staphylea trifolia* | N. America | | 1640 |
| Bramble, Double | *Rubus fruticosus* | Native | | ? |
| Broom, Evergreen | *Cytisus hirsutus* | Europe | | 1739 |
| "     Lucca ? | *Cytisus or Genista* | Europe | | – |
| "     flowering | *Cytisus scoparius* Flore Pleno | Native | | ? |
| Buckthorn | *Rhamnus cathartica* | Native | B | 1600 |
| Candleberry Myrtle | *Myrica cerifera* | N. America | | 1699 |
| Catalpa | *Catalpa bignonioides* | N. America | | 1726 |
| Cedar of Lebanon | *Cedrus libani* | Mid East | | 1638 |
| Cephalanthus | *Cephalanthus occidentalis* | N. America | | 1735 |
| Chaste Tree | *Vitex agnus-castus* | Europe | B | 1600 |
| Cineraria, maritime | *Senecio cineraria* | Europe | | 1633 |
| Climbing Dogsbane | *Periploca graeca* | Mid. East | B | 1600 |
| Cornelian Cherry | *Cornus mas* | Europe | | " " |
| Currant | | | | |
|     Gooseberry leaved | *Rubus alpinum* | Native | | ? |
| Cypress, Upright | *Cyperus sempervirens* | Europe | B | 1600 |
| Cytisus, Evergreen | *Cytisus hirsutus* | Europe | | ? |
| Dogwood, Common | *Cornus sanguinea* | Native | B | 1600 |
| "    Carolina | *Cornus florida* | N. America | | 1729 |
| Double Flowering | | | | |
|     Cherry | *Prunus avium* Flore Pleno | Native | | ? |
| Flowering Ash | *Fraxinus ornus* | Europe | | 1697 |
| Germander | *Teucrium chamaedrys* | Native | B | 1600 |
| Gooseberry, | | | | |
|     Gt. American | *Ribes oxyacanthoides* | N. America | | 1705 |
| Groundsel Tree | *Baccharis halmifolia* | N. America | | 1633 |
| Hop Hornbeam | *Ostrya virginiana* | N. America | | 1692 |
| Hop Tree | *Ptilia trifoliata* | N. America | | 1704 |
| Jersey Pine | *Pinus inops* | N. America | | 1739 |
| Judas tree | *Cercis siliquastrum* | Europe | | 1756 |
| Lady Hardwick's | | | | |
|     Shrub | ? *Aronia arbutifolia* | N. America | | 1700 |
| Lignum Vitae Tree | *Guiacum officinale* | W Indies | | 1694 |
| Maple, Scarlet | *Acer rubrum* | N. America | | 1656 |
| Medlar | *Mespilus germanica* | Europe | B | 1600 |
| Mock orange, Syringa | *Philadelphus coronarius* | Europe | | " " |
| Myrtle | *Myrtus communis* | Europe | | " " |

| POPULAR NAME | LATIN NAME | ORIGIN | | DATE |
|---|---|---|---|---|
| Nettle Tree | *Celtis occidentalis* | N. America | | 1656 |
| Olive, Sweet Wild | *Olea europaea* | Europe | B | 1600 |
| Palma-Christi | *Ricinus communis* | Africa | | " " |
| Persian Jasmine | *Jasminum sambac* | Asia | | 1665 |
| Plane | *Platanus orientalis* | SE Europe | B | 1600 |
| Raspberry, American | *Rubus occidentalis* or | N. America | | 1696 |
| | " *strigosus* | N. America | | ? |
| " Sweet Smelling | *Rubus odoratus* | N. America | | 1700 |
| Red Cedar | *Juniperus virginiana* | N. America | | 1604 |
| Red Bird Cherry | *Prunus avium* or *padus* | | | |
| | var. *rubra* | Native | B | 1600 |
| St. Peter's Wort | *Symphoricarpus glomerata* | N. America | | 1730 |
| Sassafras | *Sassafras albidum* | N. America | | 1633 |
| Saugh, Sallow, | | | | |
| various | *Salix* spp. | Native | | ? |
| Sea Buckthorn | *Hippophae rhamnoides* | Native | B | 1600 |
| Sea Purslane | *Atriplex halinus* | Europe | | 1640 |
| Service Tree | *Sorbus torminalis* | Native | B | 1600 |
| South Sea Tea tree | *Ilex vomitoria* | N. America | | 1700 |
| Spicewood Tree | ? *Tarchonanthus camphoratus* | Africa | | 1690 |
| Spindle Tree, | | | | |
| Virginian | *Euonymus americana* | N. America | | 1683 |
| Spurge Laurel | *Daphne laureola* | Native | B | 1600 |
| Sumach, Venetian | *Rhus cotinus* | Europe | | 1656 |
| Gale Myrtle | *Myrica gale* | Native | B | 1600 |
| Tacamahac | *Populus balsamifera* | N. America | | 1692 |
| Tamarisk | *Tamarix gallica* | Europe | B | 1600 |
| Thorn, Glastonbury | *Crataegus monogyna praecox* | Native | | ? |
| Tulip Tree | *Liriodendron* | | | |
| | *tulipifera* | N. America | | 1638 |
| Virginian Vine | *Parthenocissus* | | | |
| | *quinquifolia* | N. America | | 1629 |
| Virginia Blackthorn | *Prunus americana* | N. America | | ? |
| Virginia Dogwood | *Cornus ammonum* | N. America | | 1683 |
| White Beam | *Sorbus aria* | Native | B | 1600 |
| Willow, Weeping | *Salix alba* var. *pendula* | ? Europe | | ? |
| Willows, Yellow, Dwarf | | | | |
| Striped etc | *Salix* spp. | Native | | ? |

There were two species of Clematis which were grown in the eighteenth century. The native *Clematis vitalba* owes its name of Traveller's Joy to Gerard who liked its cheerful presence in the hedgerows. The French, on the other hand, called it 'Herbe aux gueux' i.e. Beggar's plant, from the practice of Parisian beggars who applied the acid juice to induce sores, thereby invoking pity and hence alms. The other species, *C. viticella* (Figure 56) came from Europe before 1600. It was particularly favoured for covering arbors. Several legumes were popular in our period, none more so than Cytisus secundus, (*Cytisus sessiliflorus*), a deciduous Mediterranean species, which has quite lost its former popularity. Two of the others, referred to as the Evergreen Broom and Lucca Broom, pose a problem. The evergreen one is probably *Genista hirsutus*. We can infer from nursery catalogues that the Lucca Broom, which was a deciduous, fair sized species, was neither ordinary Spanish Broom, nor the White or Portugal Broom, (*C. multiflorus*). A possible candidate, like *Lygos monosperma*, appears rather tender to have grown in the garden of Cullen House in 1760. We may be dealing with an arbitrary nurseryman's name for a variety of one of the more familiar species and have to leave it at that for the time being. But there was no doubt about other very popular legumes such as *Colutea arborescens* (Figure 54), the Bladder Senna, with swollen fruits which pop when squeezed, and *Coronilla emerus* (Figure 48), the Scorpion Senna. They were called Senna because the leaves are purgative, although they are botanically unrelated to true Senna, (*Cassia*).

Hawthorn was grown in vast numbers for enclosing fields, but there were also varieties for the garden such as the Double Flowering Hawthorn and the Glastonbury thorn, (*Crataegus monogyna praecox*). The latter was reputedly derived from an old thorn tree growing near Glastonbury Abbey, traditionally regarded as the result of a miracle by Joseph of Arimathea, who, one Christmas Day, thrust his staff into the ground, whereupon it burst into leaf and flower. Apart from the legend this variety was highly regarded for its flowering in mid-winter, hence the name *praecox*. The hardy American *Crataegus crus-galli* (Figure 55), the Cockspur Thorn, introduced from eastern North America in 1694, is a small tree with scarlet autumn foliage and fruit which hangs throughout the winter.

Another popular shrub was Althaea Frutex, (*Hibiscus syriacus*) (Figure 46), which, in spite of its name, is native to India and China. It is a handsome plant with several colour forms. However the flowers come late in the season and fail to open in cool and wet weather, so it must have been hard pressed to realise its potential in Scottish gardens. *Prunus nana*, the Dwarf Almond, appears to have been first recorded growing in Sutherland's garden at Holyrood. Among the less familiar species was the Chaste Tree, (*Vitex agnus-castus*), from south west and central Asia, reported as in Britain since 1570. A deciduous, aromatic shrub it was regarded in ancient Greece as a symbol and promoter of chastity although Philip Miller thought its taste and smell more likely to promote lust. There were several species of *Teucrium* including Wall Germander, (*Teucrium chamaedrys*), introduced before 1600 and valued as a cure for gout. *Teucrium marum*, known as Marum or Cat Thyme because its aromatic foliage rivalled Nepeta in feline delight. *Periploca graeca*, Climbing Dogsbane (Figure 59), a twining climber from the Balkans and the near East, was grown in Britain since the sixteenth century but is now quite forgotten.

Among the American introductions the Balm of Gilead Fir (*Abies balsamea*) was an early, favourite tree for garden planting. Introduced from Canada at the end of the seventeenth century it eventually proved unsuccessful, especially as it grew older. Its evocative name refers to its aromatic resin known as Canada Balsam, used for optical mounts and familiar to biologists for fixing cover slips to microscope slides. The Ash Leaved Maple (*Acer negundo*), on the other hand, proved a great success and came to be widely grown. It is one of the species from which maple syrup can be prepared. *Cephalanthus* or Button Bush, introduced in 1735, is a native of eastern North America and Canada. A moderate sized shrub, it grows to six feet or more. According to Harvey (1972) Lady Hardwick's Shrub may be *Aronia arbutifolia*, otherwise known as the Red Chokeberry, another eastern American. The American Euonymus referred to in the accounts etc. is probably *Euonymys americana*, introduced in 1683, but one of the spcies which did not become established. *Parthenocissus quinquefolia* was the original Virginia Creeper which was recorded in Britain in 1629. It soon

FIGURE 46
Althaea Frutex (*Hibiscus syriacus*). In spite of its specific name this is a native of Iran and China. It was a regular item in Scottish shrub accounts in the eighteenth century, although it probably often led to disappointment since its late summer flowers, of different colour, fail to open in dull and misty weather.

became very popular although ultimately largely superseded by *P. tricuspidata* from China and Japan. The American species was classed in the genera *Hedera, Vitis* and *Ampelophila* before coming, we hope, to final rest in *Parthenocissus*. It proved too optimistic to expect it to grow in Scotland. The same was true of Sassafras which was also tried. More successful were the Tacmahac or Balsam Poplar and the Tulip Tree (Figure 61). Such American species were forerunners and part of the immense importation of seeds of different species which were eagerly planted with great expectation in many gardens. Some proved both hardy and garden worthy. Many more turned out to be tender or undistinguished and quietly petered out.

The species of trees included in the list are those planted for garden ornament. There were other border-line cases like the Sweet and Horse Chestnuts and the Walnut, which might serve that purpose, but often their seeds were sown in such numbers that their potential value as timber must have been the motive. Several conifers were regularly planted such as the European Cluster Pine (*Pinus pinaster*), the Norway Spruce (*Picea abies*), the Silver Fir (*Abies alba*), the New England Pine (*Pinus strobus*) and Arbor Vitae (*Thuja occidentalis*). The seedsmen also sold their clients seeds of the Mulberry (*Morus nigra*), which grows well enough in southern England but is generally unsuited to Scottish conditions, as well as – and even more optimistically – seeds of the Cork Tree (*Quercus suber*), which was introduced to Britain in 1699.

We can round off the record of ornamental species, other than roses, grown in Scotland from mid-seventeenth to mid-eighteenth century, with a comparison of where the diffferent classes of plant originated. This is set out in the accompanying Table in percentage terms. Some regions of minor importance have been grouped under single heads. Thus Asia includes China, India and the Middle East. South America includes Mexico and the West Indies. Occasional Asian species long cultivated in Europe, from where they were introduced, to Britain, have been classed as European.

OPPOSITE: FIGURE 47
Barberry (*Berberis vulgaris*) Occurs throughout most of Europe, but is probably not native to Britain although widely naturalised. It was formerly cultivated for the astrigent fruit which was either pickled and used for garnishing meat dishes, converted into a tasty jelly or candied. Apart from its culinary virtues various compounds were extracted from the dried bark for medicinal use.

FIGURE 48
Top, Cytisus (*Cytisus sesssiliflorus*).
Bottom, Scorpion Senna (*Coronilla emerus*).
Cytisus was introduced from Italy in the early seventeenth century. It was a popular border shrub, growing to two metres. The Scorpion Senna derived its name from the purgative properties of the leaves although *Cassia* is the source of the medicinal senna.

FIGURE 49
Dwarf Elder (*Sambucus ebulus*). This is widespread in Britain, especially in waste places and may be native. It grows as an aggressive, herbaceous shrub with creeping roots. Various parts of the plant have been used in herbal medicine for the relief of dropsy and as purgatives.

BOTTOM LEFT: FIGURE 50
Trumpet Honeysuckle (*Lonicers sempervirens*). This evergreen climber was introduced from North America in the mid-seventeenth century and was one of several species of honeysuckle grown in gardens.

BOTTOM RIGHT: FIGURE 51
Great Spanish Jasmine. (*Jasminum grandiflorum*). This is closely related to the Common Jasmine, or Jessamine, (*Jasminum officinale*) which extends from Iran to China. *J.grandiflorum* is sub-tropical in origin and is more tender than *officinale*. It was popular in Italy and Spain, hence its name.

FIGURE 52

Yellow Jasmine (*Jasminum humile*) left. Persian Lilac (*Syringa persica*) right. Although *J. humile* was commonly known as yellow Jasmine there was also the yellow *J. fruticans*, which arrived in Britain before 1600, whereas *J. humile*, from Asia, came in about half a century later. It was often grafted on *J. fruticans* stock. The Persian Lilac is a hybrid shrub of great antiquity. It has been suggested by Curtis (1992) that it may be recognised as far back as 800 AD. It probably reached Europe early in the seventeenth century.

OPPOSITE: FIGURE 53

Laurustinus (*Viburnum tinus*). This Mediterranean shrub was very popular in our period of interest. It was first classed incorrectly as a kind of laurel. Sometimes it was grown in pots for indoor decoration.

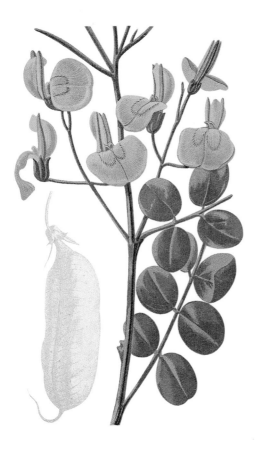

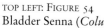

TOP LEFT: FIGURE 54
Bladder Senna (*Colutea arborescens*). From south east Europe and long cultivated it has inflated fruits which pop when squeezed. Like Coronilla, the leaves are also purgative, hence the name.

TOP RIGHT: FIGURE 55
Cockspur Thorn (*Crataegus crus-galli*). This hardy American species with the prominent thorns retains its fruits during winter.

FIGURE 56
Virgin's Bower (*Clematis viticella*). This clematis from Italy eastwards has been grown in Britain since the sixteenth century. The fragrant flowers are blue or purple. It has been used in hybridisation to produce many garden varieties.

FIGURE 57
Candleberry Myrtle (*Myrica cerifera*). This shrub was one of the earlier introductions from North America. Fat extracted from the berries, often mixed with tallow, was used to make candles. The candles were reputed to burn without smoking and give rise to a pleasant, aromatic scent.

BOTTOM LEFT: FIGURE 58
Carolina Dogwood (*Cornus florida*). This was introduced from eastern North America where it usually grows to three to five metres, rarely twice as high. The four large, white bracts account for its spring beauty.

BOTTOM RIGHT: FIGURE 59
Climbing Dogsbane (*Periploca graeca*). This attractive and easily grown climber from the Middle-east was once well known to gardeners but has been quite forgotten. It is not clear just why dogs abhor it. A related species from India was used medicinally.

LEFT: Figure 60
Cornelian Cherry (*Cornus mas*). This central and southern European shrub, with the remarkably hard wood, was formerly grown for the handsome, edible fruit which was eaten fresh or candied. It fell out of culinary favour by the late nineteenth century but its early flowers, before the leaves appear, secured it a place in the garden.

RIGHT: Figure 61
Tulip tree (*Liriodendron tulipifera*). A member of the Magnolia family, this was one of the early (c1650) introductions from North America. Hardy and quick growing it makes a substantial tree in milder parts of the country, with attractive autumn foliage.

**TABLE 7. Origins of Ornamental Plants Expressed as Percentages**

| | NATIVE | EUROPE | ASIA | AMERICA | | AFRICA |
| | | | | South | North | |
| --- | --- | --- | --- | --- | --- | --- |
| Annuals & Biennials | 10.9 | 50.0 | 20.3 | 14.1 | 3.1 | 1.6 |
| Herbaceous Perennials | 32.4 | 51.0 | 2.9 | 0.0 | 11.8 | 2.0 |
| Bulbs etc. | 13.5 | 64.9 | 16.2 | 2.7 | 0.0 | 2.7 |
| Shrubs | | | | | | |
| Frequent | 32.8 | 48.4 | 9.4 | 0.0 | 9.4 | 0.0 |
| Less Frequent | 24.3 | 24.3 | 8.1 | 1.4 | 37.8 | 4.1 |

It is particularly worth noting:

(i) The overwhelming importance of Europe as a source of garden plants of all kinds for the period concerned. There is remarkable consistency in the relative European contribution for annuals and biennials, herbaceous perennials, bulbs etc and the more commonly grown shrubs.

(ii) For annuals and biennials native species were out-numbered by introductions from both South America and Asia.

(iii) There were no South American plants among the herbaceous perennials but about a tenth of them came from North America.

(iv) For the less frequently grown shrubs, the North American contribution exceeded the proportion of shrubs derived from Europe or elsewhere.

## Roses

A reliable appreciation of what might be expected in Scottish gardens can be derived from the list of roses in Sutherland's Physic Garden in 1683 and the gardener's inventory of roses in Cullen House Garden in 1760. In Table 8 the different sorts are grouped according to their supposed affinity with the major types, recognising that the latter are usually not species but the product of complex hybridisation. In the Cullen House collection the varieties preceded by an asterisk were grown in large numbers, the rest, only as single gardeners. The spelling is that used by the gardeners.

In addition to the varieties listed, Sutherland also grew *Rosa canina* with red or white flowers, a variety without prickles, an unidentified rose he called *R. crystallina* and another he listed as 'an undescribed tree rose'. Allowing for some variation in common names the two lists are very similar. This comparison clearly illustrates the lack of change in the garden rose flora during the seventeenth and much of the eighteenth century, until the introductions from China revolutionised the scene. The collection of roses at Cullen House was entirely representative of its period. The particular favourites, grown in large nunbers, included the White, Scarlet, Monthly, Cinnamon and Centifolia roses.

**Table 8. Roses grown in Edinburgh Physic Garden (1683) and at Cullen House (1760)**

| IDENTITY | EDINBURGH PHYSIC GARDEN | CULLEN HOUSE |
|---|---|---|
| *X alba* | Common English White | * White |
| | Greater White | – |
| | Lesser White | – |
| *X alba incarnata* | Carnation or Blush | Maiden's Blush |
| | – | Virgin's Blush |
| *alba X canina* | Blush Belgick | Blush Belgick |
| *X centifolia* | Red Province | * Centifolium |
| | – | Hundred leav'd |
| | – | Dutch |
| | Great Double Damask Province | – |
| *X centifolia muscosa* | – | Moss Province |
| *X damascena* | Common Damask | – |
| | Red Belgick | – |
| | Elegant variegated Damask | – |
| *damascena versicolor* | York and Lancaster | York and Lancaster |
| *foetida* | Single Yellow | Single Yellow |
| *foetida bicolor* | Vermilion Rose of Austria | Austrian |
| *gallica* | Red rose | * Scarlet rose |
| | Double Velvet | Double Velvet |
| | – | Single Velvet |
| *gallica conditorum* | Hungarian | – |
| *gallica versicolor* | Rosa Mundi | Rosa Mundi |
| *gallica X moschata* | Monthly | * Monthly |
| *gallica X majalis* | Frankford | Frankfort |
| *hemisphaerica* | Double Yellow | Double Yellow |

| IDENTITY | EDINBURGH PHYSIC GARDEN | CULLEN HOUSE |
|---|---|---|
| *majalis* | Single Cinnamon<br>Double   " " | ⁕ Cinnamon |
| *moschata* | Single<br>Double      " "<br>Spanish    " " | Musk<br>–<br>– |
| *pimpinellifolia* | Pimpinel<br>Lesser Scottish Burnet | Scots, white, red<br>– |
| *pomifera* | Great Apple | Apple bearing |
| *rubiginosa* | Single Sweet Briar<br>Double Sweet Briar | Sweet Briar<br>Double Sweet Briar |
| *sempervirens* | – | Evergreen |
| *virginiana* | Rose with shining leaves | Early White Virginian |

⁕Asterisks indicate varieties grown in large numbers at Cullen House.

FIGURE 62
White Rose (*Rosa X alba*). Of great antiquity, and cultivated by the Romans, the White Rose is of hybrid origin. Whether this rose or *R. arvensis* was the White Rose of York is open to doubt. *R alba* is believed to have been the one chosen as an emblem by the Jacobites.

FIGURE 63
Maiden's Blush (*Rosa alba incarnata*). One of the many varieties of *R. X alba*).

Blush Belgic. This is believed to be a hybrid between *R. X alba* and *R. canina*.

Hundred Leaved Rose, Provence Rose (*Rosa X centifolia*). This famous rose is the product of complex hybridisation in which the species *gallica, phoenicia, moschata* and *canina* have contributed to its genetic make-up. It appears to have been first recognised in the latter part of the sixteenth century and was often called the Provence Rose. This led to much confusion in the literature with the much older Provins Rose (*R.gallica*).

FIGURE 66
Moss Rose (*Rosa centifolia muscosa*). This is a sport of *R. centifolia* with dense, glandular hairs distributed over the sepals, flower stems and sometimes the leaflets. Such a 'mossy' condition is not confined to *centifolia*.

FIGURE 67
York and Lancaster (*Rosa damascena versicolor*).
The Damascene Rose, of great antiquity, is of eastern origin and was probably introduced to Europe
via Egypt. The origin of the form with white, pink
or white and pink petals is obscure. It is often
confused with the Rosa Mundi of *R. gallica*.

BOTTOM LEFT: FIGURE 68
The Austrian or Vermilion Rose of Austria (*Rosa
foetida bicolor*). right. *R. foetida* is an old rose of
Asian origin, believed to have been brought to
Spain by the Moors. It was grown by Gerard.
The double form is illustrated. The Austrian Rose
is a sport of *R. foetida*; the flowers vary in colour
and are sometimes yellow.

BOTTOM RIGHT: FIGURE 69
Provins, Red or Scarlet Rose (*Rosa gallica*). Long
known and widespread throughout Europe and
beyond, this was valued for its perfume and
medical uses. It was regularly grown in monasteries
and, since there were well over thirty thousand of
them distributed throughout Europe, its ubiquity
is hardly surprising. It was grown commercially in
the district of Provins, France, hence its name and
the consequent confusion with the Provence Rose
(*R. X centifolia*).

LEFT: FIGURE 70
Rosa Mundi (*Rosa gallica versicolor*). Believed to be a sport of *R. gallica*, this was first described by L'Obel in 1581. The name has been linked, probably erroneously, with Fair Rosamond, mistress of Henry 11 of England.

BELOW: FIGURE 71
Musk Rose (*Rosa moschata*) left. Monthly Rose right. The Musk Rose is a fragrant climber of great antiquity and eastern origin. The Monthly Rose has been regarded as a hybrid between *R. moschata* and *R. gallica*. It owes its name to the production of a second, although not prolific, blooming later in the season.

## Some examples of source material

Although the lists of species which were to be found in the gardens of a particular period comprise the basic evidence about the gardening scene, they may seem a little arid unless supplemented with some human interest. To redress the balance, we have included a few examples of the kind of source material used in the compilation of species. The use of the old names and manner of presentation evoke the flavour of the times and illustrate the recurring problem of identification.

### (i) *The Earl of Morton's Account*

We start with the 'Accompt of the Earl of Morton to Mr. J.A. Sutherland Master of the Physic Garden at Edinburgh August 1691'. The collection, mostly of shrubs, was destined for the terraced gardens at Aberdour Castle. The account has been rearranged to show the price per item in Scots money, the number of plants and Sutherland's names for them. Where necessary, identification or comment has been added. The account is as follows:

| L. | s. | d. | |
|----|----|----|---|
| 1 | 10 | 0 | for 3 great wall plumes |
| 1 | 10 | 0 | to 3 best wall cherries |
| 1 | 4 | 0 | 2 Double yellow rosses – probably *Rosa hemisphaerica* which was first brought to England in 1622 |
| | 14 | 0 | 2 Scorpion – *Coronilla emerus* |
| | 16 | 0 | 2 Rid beried elder – *Sambucus racemosa* |
| | 16 | 0 | 2 Elders with whyt beries – *Sambucus nigra* var. alba |
| | 16 | 0 | 2 Cut leaved elder – *Sambucus nigra* var. laciniata, mentioned by Gerard |
| 1 | 0 | 0 | 2 Rosse elders – *Viburnum opulus* |
| 1 | 0 | 0 | 2 Shirub dwarf elder with fyne particulred lives – a form of *Sambucus ebulus* |
| 1 | 14 | 0 | 2 French tamerisks |
| 1 | 0 | 0 | 2 Figg apples ? |
| 1 | 4 | 0 | 2 Three leived Bleder nut of virginia – *Staphylea trifolia* |
| 1 | 4 | 0 | 2 Great scarlet American goussberies – *Ribes hirtellum* also known as *oxyacanthoides* |
| 1 | 0 | 0 | 2 Dwarf Medlars – *Mespilus germanica* |
| 1 | 0 | 0 | 2 Sweet American Raspes – uncertain, possibly *Rubus occidentalis*, if so, a very early record |
| 1 | 0 | 0 | 2 Mecerons – *Daphne mezereon* |
| 1 | 4 | 0 | 2 Five Lived Ivies of Virginia – *Parthenocissus quinquefolia* |
| 1 | 8 | 0 | 2 Persian Jasmine with cut leavs – probably *Jasminum sambac* |
| 1 | 0 | 0 | 2 Shrub Trefoli – *Cytisus sessiliflorus* |

OPPOSITE: FIGURE 72 Sulphur Rose (*Rosa hemisphaerica*). First recorded in India in 1503, it is a vigorous shrub whose flowers often fail to open in cooler climates.

| L. | s. | d. | |
|---|---|---|---|
| | 16 | 0 | 2 Broad lived Barbery of candar – probably a form of *Berberis vulgaris*. Loudon gives 1759 for ealiest date of introduction of a foreign species (*canadensis*) |
| 1 | 0 | 0 | 2 Silver coulred pyp trie – *Syringa vulgaris* |
| | 18 | 0 | 2 Upright thrie leive Ivie of Virginia – possibly a form of *Parthenocissus quinquefolia* |
| | 12 | 0 | 2 Whyt figes |
| 1 | 4 | 0 | 2 Yellow Jasmein – either *Jasminum humile* or *J. fruticans* |
| – | – | – | 2 Bukhan tries – uncertain, but old Scots name for beech tree was 'Buck tree' so this entry may refer to beech trees; there was no charge so they were very common items, consistent with this interpretation. |
| 1 | 4 | 0 | 2 Virginia spindle tries – probably *Euonymus americanus* |
| 1 | 16 | 0 | 2 Dwarf Almonds – probably *Prunus nana* which, according to Aiton (1789), was introduced by Sutherland |
| 1 | 8 | 0 | 2 Mok Willows – *Spiraea salicifolia* |
| | 10 | 0 | 2 Biter Sweit with whyt flurs – *Solanum dulcamara*, a rare form with white flowers |
| 1 | 0 | 0 | 2 Tries of shirub sinquefoils – *Potentilla fruticosa* |
| | 8 | 0 | 2 Bleder nutes – *Staphylea pinnata*, a native of Central Europe, long naturalised but rare in S. England |
| 1 | 8 | 0 | 2 Virginia shirub with Curan Leivs – ? *Ribes sanguineum* was not introduced until much later |
| 1 | 4 | 0 | 2 Double floured Cherries – *Prunus avium*, flore pleno |
| 1 | 4 | 0 | 2 Tries of Saint Johneswort – probably *Hypericum hircinum* |
| 1 | 0 | 0 | 2 Bla berie upright huniesucle – *Lonicera coerulea* |
| 1 | 0 | 0 | 2 Red berie upright huniesucle – *Lonicera alpigena* |
| 1 | 4 | 0 | 2 Deip purple flourd lilacs – *Syringa vulgaris* var. purpurea, later known as the Scotch lilac |
| 1 | 16 | 0 | 2 Single whyt pyp trie – *Syringa vulgaris* |
| 1 | 4 | 0 | 2 Sweet wyld olive – *Oleo europaea* or its wild progenitor *O. oleaster*, a surprising item for Scotland |
| 1 | 0 | 0 | 2 Whyt Beam tries |
| | 12 | 0 | 2 Spindle trees – *Euonymus europaeus* |
| | 8 | 0 | 2 Curan with Gousseberie leives – *Ribes alpinum* |
| 1 | 0 | 0 | 2 Red bird Chiries – *Prunus padus or P. avium* var. rubra |
| 1 | 4 | 0 | 2 Climbing dogs ban – *Periploca graeca* |
| 1 | 0 | 0 | 1 Robinns trie Acacia of America – *Robinia pseudoacacia* – the most expensive item |

(ii) *A Hypothetical Design*

The next example is both different and valuable in identifying the most popular bedding plants of the period.It occurs in correspondence between Lord Grange, brother of the Earl of Mar, and the latter's gardener at Alloa. In a discursive letter to the gardener, dated Oct. 20th, 1711, in the course of which he proclaimed: 'there is no Diversion or recreation upon earth that pleases me more than to wander in a compleat garden, wher flowers and herbes water trees and shrubs combine to make a little paradise...' However, to achieve such perfection it is necessary to arrange the plants, according to their season of flowering and their height of growth, in a manner which displays them all to best advantage, none concealing the other. He entreated the gardener to bend his mind to such a scheme and construct an appropriate plan, signing himself 'Your sincere well wisher and assured freend'. The gardener replied on Feb 11th 1714, apologising for the long delay which he attributed to his want of education, although we can surmise there were other reasons. He referred to his Lordship's request for a plan of a border with equally spaced plants, none of which concealed the other, with mild disbelief. 'I must say it is the first of that kind of Gardinerie that ever I was employed about and my Loss is I never saw it in print...' However, he enclosed a plan (Figure 76) of repeating symmetry which consists of nine rows of plants arranged on a convex bed. The middle row is made up of a repeating sequence of the tallest six species. Four rows of progressively smaller plants occur symmetrically on either side of the middle row, except that the third row is represented by tulips of different colour, which are replaced by annuals when they have faded. In each row the sequence of six different species is repeated. The plants in this scheme are as follows:

| *Single Middle Row* | *First of the parallel Rows* |
|---|---|
| White lilie | Narcisus |
| Martagen lilie | Fridelariae |
| Queen's Julyflour | Dafodill |
| Orange lillie | Junckquiles |
| Imperial | Crown Molies |
| Great Star of Bethlehem | Anemones |

| *Second of the parallel Rows* | *Third Row* | *Fourth of the parallel Rows* |
|---|---|---|
| Adonis flower | Tulips | Noble Liverwort |
| Africa Marygold | | White Jasinths |
| Larks Heale | | Double primros |
| Venus Looking- glass | | Blew jasinths |
| Botles of all colours | | Boars-ears |
| French Hunisucle | | Corocuses |
| French Marygold | | |

The chief interest of this list lies in the collection of plants deemed indispensable for an effective border at the beginning of the eighteenth century.

(iii) *Heriot's Hospital Garden*

From about 1720, the original is undated, we have 'A catalogue of flours given by James Stevenson late Gairdner to herriots hospitall for furnishing the threttie two little borders of addition which the said James Stevenson made to the said Gairden.

> Impri. One Thousand double Narsses of severall kinds
> Item One hundred settis of Snow drops
> Item One hundred crocoses
> Item Sixte orange Lillies
> Item One hundred red Martagons of Costantinople
> Item One hundred Gladelases
> Item Threttie fretelasaes
> Item Two hundred plaine coloured Tulips
> Item Threttie Bulbuserios of the small blue
> Item Two hundred of the plan coloured Auricoless
> Item Threttie whyt Lillies
> Item Sixte Settey of double Julieflour

> All the above floures are to be delivered by the above James Stevenson beside two Thousand double Spinks which are planted already in two edges of the wilderness for the decoruien of the same'.

The spelling is idiosyncratic and the script is not without difficulty but the meaning is clear enough. The small blue bulbous plants are taken to be Muscari sp. 'Sett' was the Scots for a young plant ready for transplanting. 'Spink' was the old name for the Polyanthus.

(iv) *Plants for Lord Justice Clerk*

A little later, about 1729, we have from the Saltoun papers a list of plants for Lord Justice Clerk 'to be planted at once or be spoiled'. They are as follows:

> 2 Cristmas flower – *Helleborus niger*
> 4 Autumn narcissus – *Narcissus serotinus*
> 2 Indian Colchicums – *Colchicum byzantium*
> 2 Late flowering Colchicums – *Colchicum autumnale*
> 1 Stript flag Iris – Iris uncertain but quite likely a form of *I.pallida*
> 20 Snowdrops
> 4 Hepaticas
> 4 Double saxifrage – *Saxifraga rotundifolia* ?
> 20 Daisies

6 Winter Aconites

2 Starflowers – Aster sp.

4 Gentianellas – *Gentiana acaulis*

2 Great lemon time – *Thymus X citriodorus*

2 Small leaved time – Possibly a form *of Thymus serpyllum.*

6 White March Violet – *Viola odorata*

2 Sweet Indian Scabious – *Scabiosa atropurpurea*

2 Aescyron or great flowered Peterswort – Probably *Hypericum tetrapterum*

Yellow perennial panzie – *Viola lutea*

1 Cyclamen – ? *C. coum*

Stript Perriwinkl – *Vinca minor*, a variegated form

(v) *Flowers for my Lady*

Our fifth example consists of the list of annual flower seeds sent in 1751 by the Edinburgh seedsman Patrick Drummond to Lady Drummond of Blair Drummond. The amount of seed ordered is generally given in drops, a drop being 1/16 of an ounce. For one or two species with heavy seeds the order refers to ounces.

The order is as follows:-

Drops Seeds

| | |
|---|---|
| 1 | 10 Week Stock Jullyflowers – *Matthiolaa incana* |
| 4 | Double larksheel – *Consolida regalis* |
| 6 | Nigella romana – *Nigella damascena* |
| 4 | Purple Candytuft – *Iberis umbellata* |
| 2 | Blue Convolvulus Major – *Ipomoea purpurea* |
| 1 | Scarlet Convolvulus – probably red form of *I. purpurea* |
| 2 | Giant poppy – *Papaver somniferum* |
| 4 | Small blue lupines – *Lupinus varius* |
| 4 | Scarlet lupines -? *Vicia sativa* var. fulgens |
| 1 | Matted Pinks – *Dianthus gratianopolitanus* |
| 2 | Indian Pinks – Uncertain, possibly a form of *Dianthus plumarius* or *chinensis* |
| 3 oz | Scarlet flowering bean – *Phaseolus coccineus* |
| 1 oz | White Sweet scented pease – *Lathyrus odoratus* |
| 1 | Sweet scented Marygold – a scented African marygold, long lost |
| 1 | Chinese Aster – *Callistephus chinensis* |
| 1 | Lobels Catchfly – *Silene armeria* |
| 6 roots | Italian Tuberose – *Tuberosa polianthes* |
| 4 oz | Painted lady pease – *Lathyrus odoratus*, a pink and white form |
| 1 | China aster, a repeat |
| 2 | Queens Stocks – *Hesperis matronalis* |
| 4 | Flos Adonis – *Adonis annua* |

| | |
|---|---|
| 4 | White Candytuft – *Iberis umbellata* |
| 1 | Venus Looking Glass – *Specularia speculum* |
| 1 | Scarlet Cornflower – probably *Centaurea cyanus* |
| 2 | Carnation poppy – *Papaver somniferum*, double flowered |
| 2 | Everlasting Pease – *Lathyrus latifolius* |
| 6 | Great Blue Lupines – *Lupinus hirsutus* |
| 6 | Great Yellow Lupines – *Lupinus luteus* |
| 2 | English Carnation – *Dianthus caryophyllus* |
| 1 | Pheasant Eyed Pink – *Dianthus plumarius* |
| 4 oz | Painted Lady Pease – a repeat, evidently a favourite |
| 2 | African marygold – *Tagetes erecta* |
| 2 | French Marygold – *Tagetes patula* |
| 2 | Lavatera – *Lavatera trimestris* |
| 2 | Female Balson – *Impatiens balsamina* |
| 4 | Rose Lupines – *Lupinus pilosus* |

(vi) *An Early Record of Planting*

It is a rare event to come across an early record of exactly what plants were set out in garden borders. Just such information exists for the mixed borders of the well stocked garden of Cullen House for 1760. A few examples will illustrate what the borders looked like as the gardener listed the herbaceous perennials and shrubs in order, starting at one end of a border and proceeding to the other. This kind of information is invaluable for the reconstruction of old gardens. The examples are quoted exactly as the gardener recorded them, with the variable spelling of that era, except that commas are inserted between the names for easier reading. They are as follows:

a) In the north border of the rose garden are 3 Scots roses, 1 double sweet Briar, Matted pinks, Lissimachias, different kinds of auricolos, single Carnations, sweet Williams, Columbines, Rose Campions, french Honeysuckle, primrose trees, Golden rods, Linaria or todsflax, 1 Bush clove July flowers at the upper corner, 2 bushes assyrian Baum, 2 double whyte Campanulas, Tulips, narcissas, Crocus, fretellarys, Dog tooth violet.

b) On the west border of the east wall, beginning at the north end, first row is an edging of auricolas of different kinds, second row is Crocus, Hypaticas, Jonquills, winter aconite, great star of Bethelem, Third row is Campanulas, sweet Williams, perennial poppy, piramid Campanula, Veronica, fraxinellas, Virgins Bower, Bulbous rooted Iris, double Rocket, single Rocket, Faery Speederwort, Gold Knop, purple peonies, scarlet Lichness, great blue Gentian, Tulips, autumnal Ciclamen, fourth row is Rose Campions, Narcissus, sweet Williams – Shrubs in sd border portugal Laurel, early wild virginia Rose, applebearing Rose, Evergreen rose, Rosa Mundi, scorpion Senna, Tutson of Constantinope, venetian Summack,

Lady Hardwaks shrub, hypericum, ever lasting red poppy, single yellow roman flowering sage, mountain sage, whyte Scots rose, red Scots rose, Broad Leaff'd Hypericum.

c) On the border of the north wall next the Gravel walk, beginning at the west syde – an Edge of Pinks, a Row of Heppaticas, 1 miserion, 1 monethly rose, 3 whyte roses & 3 scarlet Roses, Rose campions, whyte Lillys, Campanulas, stock Jullyflowers, sweet Williams, pinks, four Hollyhocks, Colchicums, one Ew, blue bulbs or Jaccinths, Junquls, Narcissus, Scarlet Lichness, Columbines, sweet Williams,, 4 more Scarlet Roses, Batchelors Buttons, Colchicums, Junquils, polianthus's.

FIGURE 73
Apple, Apple bearing Rose (*Rosa pomifera*) left, Burnet, Scotch or Pimpernel Rose (*Rosa pimpinellifolia*) right. The Apple Rose seems to have been grown chiefly for its large, globose, prickly hips. The Burnet Rose is a native species, most frequent on dry, coastal sites. Its white flowers are succeeded by dark purple hips. It was the starting point for the production of a great variety of Scots roses during the nineteenth century, especially by Robert Austin of Glasgow. At the peak of their popularity there were nearly three hundred named varieties.

OPPOSITE: FIGURE 74
Sweet Briar (*Rosa rubiginosa*). This is a native species with a preference for calcareous soils. It has been grown in Britain since time immemorial. It was frequently used as a hedge in the eighteenth century. The double form, shown here, was described by Parkinson.

TOP: FIGURE 75
The Virginian Rose (*Rosa virginiana*). This glossy leaved rose from eastern North America arrived in England in the early eighteenth century and was the first American rose to be grown in Europe where it became very popular. It has become widely naturalised.

BOTTOM: FIGURE 76
Hypothetical plan of a flower border designed by the Earl of Mar's gardener in 1708. This was in response to an appeal by the Earl's brother, Lord Grange, to produce a scheme which displayed all the plants to their best advantage. Its particular interest lies in the list of plants which were considered essential for the border at that time.

White lilies marked ——— o
Martagen. marked ——— δ
Queens-Juliflower. ———
Orange lilies. ——— ŏ
Imperiale-croun. ——— ‡
Great star of Bethlehem ——— ‡

Narsifus ———
Afrideloriae ———— b
Dafodils ———— c
Junchquils ——— d
Mollies ——— e
Anemonies ——— f

Tulips marked ............
Noble liberwood ———— ‚
White Jasinths ——— ₂
Double primros ——— ₃
Blew Jasinths ——— ₄
Boars-ears ——— ‚
Corocuses ——— 6

Adonis flower ———
Africa marigold ———
Larks Heell ——— r
Venus looking-glass ——— ⊥
Bolts of all colours ——— τ
French Hunisuclo ——— z
French marigold ——— ℵ

A Scale of feet.

130

*A Catalogue of New Garden Seeds to be Sold*

1681

By

M. Henry Fergussone at Blackfrier's wynd head

| **For Root seed** | **P H S** | **F S** | **Pease** |
|---|---|---|---|
| Strasburgh Onion | Succory | Branch'd Sunflower | Hotspur Pease |
| French Onion | Borage | Coventrie Bells | Hasting Pease |
| Red Spanish Onion | Double Marygold | Fox tail | Grey Rounnival pease |
| White Spanish Onion | Pot Marjerom | Iron-colour Foxglove | White Rounnival peas |
| French Leek | Summer Satorie | Nigella Romana | Blue Rounnival pease |
| Orange Carrot | | Amaranthus purpureus | Green Rounnival pease |
| Smooth Pasneep | **S H S** | Thorne Apple | Maple Rounnival pease |
| Round Turnep | Thyme | Double poppie strip | Sugar Pease |
| Yellow Turnep | Winter Sabory | Double Hollihork | Kidney Beans |
| Skirret | Sweet Marjerom | Convolvulus major | Turkie Beans |
| Scorzonera | Sweet Basil | Convolvulus minor | |
| Shallots | Rosemary | Bottles of all colours | |
| | | Blue Lupins | |
| **S S** | **D S** | Yellow Lupins | also |
| Sandwirk Radish | | White Lupins | Garden Spaces |
| Black Spanish Radish | Cardus Benedictus | Scarlet Beans | to be sold |
| French Radish | Scurvy grass | | |
| Cabbage Lettuce | Best Tobacco | Everlasting pease | |
| Roman Lettuce | Dill | Snails & Caterpilars | |
| Lumbard Lettuce | Sweet Fennel | Horns & Hedghogs | |
| Curl'd Lettuce | Cumin | | |
| Round Spinnadge | Anise | **S of T & S S** | |
| Prickly Spinnadge | Coriander | | |
| White Beet | Fænugreek | Cypress | |
| Red Beet | Wormseed | Firs | |
| Curl'd Endive | | Silver firr | |
| Italian Seleree | **F S** | Great Pine | |
| Corket | | Phyllarea vera | |
| French Sorrell | Double July-flower | Alaternus | |
| French Crosses | Clove July-flower | Pyrarantha | |
| Curl'd Crosses | Queens Gilloflower | Horn beam | |
| Round leafd Crosses | Mated Pink | Laurus tinus | |
| Sweet Chervill | Columbine | Cedar berries | |
| Purslane | Double Lark's-heel | Laurell Berries | |
| Golden Purslane | Rose Lark's heel | Yew berries | |
| Parsley | African Marygold | Spanish Broom | |
| Curl'd Parsley | Snapdragon | | |
| Asparagus | Candy Tuft | | |
| English Collyflower | Sweet Scabious | | |
| French Collyflower | Spanish Scabious | | |
| White Cabbage | White bonus looking glass | Lyme Tree | |
| Red Cabbage | White French hony Sukles | | |
| Dutch Savoy | Scarlet Lychnis | Clover-grass | |
| Melons | Marvel of Peru | | |
| Long Cucumber | Nasturtium Indicum | | |
| Short Cucumber | White Valerian | | |
| Pompion | | | |
| Gourd | | | |
| Melon | | | |

*(vii) Henry Ferguson's Broadsheet*

The early seedsmen in Edinburgh advertised their wares in the form of a single broadsheet. Henry Fergus(s)on – the extra 's' appears to have been optional – was, on present evidence, the first to do so. His first catalogue is illustrated in Figure 77. It has a great deal in common with that of the London seedsman, William Lucas (Harvey 1972), and Ferguson may have got his seeds from Lucas. Nevertheless, in its Scottish context, this list is of historical significance. Ferguson's business thrived and by 1691 he was issuing a more ambitious catalogue containing a greater variety of items for sale. The contents of this later catalogue are as follows:

A CATALOGUE of new GARDEN SEEDS
to be sold by MR HENRY FERGUSSON
A little above the head of Black-Friers Wynd, Edinburgh.

*Seeds of Sallads and Roots*

| | |
|---|---|
| Strasburgh Onion | Short Cucumber |
| Spanish      " | Long Cucumber |
| French      " | Pompion |
| French leek | Gourd |
| Orange Carrot | Mekin |
| Yellow Carrot | Corn Sallad |
| Smooth Parsneep | Spanish Cardon |
| Round Turneep | |
| Yellow Turneep | P.H.S. |
| Skirret | Endive |
| Scorzonera | Succory |
| Shallot | Borage |
| Radish | Bugloss |
| Black Spanish | Clary |
| White Spanish | Marygold |
| Cabbage Lettuce | Pot Marjerom |
| Curl'd Lettuce | Summer Savory |
| Lumbard Lettuce | Columbine |
| Arabian Lettuce | Orach |
| Savoy Lettuce | |
| Roman Lttuce | S.H.S. |
| Rose Lettuce | |
| Smothe Spinage | Thyme |
| White Beet | Hyssop |
| Beet-Rave Beet Card | Winter Savory |
| Curl'd Endive | Seet Marjerom |
| Indian Seleree | Sweet Basil |
| True Garden Rocket | Rosemary |

Sampier

Indian Cresses

French Sorrel

Candy Sorrel

Round Sorrel

Garden-Cresses

Curl'd Cresses

Sweet Chervil

Pursline

Parsley

Dutch Aspargus

Coly-flower

Red and White Cabbage

Dutch Savoy

Colewort of
  several kinds

Musk Melon

Spanish Melon

Lavender

Baum


Phy. S.

Carduus Benedictus

Scurvy-Gras

Angelica

Virginia Tobacco

Lovage

Smallage

Dill

Sweet Fennel

Cumin

Rue

Anise

Coriander

Fenugreek

Worm-Seed

Caruway

Gromer

Garden Rhubarb

*Seeds of Flowers, and other choice Plants*

Double July-flower

Clove July Flower

Stock Gillo-flower

Rose Lark's-heel

Queen's Gillo-flower

Matted Pink

Double Columbine

Double Lark's heel

African Marygold

French Marygold

Snap Dragon

Candy Tuft

Indian Scabious

Spanish Scabious

Guiny Pepper

White Venus Looking-Glass

French Honeysuckle

Non-such or flower of
  Bristol

Marvel of Peru

One grain'd Gold of Pleasure

True Woad

Thorow Eax

Yellow Mothmullen

Fine party coloured Hairy
  Campion

Sweet Oak of Jerusalem

Bucklers Mustard

English Tobacco

Great Hart-wort of Pelopenusus

Narrow leav'd spiked Madder

Macedonian Parsly

True great Century

Sweet Sage of Candy

Mithridate Mustard

True Treacle Mustard

Starry Hawkweed

Childing Pink

Great red flower'd Annual-
  Pease of Tngier

Sweet Sultan
Nasturtum Indicum
White Valerian
Branch'd Sunflower
Coventry Bells
Velvedere
Fox tail

Iron colour'd Foxglove
White flower'd Foxglove
Noli me tangere
Nigella Romana
Amaranthus Purpureus
Amaranthus tricolor
Love-Apple
Double Poppy strip'd
Thorn Apple
Double Holyhook
Lobel's catch-flie
Spanish Mollow-tree
Convolvulus Major
Convolvulus Minor
Sea Tree Mallow
Small Sweet Smelling Melilot
Shepherd's needle of Candy
Purple leav'd clary of Candy
Small Snees wort of Austria
Garden Gold of Pleasure

White Flowered Sage of Candy
Night Flowering Campion
Bladder bearing Indian Sorrel
Aethiopian clary
Swelling Collewort
Mountain Siler
Hartwort of Aethiopia
Great blue Lupins
Small blue Lupins
White Lupins
Yellow Lupins
Scarlet Beans
Everlasting pease
Snails and Caterpillars
Horns and Hedghogs
Palma Christi
Humble Plant
Sensitive Plant
With several others

*Seeds of Ever greens, and other choice Trees*

Cypress
Silver Fir
Pitch tree
Great Pine
Pinaster
Phillyrea vera
Pyracantha
Horn-beam
Alaternus
Laurus-Tinus
Laurel Berries
Cedar Berries
Bay-Berries
Yew-Berries

Sorts of Pease, beans etc.

Hasting Pease
Sandwich Hot-spurs
Barns Hot-spurs
Sugar Pease
Rose pease
Egg pease
Wing pease
Blue Rouncival
Grey Rouncival
White Rouncival
Green Rouncival
Maple Rouncival

Great Juniper-Berries
Myrtle-Berries
Lyme-tree seed
Althea Frutex
Spanish Broom
Amomum plinii
Mezereon berries
Horse Chesnut
With several others

Turky-Beans
Kidney-Beans
Hot-spur Beans

Seeds to improve LAND

Clover Grass
San-Foin
La Lucern
Canarie Seed
Hemp Seed

You may be likewise accomodated with Spades, Shovels, Rakes, Hoes, Lines, Knives, Sheers, Hedge-Bills, Chisels, Sythes, Wyre-Sives, With other things proper for the use of Gardeners; as also with Fruit Trees, Cabbage Plants &.

There is also to be sold here the Catalogue of the Plants in the Physical Garden at Edinburgh, a Work highly esteemed by all knowing Men, both at Home and Abroad.

As also there are to be sold fine Tea, Tea pots, and Tea Tables, China Dishes, and that famous Water called the Queen of Hungari's Water.

Together with both the Plain and Purging Elixirated Spirits of Scurvy-Gras, and the Pectoral Lozenge for the Cough, Shortness of Breath, or Streightness of the Breast, and Worm Powder for Children.

3

# *Fruit Trees, Bushes and Other Fruits*

In medieval Scotland the planting and care of fruit trees were to a large extent in the hands of the clergy. Roughly half the land in Scotland belonged to the Church and of that portion half was held by the monasteries, which were established on the most fertile ground, so a very large proportion of the more readily cultivable land was administered by monastic institutions. The foundations for this clerical influence were laid quite soon after the Norman Conquest. Between 1113 and 1230 thirty important monasteries were established in Scotland, belonging to seven monastic groups, together with a dozen lesser institutions. The dominant influence was French. There is no doubt that the European tradition of kitchen and herb gardening and the care of orchards travelled north with this religious invasion.

Monasteries and Abbeys had their own gardens and orchards. Monks often looked after their own plots – there is even a record of one selling kale – or collaborated in tending a communal garden. As many of the religious houses grew in importance and wealth, it became increasingly common for lay people to be employed to service the needs of the monks. This was particularly true of the Cistercians, who, together with the Augustinians, were so influential in Scotland. By precept and example the clergy taught people how to garden and care for fruit trees, laying the foundations for the subsequent Scottish distinction in these arts.

There are a number of early records and comments which reinforce this view. Giovanni Ferrerio, the Renaissance scholar who came to Kinloss Abbey to teach the young monks, noted that one of the early Abbots laboured at the uprooting and planting of fruit trees 'even to the extent of perspiration'. The famous Arbroath Oslin apple (Figure 79), very likely of French origin and esteemed for centuries, was first associated with the metropolitan See of St. Andrews and district. It has often been noted that Abbot Robert Reid in 1540 brought over William Lubais, a skilled orchardist from Dieppe, whose work and advice benefited the whole of Morayshire. The Record Book of the Cistercian Abbey of Coupar Angus includes a number of charters to tenants with conditions which demonstrate a keen interest in the maintenance of orchards. Thus in 1473 a gardener was employed for making ponds for eel and fish 'and specially with sykyr dyking and hedgyn of the orchardis to the quhickis labur and costis the Abbot sall gyfe hym for any ij bollis of meyl...' The duties of another gardener were defined thus: 'For dewe Johne Hwgonis zard four pund xiij s & xiij d; and sall have reddy to all common labour ane servand for ilk zard; and for til said dewe James zard sall furnis to the Abbot and convent caill and herbis his xv dats about; and sall haif twa beddis of herbs, sic as percell, betis, and latows; and sall furnis to the warden in the zeir, four beddis of vnzeonis (onions), bowcaill (cabbage) and the half of fructis at growis on the treis in the zeir... and about the All bounds of the said thre zardis shall hald upe the heggis and dikys sufficientlie, and sall nocht lat ane craw big within the said bounds, within his power.' 'Craws' were unpopular for a similar injuction appears in another agreement. In another contract it was 'componit with Jams Jacksoun for ane zere tak of the fowre akir of land that Thomas Jackson his fadir, brukit afore and now labourit be the said James, with hous and zard peteyng thairto; He laborand, gruband our trees and orchart in tyme of fruit and all uthir tymmes fra entree of ony bestiall, or steling of our fruct, as ane gude treu gardnir auch to do to us and our successouris etc...' And, in another entry: 'the said Andro sall mail with awys of us ane sufficiand orchard in al gudly hast he ma, with the best frut treis ma be gottin with sykkir dykin, hedgin and hanyin of the sammye.' 'Mail' means rent.

Down to the Victorian era it was recognised that the best old apple and pear trees were often to be found about ancient monasteries and abbeys. McPhail, in his History of the Religious House of Pluscarden (1881), noted that the fruit trees there were planted over circular causeways of flat stones to prevent the roots striking downwards and to promote horizontal growth. Cosmo Innes in 1860, reported that about a hundred years earlier, the last of the old pear trees at Kinloss were blown over in a storm, revealing that they were planted over flat flagstones 'after the most approved manner of orchard cultivation'. Indeed this practice did not die out until early in the present century with the advent of improved dwarfing rootstocks.

Patrick Neil, in his report on Scottish gardens and orchards (1813), noted that the Oslin apple had long been known from the vicinity of the Abbey of Aberbrothwick in Fife. The old Jedburgh orchards, laid down by the monks, still contained many very old trees, especially pears, which he thought were of French origin. Some of them had grown to a great size, up to forty feet or more, with immense trunks and wide spreading branches. They were believed to be about two hundred years old, which would date their planting from about 1600. They included a Red Honey pear, fifty to sixty feet high, with a bole of nine feet circumference. Many of these ancient trees had to be supported by posts but continued to bear great crops of fruit. He identified the pears as the ancient varieties known as Auchan,

Longueville, Crawford, Lammas, Warden, Bonchhretten, Bergamot, Gallert and Jargonelle. The Warden, a baking pear, had been known to yield thirty to forty bushels. In other Jedburgh orchards he encountered further old varieties such as St Catherine, Green Chisel, Drummond, Grey Gudwife, Pound Pear, Grey Honey, Mother Corse and Green Yair. Of these, at least Auchan and Green Yair were of Scottish origin. At Melrose a couple of old Thorle pear trees, of monastic origin, produced up to sixty thousand pears in a season. About the ruins of Lindores Abbey he came across old varieties of apple for which gardeners could no longer find a name. Further north, at Beauly Priory, there was once a large orchard. Many of the monastery orchards were established with trees from sister institutions in either England or, very often, France.

As far back as we have records fruit trees came in many varieties. Pliny accounts for twenty three sorts of apple, Parkinson listed some fifty and noted there were many more. Loudon, in 1826, relying largely on William Forsyth's 'A Treatise on Fruit-trees' (1802), listed two hundred and twenty eight varieties, excluding twelve sorts of cider apples. Trees like the apple do not breed true from seed so seedlings from a single trees may vary in growth and quality of fruit. If one or other of the seedling trees happens to take the grower's fancy he gives it a name, and propagates from it by grafts. If it is widely distributed it generally acquires a number of synonyms over the years so that the origin often becomes obscure. At least that is what used to happen in the past.

As a consequence, the naming of varieties of fruit tree is notoriously chaotic. Some old apple types have dozens of synonyms. Different names were sometimes given to trees of the same variety growing in the same orchard, simply because they were brought in from different places. We can echo the sentiments of James Gordon, an Edinburgh nurseryman, who published an excellent pocket guide to gardening in 1774. He included a long list of the names of apples with the comment: 'Perhaps all the kinds mentioned in the preceding lists are not different species; but they are all in the nursery-catalogues from England, and many more, which are here suppressed, as also that inundation of names that is poured upon us from all quarters of our own country: many gardeners naming the kinds they are unacquainted with after the places they had them from, or according to their own fancies. This is an abuse which cannot be tolerated; it confounds people, and prevents them knowing their right names. It is therefore to be wished, that this practice was at an end, and that gardeners, if they cannot give proper names to their fruits, they would give them none at all, till from more skilful hands they learn the proper names, so they may answer the commissions entrusted to them'.

Dr John Gibson, a Scottish naval physician, who in 1768 published a book on fruit growing based on twenty years experience, was of a similar mind. He confirmed that 'The same kind of fruit bears a multiplicity of names and the same name is likewise often given to fruit of very differernt

FIGURE 78
In 1682 the Earl of Crawford completed an inventory of the variety and quality of the fruits being grown on estates in southern Scotland. He dealt with apples, pears, plums, cherries, peaches, nectarines, currants, gooseberries, strawberries and even filberts. His account is valuable not only for the record of different named varieties but also for the names of the estates where there were orchards and no doubt gardens in the seventeenth century. The illustration reproduces a fragment of the original text.

kinds. Hence the confusion must always remain among planters, till a proper manner of ranging and ascertaining each kind shall be found out; for hitherto there are few kinds that are known by one proper name.' One of the consequences of this confusion was that, quite often, whatever a person ordered from a nurseryman might have little relation to what was supplied. According to Gibson, a nurseryman would frequently meet the order from his limited stock of varieties and it would be several years before the deceit came to light, when it would be too late to do anything about it.

Faced with such critical scepticism about identity we might well wonder how best to proceed with an account of what kinds of fruit trees were grown in the period concerned. All we have to go on are the names which have come down to us so we have no choice but use them, not forgetting the uncertainty which may attach to many of them. A vivid picture of the variety of fruit trees has been left to us by the Earl of Crawford, who went round the country sampling the fruit on different estates. In 1692 he set down a list ranked according to his order of excellence (Figure 78). This list includes twenty-two sorts of apple, forty pears, thirty-six plums, eighteen cherries, eight peaches, two nectarines, six apricots, eight gooseberries, four currants, four strawberries, two raspberries, two filberts and three artichokes. They were 'in order sett down as I esteem them according to ye

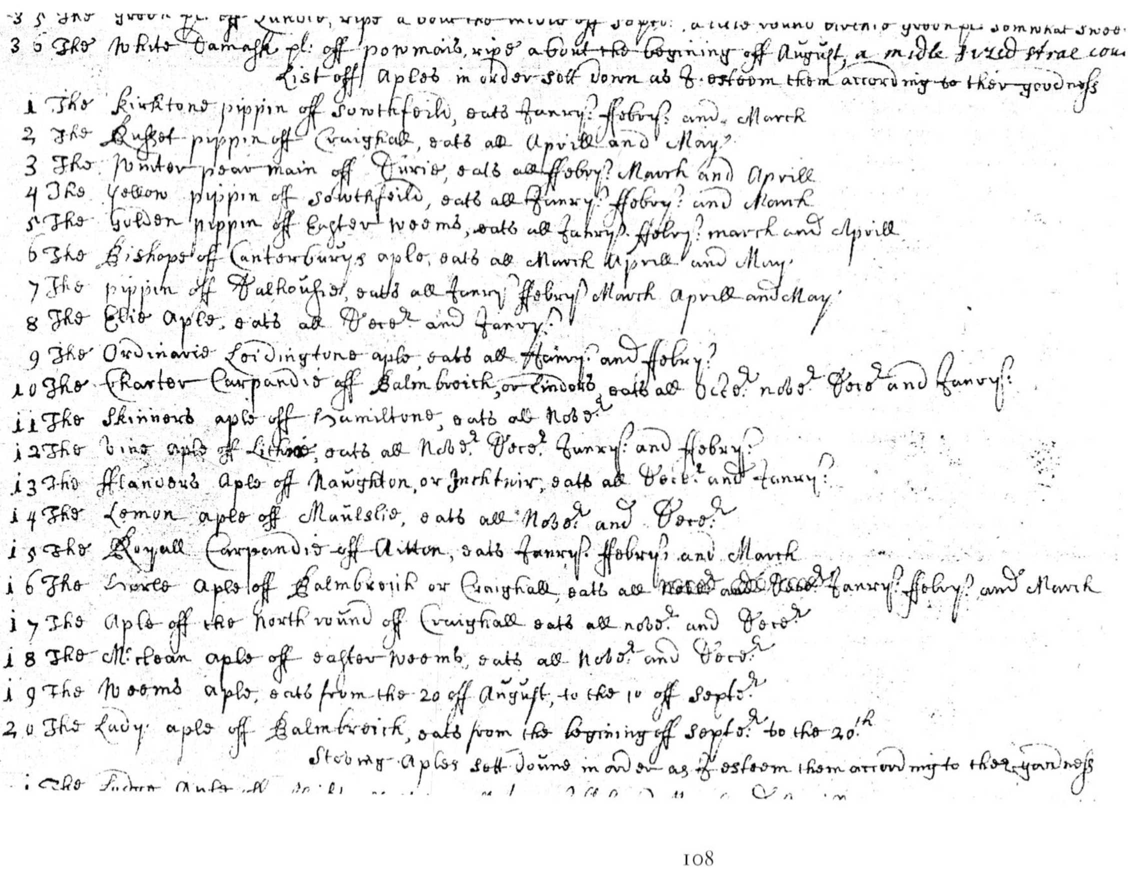
36 The White Damask pl: off Powmais, ripe about the begining off August, a midle sized strae cou
List off Aples in order sett down as I esteem them according to their goodness
1 The Kirktone pippin off Southfeild, eats Janry: Febry: and March
2 The Russet pippin off Craighall, eats all Aprill and May:
3 The Winter pear main off Durie, eats all Febry: March and Aprill
4 The Yellow pippin off Southfeild, eats all Janry: Febry: and March
5 The Golden pippin off Easter Weems, eats all Janry: Febry: march and Aprill
6 The Bishops off Canterburys aple, eats all March Aprill and May.
7 The pippin off Dalhousie, eats all Janry: Febry: March aprill and May
8 The Elie aple, eats all Decr: and Janry:
9 The Ordinarie Loidingtone aple, eats all Janry: and Febry:
10 The Charter Carpandie off Balmbreich, or Lindores, eats all Octr: Novr: Decr and Janry:
11 The Skinners aple off Hamiltone, eats all Novr:
12 The Vine aple off Lithrie, eats all Novr: Decr: Janry: and Febry:
13 The Flanders aple off Naughton, or Inchtuir, eats all Decr: and Janry:
14 The Lemon aple off Mauldslie, eats all Novr: and Decr:
15 The Royall Carpandie off Aitton, eats Janry: Febry: and March
16 The Gowks aple off Balmbreich or Craighall, eats all ~~Novr: and Decr:~~ Janry: Febry: and March
17 The Aple off the north yard off Craighall eats all Novr: and Decr:
18 The Mr Loan aple off Easter Weems, eats all Novr: and Decr:
19 The Weems aple, eats from the 20 off August, to the 10 off Septr:
20 The Lady aple off Balmbreich, eats from the begining off Septr: to the 20th
Stoving Aples sett downe in order as I esteem them according to their goodness

goodnesses'. He also noted the months when they were best eaten, which pears were for storing, which were second rate etc. For example: 'The Lemon aple of Maulslie, eats all Nove(mbe)r and Dece(mbe)r'; 'The petit muscat pear of Culrose eats from the beginning of July to the middle'; 'The Queen Mother plume, ripe about the beginning of Sep(temb)er; a liile red plume stript with green from the sun'; 'The Amber Ch(erry) of Struthers, ripe about the midle of Julie, a lairg amber ch: a very ill bearer' and so forth.

Dealing first with the apples, Crawford's list is as follows:

1   The Kirkton pippin of Southfeild
2   The Russet pippin of Craighall
3   The winter pearmain of Durie
4   The yellow pippin of Southfeild
5   The Golden pippin of Easter weems
6   The Bishop of Canterburys aple
7   The pippin of Dalhousie
8   The Elie aple
9   The Ordinarie Leidingtone aple
10  The Shorter Carpandie of Balmbreich
11  The Skinners aple of Hamilton
12  The wine aple of Lithe
13  Flanders aple of Naughton
14  The lemon aple of Maulslie
15  The Royal Corpendie of Aitton
16  The Sorle aple of Balmbreich
17  The aple off the north round of Craighall
18  The M'clean aple of easter weems
19  The Weems aple
20  The Lady aple of Balmbreich

Storing aples sett down etc.
1   The Ludge aple of Kirkton
2   The Graycheek aple of Monymeall

Only seven or eight of these are recognisable. Taking the names at their face value, the Russet is an old English apple recorded in 1597 but probably grown a long time before that. The Kirkton pippin may have been the same as the Kirton or Cracked pippin identified by Loudon as of Scottish origin. The Sorle of Balmbreich perhaps should have been written as 'Thorle' since that is the name of another very old Scots variety. According to the National Apple Register, the Winter Pearmain has been utterly confused with the Summer Pearmain (Figure 82), which goes back to the 1200s, so there is uncertainty about which was meant. The Golden Pippin (Figure 80) was recorded in 1629. It was very popular in the seventeenth and eighteenth centuries, during which time it acquired dozens of synonynms. Corpandie was the Scots version of Court-pendu (Figure 81), of which there was more than one kind. The original was of French origin and may have existed since Roman times. The Lemon or Lemon Pippin (Figure 83) is thought to be English or Norman in origin. The Ledington was a Scots cooking apple from the vicinity of Haddington. It is possible that the Yellow Pippin of Southfield refers to the Arbroath or Summer Oslin, later often called the Mother apple in Scotland, which, as already noted, can be traced back to the ecclesiastical institutions about St. Andrews, once the Metropolitan See of Scotland. It probably came from France, named after a French village. In 1810 there was a contribution to the Memoirs of the Royal Caledonian Horticultural Society in which a Dr Duncan suggested that this apple may be the Aurea Mala of the Romans and, in a further, wild flight of classical fancy, he thought it might even be the golden apple grown in the garden of the Hesperides. As for the rest of the list uncertainty prevails. Certainly some of them were of Scots origin like the Maclean and the Elie, which turn up in later lists, although they were not included in the comprehensive tabulation of apple varieties in Loudon's Encyclopedia of Gardening (1826), so they evidently dropped out of the nurserymen's lists about the end of the eighteenth century.

The Earl of Crawford's account is significant for another reason. From the list of places which appear in his notes for apples, pears and plums, and bearing in mind that his survey of Scottish orchards was by no means complete, we can infer that there was no shortage of well established orchards in Lowland Scotland at least from the second half of the seventeenth century. Where there were orchards there were also gardens and gardeners to care for them. From this evidence alone we can infer greater gardening activity in Scotland from the second half of the seventeenth century than has been hitherto supposed.

From 1697 we have a particularly valuable gardener's list of fruit trees growing at Scone. It is an exact record of the apples, pears, plums and cherries he had in the orchard. The list of apples includes a number of the names noted by the Earl of Crawford. The varieties of apples at Scone, listed in order of the numbers grown (in brackets), and in anglicised spelling, are as follows:

| | |
|---|---|
| Maclean (20) | Gray Cheek (18) |
| English Courtpendu (17) | French Russet (16) |
| Pearmain (16) | Elie (15) |
| Golden Pippin (15) | Ladies Apple of Wemys (12) |
| Lemon (10) | Bishop of Canterbury (9) |
| Long Apple of Ledington (9) | Shorter Courtpendu (7) |
| Bambreich Court-pendu (7) | Skinner's Apple (5) |
| Apple of Monniemeal (5) | Russet (4) |
| Pippin of Pitreive (3) | |

The remaining varieties, represented by only one or two trees, include:

| | |
|---|---|
| Apple Balbirrney | Kentish Pippin |
| Kinnoulton | Pippin Ludge |
| St. John's Apple | Winter Apple of Balcomie |
| White Apple of Moncrieff | English Rennet |
| Golden Money | Briar Bush |
| Apple of Balbeirrie | Pursans Pippin |

With a total of some two hundred apple trees and thirty nominally different varieties this was a very respectable collection. The gardener's list is also, like Crawford's, significant in the record of names of different estates where there were other orchards and hence gardens.

In the lists of apples purchased from London the names are generally different. Thus in 1729 the following varieties were sent to Drummond of Blair Drummond:

| | | |
|---|---|---|
| Nonpareil | Perells (?) | Cockle Pippin |
| Golden Pippin | Horton Pippin | Golden Munday |
| Autumn Red Pearmain | Scarlet Pearmain | Royal Russeting |
| Mr Costare | Kentish Pippin | Hartfordshire Pearmain |
| Kentish Rennet | Silver Pippin | |

In 1740 the followwing were supplied from London for Abercairney:

| | | |
|---|---|---|
| Janneting | Margeting | Summer Pearmain |
| Royal Pearmain | Loan's Pearmain | Scarlet Pearmain |
| Transparent | Spencer Pippin | Holland Pippin |
| Hereford Pearmain | Royal Russet | Harvey Apple |
| Wheeler's Russet | Catshead | Monstrous |
| Nonpareil | Golden Pippin | |

All the Abercairney apples were on Paradise stocks. Paradise was a very old apple, recorded in 1472 and of inferior fruit quality although it long continued in use as a stock to which better varieties could be grafted. However the name Paradise was also used loosely for stocks of ancient, and uncertain origin. Although the names among the apples sent from England generally differ from those grown at Scone, there are a few in common, such as Golden Pippin and Russet. Catshead was an English apple of irregular shape known in the 1600s; Monstrous was a synonym according to the National Apple Register. Janneting is a corruption of June-eating. Nonpareil was an old French apple introduced into Britain about the middle of the sixteenth century. Transparent may have been the White Astrachan introduced from Sweden or Russia in mid-seventeenth century. Margareting or Margaret was another English apple recorded in 1665.

It is instructive to round off this account with the list of apples extracted from the gardener's inventory for the garden of Cullen House in 1760. Each tree was recorded, so we can rank the varieties in order of the numbers grown. There were thirty-nine different named sorts of which eight were each represented by from twenty to as many as seventy-five trees. The rest were present mostly in single numbers. The most abundant sorts were as follows:

| | |
|---|---|
| Mother | Apple Russet |
| White Wine | Summer Permain |
| Autumn Permain | Summer Ledington |
| Nonpareil | White Ledington |

The rest, represented by only a few trees, included:

| | |
|---|---|
| Crab | Dutch Pippin |
| Summer Oslen | Oslen |
| Dutch Codlin | Golden Pippin |
| Lemon | Golden Rennet |
| Summer Codlin | Kentish Pippin |
| Winter Oslen | Summer Scarlet |
| Painted Lady Pippin | Codlin |
| Nonsuch | Dutch Rennet |
| Permain | Transparent |
| Winter Scarlet | Summer Sweet |
| Bitter Sweet | Red Rennet |
| Summer Jeanlet | |

OPPOSITE: FIGURE 79
The Oslin, also known as the Arbroath Oslin or Mother Apple, can be traced back to the ecclesiastical institutions about the Metropolitan See of St. Andrews. It probably originated in France where it was named after a village. It was widely grown in Scotland and, even as late as 1760, it was the most abundant apple in the orchard of Cullen House.

This list illustrates the tendency for an original variety to give rise to several derivatives, like the different Oslens or Oslins and the Ledingtons. Gibson recognised five sorts of the latter: the Grey, the Stoup, the Green, the White and the Scarlet Ledington, not to mention the Summer Ledington referred to here. The Cullen list shows an increase in the proportion of English apples. As the century wore on many apparently new varieties came in from south of the Border but some of the old Scots apples held their own. Thus the Mother apple, known also as Arbroath or Summer Oslin, with seventy-five trees, was by far the most numerous type at Cullen. In spite of its medieval origin it was the backbone of this large orchard. Even as late as 1778 Dickson and Brown's (Perth) catalogue included a number of the old Scots names such as Wine, Maclean, the Lady Apple of the Wemys, Transparent and the White Apple of Hawthornden, which came in after the period we are concerned with.

TOP LEFT: FIGURE 80
The Golden Pippin, known since the early seventeenth century, was one of the most esteemed apples, acquiring many synonyms. The nineteenth century original for the illustration was very close to the true Golden Pippin, which had become scarce by then.

TOP RIGHT: FIGURE 81
The Courpendu was an apple of great antiquity, possibly grown since Roman times. The French name was converted to 'Corpandy' by the Scots gardeners.

FIGURE 82
The Summer Permain has, according to the National Apple Register, become hopelessly confused with the Winter Permain. At least we know that an apple called Permain was known to gardeners in the thirteenth century, probably originating in France. It was both good to eat and suited for the making of cider.

TOP LEFT: FIGURE 83
The Lemon Pippin was known before 1700 and probably a deal earlier. Since the term 'lemon' was applied to other varieties there is some uncertainty on this score.

TOP RIGHT: FIGURE 84
The Nonpareil is another apple of French origin which probably came to Britain in the mid-sixteenth century. A dessert apple of high quality, it gave rise to many synonyms.

**Pears**

Like the apple many varieties of pear have been known since Roman times. All the qualifications about identity of synonyms and the general confusion about the names of apples apply equally, if not more so, to the pears grown in seventeenth- and eighteenth-century Scotland. The Earl of Crawford listed forty sorts of which a number were recorded from several orchards, confirming that they were well recognised varieties at that time. His account showing the usual inconsistency of spelling and the arbitrary use of capitals, is as follows:

1  The Bargamond pear of Southfeild, or wester weems
2  The Swan egge of Newark, or Red house, or Gosfourd
3  The Goosegge pear of Kersy, Green pear of Culrose, or pippersdron of Gosford
4  The St. Andrew pear of Dalhousie, Red house, or Gosfourd
5  The Red pear of Achens
6  The Enderleeth pear of weems, or Drumond
7  The summer Bungreson of Beill, or Dalhousie
8  The John Monteith pear of Struthers
9  The Sheephead pear in Balzie Chahouns yaird in Glasgow
10  The Sorrell pear of Ava or L; Colvils pear
11  The Kings pear of Dunnibirse est from the chapile of Weems
12  The Longvill pear of Tulliallane
13  The white breir bush of Newark
14  The pear Vaingorous of paisley, or Deserse
15  The Greenish Drumond of Steivenson
16  The Red Breir bush of Milton, or Newark
17  The Red Drumond from James Clep'ans yaird in Couper
18  The Muray pear of Kennett
19  The Russelet from the K's garden at London
20  The Qwince pear of Tininghame
21  The Red Buchanan of red house
22  The green pear of Kilwining
23  The Lindsays pear of Alaways
24  The Red pear of Stirling from Culrose
25  The pippin pear of Blackston
26  The whauks (?) sumer Bargamond
27  The lawrence pear of Culrose
28  The manifesto pear of Barniclugh
29  The petite muscat pear of Culrose
30  The Gray pear of Kirkton
31  The Long keeping pear of Ed(inburgh)
32  The Brethren pear of Kenett
33  The Nonsuch pear of Hamilton, or long lest (lost?) of Red house, or Newark

34  The Green Buchanan of Struthers
35  The E: David of Wester Weems
36  The Crawfourd pear
37  The Warden of pitliver
38  The pond pear of Cambusnethin
38  The pear Winnid(?) of Kirktone, or Lewchers, Kinnaird,
    or Struthers
40  The winter Drumond of Lewchers, Kinnaird or Struthers

The last four are all storing pears. The Earl of Crawford did not miss much, witness the reference to the pears in Baillie Colquhon's and James Clephan's 'yairds' in Glasgow and Couper respectively.

To compare the popularity of different sorts of pear at the beginning and end of the eighteenth century we can compare the names of pears grown in the Scone orchard (1697) with those in Crawford's list (1692), the pears at Cullen House (1760) and those recorded as growing in the Carse of Gowrie in 1813. The pears growing at Scone are listed in order of declining frequency in the orchard. Down to 'Orleans' there were about a dozen trees of each. From 'Airlie' downwards there were only one or two. About a quarter of the pears at either Scone, in Crawford's list or at Cullen House were still being grown in the Carse of Gowrie, although they were not all the same varieties. The comparisons, with anglicised spelling, are as follows:

| SCONE (1697) | CRAWFORD (1692) | CULLEN (1760) | GOWRIE (1813) |
| --- | --- | --- | --- |
| Swan Egg | + | + | + |
| Achan | + | + | + |
| Pound | + | + | + |
| Colmer | + | − | + |
| James | − | − | + |
| Sheep's Head | + | + | − |
| Beurre | + | − | + |
| Elshine Haft | − | − | + |
| Golden Knapp | − | − | + |
| Longueville | + | + | + |
| Katharine | + | − | − |
| Orleans | − | − | − |
| Airlie | − | − | − |
| Beurre de Roi | − | − | − |
| Burgoniond | − | + | − |
| Royal Russian | − | − | − |
| Quince | − | + | − |
| Bergamot | + | − | + |
| Burgamon | − | + | − |
| Bon Chretien | + | + | − |

Brown Beurre Pear.
This was the first of the
varieties called Beurre
from the consistency
of the flesh and was
recognised by 1608.
It gave rise to several
variants with either gray,
red or gold coloured
fruit. It was known to
the Scots gardeners as
the Burry or Bury Pear.

RIGHT: FIGURE 86
The Summer Bon
Chretien was another
old French pear of
excellent eating quality.

| | | | |
|---|---|---|---|
| Cuisse Madam | – | – | + |
| Jargonelle | + | – | + |
| Nonsuch | – | + | – |
| St Andrews | – | + | – |
| Verdun | – | – | – |
| Yellow Pear of Bumbreith | – | – | – |

A substantial number of the pears in these four lists were probably of Scottish origin. The ones which can be confidently identified as such include the Achan or Auchan, which came in several forms such as the Red, Grey and the Winter or Black Achan, the James, the Elshine Haft (elshine was the Scots word for awl), the Longueville, obviously French but grown since early times in Scotland, the Orange Bergamot, the Red Buchanan, the Briar Bush, both red and white and the John Monteith. To these we can add, from other evidence, the Muirfowl, the Yair or the Green pear of the Yair, the Early and also the Late or Grey Carnock. Large orchards generally contained the Swan Egg, Pound, Colmer, Beurre (Figure 85), of which there were several varieties, inncluding a white and a brown, the Bergamot which, by the early nineteenth century had acquired six or seven presumed derivatives, including the Scots Orange, the French, Swiss, Summer, Autumn and Gorell's Bergamot, the Cuisse Madame and Jargonelle. In the

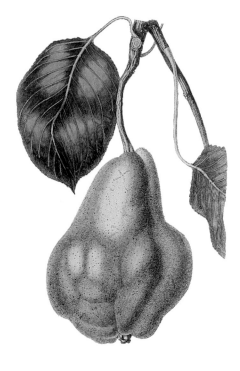

Table of camparisons the spelling is anglicised but in the original records the names often appear rather different since the gardeners converted French names into more familiar versions. Thus Beurre became Burrie or Burry, Bon Chretien (Figure 86) became Boncreitton, Cuisse Madam, politely translated as lady's thigh, ended up as Cush Madam while Royal Russian appeared as Roall Rossan.

## Plums

The Earl of Crawford's list runs to thirty-one entries but many of these were evidently small dark plums of uncertain status and poor quality and there seems little point in listing them all. It is suffiicient to examine the lists from Scone and Cullen House and note that about a dozen of them also appeared in the Earl of Crawford's list. The comparison is set out in the Table below.

| ENGLISH NAME | SCONE | CRAWFORD | CULLEN |
|---|---|---|---|
| Imperial | + | + | + |
| Bonum Magnum | + | + | + |
| Mussel | + | + | + |
| Orleans | + | − | + |
| White Perdigon | + | + | + |
| Queen Mother | + | + | − |
| Chestnut | + | + | − |
| Damask | + | + | − |
| Violet Damask | + | + | − |
| Green Gage | − | + | + |
| Cherry | − | − | + |
| Fotheringham | − | + | + |
| Gascon | − | + | + |
| Cornelian | − | − | + |

It is unclear how far the varieties Imperial and Bonum Magnum differed. There was a well recognised Red Bonum Magnum, perhaps the same as the Bonum Magnum in Crawford's list. Mussel was a very old plum which later was used as a stock to which other varieties were grafted. Orleans was an old French plum dating from the second half of the seventeenth century. The Green Gage was another French plum, also called Reine Claude after the wife of Francois I. Sir Thomas Gage introduced it to Britain, hence the name. The Damask was yet another French plum. The Violet Damask was presumably a derivative. Fotheringham was an old plum of English origin. The Cherry Plum or Myrobalan belongs to the species *Prunus cerasifera*, native to western Asia, and recognised as one of the parents in the hybridisation with the blackthorn, *Prunus spinosa*, which gave rise to the cultivated plums.

## Cherries

A surprisingly large number of cherries were grown even in the north of Scotland, very often against walls. Crawford lists eighteen sorts; at Scone fifteen kinds were grown. At Cullen House, although there were not so many different kinds, the orchard included just under seventy trees. The accompanying Table shows those sorts in Crawford's list which were also grown at either Scone or Cullen. Similarity of name may not always imply identity of variety.

| ENGLISH NAMES | SCONE | CRAWFORD | CULLEN |
|---|---|---|---|
| Amber | + | + | + |
| Kentish | + | + | + |
| Black Heart | + | + | + |
| Carroun / Coron | + | + | − |
| Flanders | + | − | − |
| Heart | + | − | − |
| White Heart | + | − | − |
| White Spanish | + | + | − |
| Morello | + | − | − |
| Red Heart | − | − | + |
| May Duke | − | − | + |
| Cluster / St. John's | − | + | + |
| Double Blossomed | − | + | + |
| Cornelian | − | − | + |
| Bird | − | − | + |

OPPOSITE: FIGURE 87
Cherries. Two species were ancestral to the cherries. *Prunus avium*, the gean, with coloured juice, gave rise to the sweet cherries, while *P. cerasus*, with colourless juice, was the parent of the sour Morello type. Among the former, the Bigarreau cherries, there were both round and heart-shaped forms. The Duke and May Duke cherries are believed to have arisen by hybridisation between the two species or their derivatives. *P cerasus* is a bush or small tree while *P. avium* can grow to twenty metres.

The additional names in Crawford's list include : Black Orleans, Archduke, Luckwood, Cligibborriolin (of the King's garden), Carnation, Spanish, Bleeding heart, Mumurance, Airlie Flanders, Spotted corner'd, Maister Millen and May.

The cherries present the now familiar confusion about names. Two species are involved, *Prunus avium* or Gean which gave rise to sweet cherries of various shape and colour, and *Prunus cerasus*, the ancestor of the sour cherries, the Morellos or Amarelles. They are distinguished by having respectively coloured or colourless juice. Hybridisation between these two species led to varieties termed Dukes, which appear to have arisen in England. Like the apple and pear, cherries have a long history. Gibson thought he could identify some existing varieties as the same as those known to the Romans. He might have been right.

The sweet cherry, Amber, was synonymous with a variety known as Graffion or Kentish Bigarreau, of dubious origin, but probably southern European, possibly Italian. Kentish may have been the same as what was known as Kentish Red, which was close to the Flanders or Flemish, derived from *Prunus cerasus*, and likely ancestor of the various Heart cherries, of which three sorts, red, white and black are mentioned here. The Bleeding

Heart originated in Gascony a very long time ago. The Spanish and the May were among those believed to go back to Roman times. Caroon was a sweet cherry which came fairly true from seed and embraced many minor variants. May Duke and Archduke were English varieties of hybrid origin. The Cluster cherry was not far removed from the wild gean. The 'Bird' cherry of those days would probably have referred to the wild gean rather than *Prunus padus*, as in later usage. The Cornelian Cherry, grown at Cullen House, was not a cherry but a member of the Dogwood family (*Cornus mas*). As noted earlier, its tart, red cherry-like fruits were once esteemed for making preserves. There is little point in speculating about the other names in Crawford's list.

## Apricots

Crawford lists six varieties of 'Apricock', namely the Orange, the Masculin, the Red, the Algeir or Earlie, the Roman and the Smooth, of which all but the Red and the Smooth appear in Loudon's Dictionary (1826), apart from some spelling differences.The Apricot was not mentioned in the *Capitulare de Villis* since it was a comparative newcomer to European gardens. It is reported (Roach, 1985) that it was brought to England in 1524 by a priest

FIGURE 88
The Roman Apricot was probabaly the first variety of Apricot commonly grown. As the name implies it can be traced back to antiquity but was superseded by superior varieties from the late eighteenth century onwards.

who was employed as gardener by Henry VIII. It was taken up widely in England during the sixteenth and seventeenth centuries. Being a tender tree it was grown in sheltered sites on south and east facing walls. It hardly seems adapted to the Scottish climate. Crawford names five estates where apricots were grown: Steivenson, Hamiltone, Crighall, Culrose and Tininghame, to use his spelling. Both Hamilton and Craighall grew two varieties. Between 1707 and 1710, in a large consignment of fruit trees from Brompton Park, London, delivered to Panmure in Fife, there were four sorts of apricot, including Masucline, Orange, Roman and Turkey. One would like to know what kind of success they had. Apricots were not mentioned in the Scone and Cullen lists.

## Peaches and Nectarines

These fruits, although of ancient cultivation in China, were probably not introduced to Britain until the thirteenth century. By Parkinson's time twenty-one varieties were recognised. Crawford lists eight different peaches, three from the King's garden at London. These were the Madona, the Savoy and the Bollito. The other five included: 'the Malcotton, the Pavie, the Rambuillon, the Newingtone, and the White nuttmeg'. Since peach and nectarine require the same kind of care and shelter as the apricot it was not surprising that Crawford mentioned only five estates where they were grown. They are Hamilton, Leslie, Tiningham, Durie and Hatton. At Leslie there were three sorts of peach, the Pavie, the Rambuillon and the Newington, while only Durie grew nectarines, both the Roman and the Tawny. At Cullen only Newington and Honey peaches were grown, while at Scone there is no reference to peaches or nectarines in the gardener's record, although five sorts of peach were included in the consignment to Panmure noted above.

## Gooseberries

Gooseberries were very popular from early times. Parkinson lists eight varieties, the same number as in Crawford's list, which is shown in the accompanying Table, together with the varieties of gooseberries at Cullen House:

| CRAWFORD'S LIST | CULLEN HOUSE |
| --- | --- |
| Red | Red |
| Yellow | Yellow |
| White | Globe Green |
| Long Red | Italian Cristal |
| Amber | Walnut |
| Hedge- hog | Scots Black |
| Small Round | Red Scots |
| Long Green | Rough |

At Cullen House gooseberries were grown in such large numbers they must have been sold off the estate. They are not mentioned in the Scone inventory although no doubt they were grown. At Cullen about one hundred and forty bushes of both red and green were being harvested, with a further eighty or so Cristal and Walnut, about thirty Scots black and one simply termed Scots. Only seven yellows were mentioned. Towards the end of the eighteenth century the varieties of gooseberries escalated in number. Loudon (1826) refers to eighty to one hundred kinds, while some of the Lancashire growers offered more than three hundred.

### Strawberries

The Earl of Crawford lists four sorts: the Small Wild, the Great Red, the Green and the Virginian strawberry. The fist of these is *Fragaria vesca*, the wild strawberry of the woods. The second was most likely *Fragaria elatior*, also known as *F. moschata*, the Hautbois (Figure 89), a European species which was being cultivated in the sixteenth century. Later shown to have the sexes on separate plants it was selected to produce a number of different cultivars. The green was probably a mutant form of *F. vesca*, familiar to Parkinson and esteemed by Philip Miller. Green or white colour may turn up by mutation in any strawberry. The Virginian was the variable and widespread North American *F. virginiana*, which had been cultivated by the American Indians, who recognised different varieties, including some with either red, yellow or white fruit. Jean Robin, botanist to the King of France, first described this species in 1624. It became very popular. The Cullen list included both the Hautbois and the Chilean strawberry. The latter was *F. chiloensis*, with a vast distribution in both North and South America, although the first introduction to France in 1714 was from South America. Philip Miller imported it in 1727. A derivative of this species, with larger fruits and a characteristic flavour, was first described by him in 1760. It became known as Ananas, the Pine or Pineapple strawberry (Figure 90). It is particularly interesting that the latter was being grown in the garden at Cullen House in 1760; the gardener had brought plants from London. Hybridisation between *F. virginiana* and *F. chiloensis* later gave rise to modern strawberries.

### Raspberries

The cultivation of raspberries dates from the early seventeenth century. Before then they were simply gathered from the wild. 'Raspes' in the Earl of Crawford's list were of two kinds, white and red. No doubt these were forms of *Rubus idaeus*, the European wild raspberry, which had been selected for stronger and fewer canes and larger fruit. At Cullen House there was a large stand of rasps which were mostly *R. idaeus*, but there was also mention of American rasps which may have been the North American *R. occidentalis*.

LEFT: FIGURE 89
Hautbois Strawberry (*Fragaria elatior*). The Hautbois is native to central Europe
and has been cultivated since at least the sixteenth century. The plant is larger than
the native Strawberry (*Fragaria vesca*). Its fruits stand clear of the foliage and taste
a little different.

RIGHT: FIGURE 90
Carolina, Old Pine Strawberry (*Fragaria chiloensis*). This species has an immense
distribution in both North and South America. It was imported from Holland by
Philip Miller in 1727. A derivative was developed in France, with larger fruits and
a characteristic flavour, which became known as the Pine or Pineapple strawberry.
It was being grown about 1760 in Cullen House garden. Hybridisation between
this species and the fine flavoured *F. virginiana*, which came in earlier, gave rise
to modern strawberries.

## Currants

Seventeenth century accounts have frequent reference to 'currans', i.e. red currants which were very popular in Scotland and widely grown. In early records they were sometimes called 'risearts' or variants of that name. Crawford mentions four sorts of currant: the Great Dark Red, the Great Bright Red, the White and the Black. It is likely that the first three are derived from the West European *Rubus sativum* while the black currant refers to *R. nigrum*, with a much wider distribution across Europe and Northern Asia. Currants were grown at Cullen in such numbers that, like gooseberries, they must have been sold as a source of income for the estate. There were nearly two hundred bushes of white currants, more than a hundred black and some thirty red currants.

In addition to the familiar fruits one or two varieties of fig were quite often grown. Hazel nuts or filberts, often imported from Holland, were planted extensively during the eighteenth century on some estates like Hamilton. Crawford refers to both white and red filberts grown at Struthers. Walnuts were also planted, often in large numbers, presumably for the timber rather than the nuts. Quince and medlar were mentioned only very rarely. Almonds were referred to a little more often. Of course, later, when glasshouses became available several sorts of vine were widely grown. As observed earlier, the occasional optimist ordered mulberry seeds, of either the black or white species.

We can fill in the picture of the gentry's interest in orchards and fruit with sundry additional observations which have come to light in the records. The Duke of Hamilton's orchards were the finest in the country. In the journals of Lauder of Fountainhall, 1665-76 we read how 'we took horse at the Gallogate to go for Hamilton 8 miles from Glascow... went and saw the yards: great abundance of good wines, peaches, apricoats, figs, walnuts, chaistinis (chestnuts) , philberts etc., in it as in any part of France; excellent Bon Crestien pears, brave palissades of firs, sundry fisch ponds. The walls are built of brick which conduces much to the ripening of the fruits: their be 20 ackers of land within the yeardes...'

Lauder was well placed to compare the produce of his own country with that of France, where he had travelled extensively. He reported that 'our peirs that growes at home are all out as delicious vitness the carnock as any we have eaten in France tho they grow in greater abondance. As to the apples we most not contest wt them, since besides many brave sorts, they have the Pipin, which I conceive most be that they call Reynett, brought unto France from Italy, by Queen Blanche, mother of St. Louis; it was first found in Africk. The Pomme Minion is better than any of ours: our Marican Seines to be a degenerat sort of it'. In another comment he mentions that in France they have apples without seeds in them, also the best sort of peach, the Great Pavies, and describes how they are grafted to produce such fine fruit.

In 1674 Hew Wood, many years the gardener at Hamilton and a man who had a considerable reputation among his contemporaries, sent a parcel of twenty two pear trees to Sir William Bruce of Balcaskie to his lodging at the Abbey of Holyrood House, where he was engaged in the restoration and extension of the palace. The covering letter refers to '8 swan-eggs, 8 english bergamots, 2 Carnocks – 2 pear dangerous, as for the rest of the trees I could get non except 2 of the keeping pund pear of Cambusnathen for there is hardly any nurseries here besides our own, and also those few they have hardly know their names, so that if one should buy them they can not be sure of the kinds they call for.' The Duke of Hamilton's enthusiasm for planting is evident in the record of more than ten thousand trees transplanted from the nursery between 1702 and 1722. These were mostly forest and amenity trees but the point is made.

We have already noted the consignment of fruit trees to Panmure comprising ten sorts of plum, seven of pear, six of peaches, four of cherries and four of apricots. In 1722 a statement by Sir John Clark, for the sale of Cammo, near Edinburgh, specified the numbers of different kinds of fruit trees and bushes as follows: apples – 34, pears – 44, plums – 13, cherries – 2, peaches – 2, apricots – 2, nuts – 4, gooseberries – 3, currants – 2, together with medlars, vines, almonds and walnuts. 1712 was quoted as the date of planting of this orchard. In 1720 one hundred and twenty-six dwarf fruit trees were sent to Blair Drummond comprising fifty-four apples of fourteen kinds, twenty-four pears of eleven kinds, twenty-four cherries of eight kinds, twelve peaches of nine and twelve apricots of five kinds.

From 1741 we have a list of fruit trees sold by William Miller from the Abbey nursery. The large number of different named sorts included: apples – twenty-eight, plums – eleven, pears – thirty-three, cherries – eleven, apricots – seven, peaches – twenty-two, nectarines – seven, to which list we can add two sorts of fig, seven kinds of vine and even almonds and Dutch grafted filberts. Scottish varieties of apples, pears and plums were conspicuously absent. Evidently Miller obtained his stock from England as well as Holland. Thus the *Edinburgh Evening Courant* for Jan 18–2 2, 17 2 2, contained the following advert, which was repeated in other issues: 'There is just come from Abroad Varieties of the very best of new garden Seeds, with several sorts of Fruit trees, Dutch Allers; and Gardners Tools to be sold by William Miller Gardner, at the Abbey of Edinburgh. As also, of his own propagation, several Sorts of Fruit trees, Forrest trees, and Evergreens, and Thorns for Hedges, with different sorts of Linnen Cloath; all sold at the very lowest prices.' 'Allers' refers to alders.

In 1749 the Duke of Argyll, who operated on a lavish scale, received from London one hundred dwarf fruit trees for his orchard at Inveraray. The number of varieties included: apples ten, pears ten, plums nine, cherries eight, apricots eight, peaches seven, and nectarines seven. In most cases the names of the varieties supplied do not appear in earlier records of trees in old established Scottish orchards.

Orchards were not confined to country estates. Even within the confines of Edinburgh there were gardens with many fruit trees, and, of course, we must not forget the Earl of Crawford's reference to the Sheephead pear in 'Baillie Chahoun's yaird' in Glasgow and the red Drummond in 'James Clep'an's yaird' in Couper. In 1646 the gardener's inventory of Earl Murray's garden in the Canongate included some two dozen apple trees, about sixty plums and about eighty cherries, some of which were geans. Many of these trees were termed 'great' and must have been quite old. One wonders how much of the cherry crop was recovered and how much the birds got. There was also a damson, a quince, five apricot trees and a fig. In another inventory, from the next century, 1730, The Duke of Roxburgh's garden, also in the Canongate, contained forty apples, of different kinds, forty plums, a hundred and fifty gooseberry bushes (!) and fifty white and also red currant bushes.

Taking all the evidence into account, it is clear that orchards were widespread in Lowland Scotland during the seventeenth century, certainly in the second half at least. Bearing in mind the important, early role of the abbeys and monasteries in establishing orchards and the comments of early travellers, we can infer an unbroken tradition in the planting and care of fruit trees from the twelfth to thirteenth centuries onward.

# 4

# *The Physic Garden*

In our time we are so used to pills and solutions prepared by the pharmacists for the treatment of our ailments, that it takes an effort of the imagination to appreciate how much our ancestors relied on herbal medicines. In the period we are concerned with, botany and medicine were so interwoven that familiarity with plants and their uses was an essential part of a medical education, at least in more enlightened circles. It is only in comparatively recent times that all trace of botany has been deleted from the medical curriculum. But in the seventeenth century for a medical institution to create a physical garden was sign of a progressive outlook. According to Guthrie (1960) the first such institutional garden in Scotland was established in 1656 under the auspices of The Incorporation of Surgeons and Barber Surgeons, founded in 1505. On Oct. 27th 1656 the Edinburgh Town Council granted a licence to the Chirugeons 'to cast five hunder devotts... for their use of the garden in Curryhill Yard', whereupon two of the Surgeon Apothecaries planted medicinal plants at an expense of two hundred pounds Scots within the confines of the Yard. A little later, in 1661, the Governors of Heriot's Hospital decreed that part of their grounds should be set aside for the planting of 'all sorts of physical, medicinal and other herbs such as the country can afford', and that it should be open to anyone who wished to study the plants. There appears to be no record of the size of this garden nor of what medicinal plants it contained.

The next move lay with two Edinburgh physicians Robert Sibbald and Andrew Balfour, the most distinguished Scottish physician of his day. Sibbald, concerned at the ignorance of those practising what passed for medicine in Edinburgh at that time, set up a private garden for medicinal herbs. He had a friend in this undertaking in the Laird of Livingstone, Patrick Murray, who had brought together nearly a thousand plants in his garden at Livingstone. Tragically he died while travelling in France in 1671. In 1670 Balfour and Sibbald arranged the lease of a piece of ground in the North Yard of Holyrood Abbey from a tenant market gardener. This was quite small, being only forty feet square, although between eight and nine hundred plants, drawn from Sibbald's and Murray's collections, were packed into it. Both Sibbald and Balfour were busy men and needed some-one to look after the garden. They were fortunate in finding a young man with a good knowledge of plants. He was James Sutherland, about whom we shall have more to say later. The collection soon required better accomodation and in 1675 another plot of land was leased from the Town Council, with James Sutherland, herbalist, in charge. This was attached to Trinity Hospital, approximately where Edinburgh General Post Office once stood. It was much bigger, three hundred by one hundred and ninety feet, and was later known as the Physic garden. In 1695 Sutherland took over the supervision of part of the Royal garden at Holyrood known as the King's garden where he grew vegetables and medicinal herbs.

The Trinity garden was divided into six separate plots in which the plants were arranged systematically in genera and species. It was already more like a botanical garden and was often known as the Edinburgh Botanical Garden. Only one of the plots was devoted to physical herbs, which Sutherland arranged in alphabetical order to make it easier for medical students to remember the names. The garden contained a number of tender plants, protected by belljars or small frames, and contained many fine shrubs growing against the walls, but lacked a greenhouse. Without proper fencing it was subject to trespass by both man and beast and, with only a wall and an earth mound between it and the end of the Nor' Loch, it was devasted by flooding when the Loch was drained during the seige of Edinburgh castle in 1689. Nonetheless it flourished under Sutherland's guidance and, in 1763, the contents of the garden were transferred to a five acre (English) site in Leith and the foundations of the Royal Botanic Garden of Edinburgh were truly laid. But that is a different story and we must return to the physical herbs.

It is difficult to discover to what extent medicinal plants were grown in private gardens. The occasional reference to the 'physic garden' suggests that part of the ground or yard was set aside for medicinal herbs. We know that part of the garden of Cullen House was used for medicinal plants but we have no clear idea how often this was the case. On Dec 23rd 1725 Lord Grange, whom we have met before, wrote to Philip Miller, Botanist Gardener at Chelsea, with another of his proposals. He suggested that Miller, following on the success of his Dictionary, should prepare a similar account of purely medicinal plants, since this would be a great help to practicioners of Phsyick or Pharmacy. Such information would be 'an additional Profit for the honest and industrious Gardner. It would also be agreable to the Nobility and Gentry some of whom I have known inclines to have a Compartment as a Curiosity, in the garden for Physical Plants; but they were discouraged from attempting and because neither they nor their Gardeners knew them sufficiently nor how to cultivate them'. He went on: 'Such of them as were to be gathered as they grow wild and out of gardens, it may be fit to acquaint us whether to look for them in Meadows, Woods, Hills, Fields, Heaths etc., and at what season according to their

Leaves, Stalks, Flowers, Roots, Seeds are to be used. But any of this sort which may be improved by culture, or of which it may be fit to have a Plant or two in the Garden that a Learner may know them, it would seem proper to direct us how to bring them into the Garden and to manage them in it.' This earnest, laboured and rather ungrammatical appeal fell on deaf ears. If we are to believe Lord Grange it appears that private physic gardens were not common, although perceived as an asset in view of the reliance on herbal remedies for the cure of disease.

Probably the majority of the species of plants grown in medieval gardens were there on account of their culinary value or assumed virtue in the treatment of disease. This would have been particularly true of the gardens of the abbeys and monasteries. If these plants had attractive flowers, a fine aroma or shapely form they were likely to retain their place in the gardeners' affection even when their utilitarian qualities had been superseded or forgotten. Of course, there is a hard core of species which have only been grown for their medicinal value, but there are others, now regarded as purely ornamental, which were first grown for other reasons. Such distinctions are illustrated by comparison of the kinds of plants growing in William Miller's garden at the Abbey of Holyrood in 1740. Altogether some one hundred and twenty species were grown of which some fifty percent have been put to medical use and are listed in the pharmacopoea. Among the latter we find plants we now regard as purely ornamental such as Love Lies Bleeding, Asarum, Cyclamen, Larkspur, Dwarf Elder, Solomon's Seal, Wolf's Bane, Stock, Hart's Tongue Fern, Royal Fern, Spindle Tree, Daphne, Butcher's Broom, Black Hellebore, Hepatica and Physalis, to mention the most unexpected examples. Therefore compilation of a comprehensive list of physical herbs encounters border-line cases and meets the problem of where to draw the line.

In the present instance we have relied for our information about medicinal plants, used in Scotland during the seventeenth and eighteenth centuries, on accounts rendered by apothecaries to members of the gentry and on family recipes. The origin of such recipes for medicines is generally unknown. They may have been copied from a medical manual, usually into a carefully written note-book, or they may have been handed down from previous generations. In either case we have no reason to doubt that these remedies were being used in the period concerned, for which we have compelling evidence, from 1627, in a personal diary of their practical application in the treatment of disease.

The apothecaries' lists of medicines supplied to members of the gentry and their households refer to many different kinds of physical herb, very often to be used in so many 'handfuls' of leaves or whole plants, suggesting they were gathered fresh and readily available. Also the constituents of medicines include oil of such plants as Chamomile, Rose, Lily, Rue etc. or the roots of Horse-radish, Comfrey, Knot-grass, Fennel, Rhubarb or Asparagus. Quite often the recipe refers to 'water', i.e. an aqueous extract of such plants as Rose, Bean, Cumin, Woodbine, Fumitory, Carduus, Plantain, Dragons etc. Sometimes alcoholic extracts were used and these might be distilled to produce oils. It is likely that dried preparations of whole plants or parts of them like the roots or seeds were part of the apothecary's stock in trade and were articles of commerce. But in the majority of cases the instructions imply the gathering of fresh material. No doubt such sorts of plant as Dandelion, Groundsel, Ground Ivy, Self-heal, Pearlwort, Eyebright etc. would have been collected in the wild, probably by a herb collector, but often it would have been more convenient to have the more commonly used species growing nearby in a garden. In any case, a number of the species used were not native and, if not commonly naturalised, must have been grown for use.

The compilation of medicinal species includes a substantial number which were also culinary herbs. They had dual status and included such species as Angelica, Dill, Pot Marjoram, Anise Endive, Sage, Asparagus, Fennel, Sorrel, Caraway, Horse-radish, Spearmint, Chervil, Mint, Tansy, Cucumber, Penny Royal, Thyme and even Cress. From the early eighteenth century we have, in the Saltoun papers, an extensive list of medicinal herbs which singles out those considered 'most essential and sufficient' for a small garden. Except for Penny Royal such essential herbs include all those in the list above. In the species set out in Table 9, derived from the various sources already considered, a (+) sign shows it was included in the record of essential species for a small garden. An asterisk before the specific name indicates its mention in the *Capitulare*. The common names quoted are those which appear in the recipes and apothecaries' accounts, except that the often idiosyncratic spelling has been converted to modern style. A number of names appear which have been mentioned before either as garden plants or culinary herbs, for the reasons already noted.

## TABLE 9. Plants used in Scotland for medicinal purposes at least from the early seventeenth century

| COMMON NAME | | LATIN NAME | ORIGIN |
|---|---|---|---|
| Alexanders | | *Smyrnium olusatrum* | Native |
| Agrimony | | *Agrimonia eupatoria* | Native |
| Archangel | | *Lamium album* | Native |
| Arum | | *Arum maculatum* | Native |
| Asarabacca | + * | *Asarum europaeum* | Europe |
| Balm | + | *Melissa officinalis* | Europe |
| Bastard Saffron | + | *Carthamnus tinctorius* | Asia |
| Bay berry | + | *Myrica cerifera* | N. America |
| Bear's Foot | | *Alchemilla vulgaris/* | Native |
| | | *Helleborus Foetidus* | Native |
| Betony | | *Betonica officinalis* | Native |
| Birthwort | | *Aristolchia clematitis* | Europe |

| Common Name | | Latin | Name Origin |
|---|---|---|---|
| Bistort | + | *Polygonum bistorta* | Native |
| Bramble | | *Rubus fruticosus agg* | Native |
| Broom | | *Cytisus scoparius* | Native |
| Bryony, White | | *Bryonia dioica* | Native |
| Bugle | | *Ajuga reptans* | Native |
| Burnett | | *Sanguisorba officinalis* | Europe |
| Calendula | + | *Calendula officinalis* | Europe |
| Caper | | *Euphorbia lathyris* | ? Native |
| Carduus | + | *Cnicus benedictus* | Europe |
| Celandine | | *Chelidonium majus* | Native |
| Centaury | + * | *Centaurium erythraea* | Native |
| Chamomile | + | *Chamaemelum nobile* | Native |
| Chaste Tree | | *Vitex agnus-castus* | Europe |
| Chickweed | | *Stellaria media* | Native |
| Cinquefoil | | *Potentilla reptans* | Native |
| Coltsfoot, Foal's Foot | | *Tussilago farfara* | Native |
| Comfrey | + | *Symphytum officinalis* | Native |
| Cowslip | | *Primula veris* | Native |
| Cumin | | *Cuminum cyminum* | Africa, Asia |
| Daisy | | *Bellis perennis* | Native |
| Dandelion | | *Taraxacum officinale* | Native |
| Deadly Carrot | | *Thapsia garganica* | N. Africa |
| Dragons | * | *Dracunculus vulgaris* | Europe |
| Elecampane | | *Inula helenium* | Asia |
| Eyebright | | *Euphrasia officinalis* | Native |
| Fenugreek | * | *Trigonella foenum-graecum* | Europe |
| Feverfew | | *Tanacetum parthenium* | Europe |
| Filipendula | | *Filipendula ulmaria* | Native |
| Fleawort | | *Conyza canadensis* | N. America |
| Fumitory | | *Fumaria officinalis* | Native |
| Gentian | | *Gentiana lutea* | Europe |
| Germander | | *Teucrium chamaedrys* | Native |
| Ground Ivy | + | *Glechoma hederacea* | Native |
| Groundsel | | *Senecio vulgaris* | Native |
| Hart's Tongue | | *Phyllitis scolopendrium* | Native |
| Henbane, White | | *Hyoscyanus albus* | Europe |
| Henbane, Black | | *Hyoscyanus niger* | Native |
| Hog's Fennel | | *Peucedanum officinale* | Native |
| Hollyhock | | *Althaea rosea* | Asia |
| Honeysuckle, Woodbine | | *Lonicera periclymenum* | Native |
| Hops | | *Humulus lupulus* | Native |

| COMMON NAME | | LATIN | NAME ORIGIN |
|---|---|---|---|
| Horehound | + | *Marubium vulgare* | Native |
| Hound's Tongue | | *Cynoglossum officinale* | Native |
| Hyssop | | *Hyssopus officinalis* | Europe |
| Juniper | | *Juniperus communis* | Native |
| Knot-grass | | *Polygonum aviculare* | Native |
| Lavender | | *Lavendula X intermedia* | Europe |
| Lavender Cotton | + | *Santolina chamaecyparissus* | Europe |
| Lily, White | + * | *Lilium candidum* | Europe |
| Liquorice | + | *Glycyrrhiza glabra* | Europe |
| Liverwort Ash coloured, | | *Peltigera canina* | Native |
| Lovage | * | *Levisticum officinale* | Asia |
| Lungwort | | *Pulmonaria officinalis* | Europe |
| Maidenhair | | *Adiantum capillus-veneris* | Native |
| Mallow | + * | *Malva sylvestris* | Native |
| Mandrake | | *Mandragora officinalis* | Europe |
| Marsh Mallow | + * | *Althaea officinalis* | Native |
| Masterwort | | *Peucedanum ostruthium* | Europe |
| Melilot | + | *Melilotus officinalis* | Europe |
| Mints | + | *Mentha spp.* | Native |
| Mercury | ? | *Mercurialis annua* | Native |
| Moneywort | | *Lysimachia nummularia* | Native |
| Motherwort | + | *Leonurus cardiaca* | Europe |
| Mouse Ear | | *Pilosella officinarum* | Native |
| Mustard, White | * | *Sinapis alba* | Europe |
| Oculus Christi | | *Salvia verbenaca* | Native |
| Pearlwort | | *Sagina sp.* | Native |
| Pellitory of the Wall | | *Parietaria judaica* | Native |
| Pimpernel | | *Angallis arvensis* | Native |
| Plantain | | *Plantago major* | Native |
| Polypodium | | *Polypodium vulgaris* | Native |
| Poppy, Red | | *Papaver rhoeas* | Native |
| Poppy, White | + * | *Papaver somniferum* | Asia |
| Rhubarb, Monk's | + | *Rumex pseudo alpinus* | Europe |
| Ribwort | | *Plantago lanceolata* | Native |
| Roman Wormwood | + | *Artemisia pontica* | Europe |
| Rose, Red | + * | *Rosa gallica* | Europe |
| Rose, White | + | *Rosa damascena* | Europe |
| Rosemary | + * | *Rosmarinus officinalis* | Europe |

| Common Name | | | Latin | Name Origin |
|---|---|---|---|---|
| Royal fern | | | *Osmunda regalis* | Native |
| Rue, Herb of Grace | + | * | *Ruta graveolens* | Europe |
| Saffron | | | *Crocus sativus* | ? |
| Sage | | | *Salvia officinalis* | Europe |
| Sanicle | | | *Sanicula europaea* | Native |
| Saxifrage | | | *Pimpinella saxifraga* | Native |
| Savin | | * | *Juniperus sabina* | Europe |
| Scabious | | | *Knautia arvensis* | Native |
| Scurvy grass | + | | *Cochlearia officinalis* | Native |
| Self-heal | | | *Prunella vulgaris* | Native |
| Shepherd's Purse | | | *Capsella bursa-pastoris* | Native |
| Siberian Larkspur | | | *Deplhinium ? elatum* | Russia |
| Smallage | + | | *Apium graveolens* | Native |
| Southernwood | + | * | *Artemisia abrotanum* | Europe |
| Speedwell | + | | *Veronica officinalis* | Native |
| Spurge | | | *Euphorbia lathyris* | Native |
| Stitchwort | | | *Stellaria holostea* | Native |
| Stonecrop | ? | | *Sedum acre* | Native |
| St. John's Wort | | | *Hypericum perforatum* | Native |
| Succory | | * | *Cichorium intybus* | ? Native |
| Tamarisk | | | *Tamarisca gallica* | Europe |
| Tormentil | | | *Potentilla erecta* | Native |
| Valerian | + | | *Valeriana officinalis* | Native |
| Vervain, Berbine | | | *Verbena officinalis* | Native |
| Violet | | | *Viola odorata* | Native |
| Wallflower | | | *Erysimum cheiri* | Europe |
| Water-purpie | | | *Veronica beccabunga* | Native |
| Woad | | | *Isatis tinctoria* | Europe |
| Wormwood | + | | *Artemisia absinthum* | Native |

A few names appear in the recipes which cannot be identified with confidence or await identificatiion. They include the following: 'Prosper' which turns up occasionally and, in one instance, is given as an apparent substitute for Purslane, suggesting it may be *Atriplex portulacoides*. 'Suncropt' looks like a corruption of Stonecrop; 'Capon's grass' may be *Valeriana officinalis* but that is quite uncertain. 'Couch grass' may be the familiar garden weed or perhaps is another name for the Knot-grass; 'Little Fenbin' might refer to Henbane; 'Mercury' could refer to *Chenopodium bonus-henricus*. 'Pimpernel' might be another name for *Pimpinella saxifraga* while 'Broad grass' might be *Plantago major*.

One of the most interesting plants in the list is 'Carduus', the Blessed Thistle. This was an invariable item in the seed accounts until late in the eighteenth century. This attractive annual from southern Europe has been in Britain since medieval times at least. It was a plant traditionally believed to cure the plague and alleviate all manner of other ills and diseases, including fevers and cancers; it was a kind of cure-all which could be eaten like cress or dried and taken as a powder or an infusion. But, alas, by 1836 in Loudon's Encyclopedia of Plants, it was dismissed as 'in no estimation whatever'. It is worth noting that about sixty percent of the plants in the above list are native, compared with only thirty-three percent for herbs which were used entirely or in part for culinary use. This suggests an ancient reliance on native species for medical purposes.

Evidently an immense number of different kinds of plant were recommended for treating diseases. It is worth taking a look at a few examples of how some of them were actually used during the period which concerns us.

The recipe for the cure of rickets in a child made use of quite a number of herbs which were added to the crushed bones of either a fox or black faced sheep's heads. First the bones were put into a great 'boyler or two pots in faire water and lett boyle Half an Houre, then close up the pots very close and lett it boyle very Easily for twenty four Hours then take itt and Strane itt and put in into the pots with Spearemint and Rosemary, Suthernwood, Harts Tongue, Liverwort, Strabery Leaves, Sweet Marjoram, Violett leaves… of Iach a good Handful and let them all boyle… till the Coller of the Hearbs be changed but if you can gett March Mallows that growes att the sea Side put in a good quantity.' The child was then to be immersed to the chin in this soup for half an hour or longer, then put to bed in clean linen. The sweating, produced by the immersion, and thereafter would 'purge' the disease. The child was then to be given a drink of mild ale with a little white wine vinegar, to which had been added Harts Tongue, Liverwort, Aniseed, powdered Liquorice and sugar candy. As so often in such recipes, the prescription ends with a confident assertion that it will cure the ricketts 'w/t out fail'.

A recipe for scurvy dating from 1666 is more soundly based, judged by our standards. It runs 'Take ane Handfull of Scruvie Grass, half ane Handfull of Wormwood and a Handfull of Water Purpie, 2 Oranges and 2 lemmon Citrons, cut the orange and Citrons in slyces and steep all amongst ane quart of white wyne either in quart stoup or any wide mouth't vessell' across the mouth of which was tied a 'clean lining cloath' through which the liquid extract was strained. The patient was instructed to drink a mutchkin (4 Scots gills or 0.4 2 litres) of the liquid, hot or cold, every morning before eating and fasting for two hours thereafter for the 'space of the spring and harvest'. It is noted also that if oranges and lemons cannot be got 'three cropts of a firr tree' may be substituted. Presumably 'cropts' refers to the very top shoots of the tree. The reference to 'Water purpie' poses a problem. 'Purpie', as used in the vegetable seed lists refers to purslane, as we have already noted. The Concise Scots Dictionary identifies water purpie, probably correctly, as Brooklime (*Veronica beccabunga*), a common native wild plant of ditches and small streams.

A recipe for 'Shortnes of the Braith' included four ounces each of Aniseed and green Liquorice and an ounce of Cumin seed. A recipe for weakness in the knees, palsie, dropsy and wounds called for '3 chopines (a chopin was equivalent to two Scots mutchkins or 0.848l) of wheit wyne putt... in a quart stoup Then take as much of ye tops of broom without ye floure small shorn as will fill up ye haill quart stoup.' Another concoction, apparently for coughs and consumption, was made from Mouse-ear Hawkweed. We learn that the apothecaries of the Low Countries made a syrup from the juice of this plant. Another recipe referred to Elecampane roots.

The medicine of 1716 to cure fits in young Lady Stairs is little short of hair-raising. A lot of herbs were used, namely two handfulls each of Angelica, Greater Celandine (referred to as 'Sallandine' and identified as *Chelidonium majus*), Woad (*Isatis tinctoria*), Sorrel, Agrimony, Betony, Carduus and the inner rind of bearberry bark, one handful of Rosemary tops and flowers, three handfuls of Bearsfoot (*Alchemilla vulgaris*) and one and a half handfuls of red dock root, after removal of the pith. These were added to an extraordinary concoction which required a peck of garden snails which were put in the oven 'as hot as for cheese cakes' and cooked until they had 'done making a noise'. They were then taken out and washed well in beer. Next two quarts of great earthworms were slit and scoured in water and salt, washed well in beer and allowed to drain. Snails and worms were then ground in a stone mortar. Angelica was laid in the bottom of a cooking vessel (lembeck), the herbs were mixed, chopped and added, keeping a little back to add to the snail-worm mix. Then the dock root went in followed by the snail-worm mix then three ounces of broken cloves, and one ounce each of tumeric (*Curcuma longa* from southern Asia) and fenugreek, followed by saffron to the weight of one shilling, and six ounces of hartshorn shavings. To this was added three gallons of good strong ale and three quarts of canary. The top was closed and it was all allowed to stew for twelve hours. This elixir was recommended for convulsion fits and was to be administered at the rate of three spoonfulls to man or woman, at the time of the fit, and to children '3 of its own litle spoonfils'. This gem of herbalist ingenuity was labelled 'The receipt of ye Snail Water'.

Asarabacca or *Asarum europaeum*, a probably introduced species, was recommended for deafness. It was to be dried in heat until it crumbled and then three or four grains were to be sniffed up the nose when retiring at night. For the dropsy Dr Stanford of Andover's Receipt required three handfuls of bruised artichoke stalks, a quart of bruised Juniper berries, one handful of Horse Radish, two handfuls of tops of green firs, 'bruised small' plus two table spoonfuls of white mustard, similarly bruised. The mixture was then boiled in two gallons of water until reduced to one gallon and, after cooling and straining, the patient was to take a pint night and morning. Another, later, recipe for dropsy required green broom to be oven dried and then burnt to ashes, two ounces of which was added to a quart of Rhenish wine. Three glasses were to be taken daily, filtering the liquid through muslin. White poppy was used in another recipe. Dr Burnett's recipe also used many herbs i.e. Penny Royal, Feverfew, Mugwort, Balm, Wormwood, Mint, Rue, Borage, Agrimony, Juniper berries, Anise, Fennel seed, Germander, and Savin, of which the tops were used. A cure for trembling fevers specified a handful of Carduus, the ever popular Holy Thistle, a handfull of Marigold leaves together with the skin of an orange. Handfuls of leaves of Pellitory of the Wall, Fennel (finkle) and Chamomile featured in another recipe for the Laird of Pennicuik. A remedy 'against Iliack Passion or Colick' called for Chamomile flowers, Juniper berries, Laurel berries, boiled in water to which was added seed of Sweet Fennel, Caraway, Cumin and Anise. Garlic was often used as in Dr Boerhave's cure for worms, in which a head of garlic was bruised and mixed with French brandy, to be taken every morning for nine mornings followed by a dose of salts. White Mullein leaves were used in a cure for piles. Another cure for worms used powder of Indian Pink which, however, is not the Dianthus grown in the flower border but an American physical herb called *Spigelia marylandica*. For curing smallpox, after bleeding with loch leeches, the patient was given syrup of white poppies to induce sleep. After the pox appeared a handfull of sheep's purles i.e. dung pellets, were to be steeped in a large mutchkin of Carduus or Hyssop water or fountain-water for between five and six hours. The extract was poured off and sweetened with syrup of red Poppies. The patient was to take a spoonful or two of this every four or five hours and increase the dose rate if the pox on the face got worse. At the end of the disease a fine oil was recommended like spirit of Hartshorn in syrup of Violets.

A recipe to 'staye ye abundance of flux' called for browne mints (?) and cloves bruised and a quart of ale into which was put 'i spoonful of ye powder of a pikes jaws seeth (boil) them together, also bind both ye armes about ye brannes with ribbin something hard, allso parsley stampt (ground) and bounde to both ye great toes use all thes at once, if need be…'

The Edinburgh Evening Courant often carried advertisements for Dr So and So's tincture, pills or elixir. Herbs were often mentioned. Thus on Tuesday, Feb. 2nd 1725, it was announced that: 'A great quantity of Eyebright and other useful Herbs, exceeding good for preventing Giddiness in the Head, of great Beneift for the Sight, and an immediate Cure for the Pain in the Stomach and Ague, are to be sold at easy and reasonable Rates, Enquire from Mary McIntosh at the House, first Stair bewest the Foot of the Cattl Wynd in the Grass-Market, Edinburgh'. In September of the same year Dr Bateman's 'Spirit of Scurvy-Grass', both golden and plain, was advertised as a cure for scurvy and also for purifying the blood. Dr Robert Eaton made a bold claim for his 'Balsamick Styptick' which reputedly stopped bleeding. It had even arrested the flow of blood from a dog with a severed jugular. There were many more advertisements in similar vein.

Our forbears were greatly exercised by the risk of being bitten by a mad dog and recipes for an antidote abound. Thus one 'infallible cure' used cleanly picked Rue, peeled and bruised garlic and 'Venise treacle', apparently an electuary containing many ingredients. To this was added filed pewter or scraped tin and the whole was boiled in best ale in a tightly stoppered vessel. After straining, eight or nine spoonfulls were to be given to a man or woman and less for a child or one of weaker constitution while, for a horse or bullock twelve spoonsfuls were needed and three to five for a sheep, hog or dog. In another recipe you were to take six ounces of Rue, without the stalk, four ounces of Garlic 'pickd from the skins and well beat' and a similar quantity of mithridate and dust of English tin. To this was added a handfull of ash coloured liverwort, familiar to many of us as a pest of old lawns. This mixture was boiled in old ale, strained and, for a man, taken in seven spoonfuls, warm in the morning. In yet another recipe against biting of mad dogs, from late seventeenth century, leaves of Rue, Vervain, Sage, Plantain, Polypody, Wormwood, Mint, Mugwort, Balm, Betony, Hypericum and Centaury were gathered when they are 'in ye greatest growth qu/h (which) is about ye full moone in June and speedily dryed in a hott sun to be kept for use and to be yearly renewed not bating ym to pouder till you have use for ym.'

On April 11th 1738 *The Edinburgh Evening Courant* reported 'For the Benefit of the Publick and lest any Accident Should happen at this critical Time when they are killing all the Dogs in Town, we shall present our readers with three following Receipts for the Cure of the Bite of a Mad Dog: the first is by the celebrated Boerhave, the Second by the Eminent Dr Mead, and the Third by a French Physician, who says it is infallible, and that he has seen it often tried in France, even a person condemned to be smother'd between Feather Beds, and never known to fail of success'. Boerhave's receipt was the one noted already, with Rue, Garlic and Liverwort. Mead's version also used Ash Coloured Liverwort but also used Black Pepper. The Frenchman's recipe was wildly different and used 'shells of male oysters' of which the inner parts were calcined and then ground to powder which was sieved and added to 'right neat white wine'. This the patient was to drink without taking other liquids, avoiding anything oily. It is interesting to speculate which of these alternatives the public favoured.

The ash coloured lichen had a considerable reputation. In 1735 a correspondent of The Edinburgh Evening Post, signing himself Philanthropos, reported that Dr Mead had successfully treated more than five hundred patients bitten by a mad dog with the aid of the lichen powder. However, among some family papers, there was a note anent mad dog bites in which the writer observed that in the gathering of the lichen a good deal of moss or 'fog' may be included and he wondered, with commendable scientific scepticism, whether it might not be the moss rather than the lichen which contained the principal, efficacious ingredient. This was as footnote to yet another recipe which specified Jews ear (the fungus), powdered reed and brimstone. As a last example of the endless cures there was in 1739 a report of 'an Easy remedy for the Bite of a mad dog so much experienced by a certain country physician in England that he would willingly go amongst mad dogs to be bitten only to show the value of the remedy'. The remedy consisted simply of salt and water, one pound of salt to an English pint, which was used to bathe the wound for three hours followed by adding some salt to the wound which was bound up. There we must leave the remedies with some doubt as to whether the dogs in question were quite as mad as they seemed.

Finally, one last tailpiece, not wholly out of place in the context of some of the more extravagant claims we have just noted. In an issue of the Edinburgh Evening Courant for 1741 appeared the following notice: 'People of Broughton are just now under a terrible Panick by Reason of a Female Ghost, which they say, publicly Haunts the House of one George Ball a Blacksmith and Vents her Rage on the Good Woman of the House and the two penny bottles. The Chimaera draws a concourse of people to the House'. The press never changes.

# 5

# *The Evidence for Gardens in Sixteenth- and Seventeenth-Century Scotland*

We have already dwelt on the pre-eminent role of monastic institutions in promoting and sustaining the European tradition of gardening in Scotland. After the dissolution of the monasteries in 1560, skills in orchard management and kitchen gardening, once promoted by the Church, would now have been vested in the lay workers who formerly supplied the abbeys and monasteries with fruits and garden produce. Bearing in mind the extent to which Church properties were taken over by members of the nobility, the gardeners would have found themselves working for new masters. As the seventeenth century wore on there was increasing recruitment to the land-owning class by non-aristocratic merchants and members of the professions who aspired to the status of country-gentleman. Orchard and garden were essential hallmarks, so there would have been an expanding demand for trained gardeners and job prospects for apprentices would have been encouraging.

The other important way in which the European mediaeval tradition was sustained in Scotland was via the royal house. In Edinburgh the King's gardens were located on the south and west aspects of the Castle and the outlines of the terraces were still apparent, at least in 1925. The great royal orchard stretched southeast from the Green Market to the precincts of Liberton in the east and to the King's farm at Dalry in the west. Although referred to as an orchard it was, in part at least, more in the nature of a park where people played games and took their ease in summer. It was in the adjacent forest where David I escaped from the stag and, as a thank-offering, presented large tracts of land in and about Edinburgh to the Augustinian order. The royal grounds provided the food supply of the royal household and included crops, cattle, fish ponds, rabbit warrens and dovecots. From the Exchequer Rolls we learn that the produce included onions, leeks, syboes, cabbages, peas, beans and garlic, while apples, pears, plums and strawberries were the fruits commonly grown. No doubt culinary and medicinal herbs were grown as well. Roses, gilliflowers, cinnamon flowers (?), crocuses and primroses adorned the royal garden, while violets were grown to eat as a salad along with garlic and lettuce.

The centre of Edinburgh appears to have been largely taken up with garden ground. Apart from the extensive royal gardens around the Castle, there was the monastic garden of St. Giles which extended from the church to the Cowgate, as well as the Black Friars' garden which occupied the area roughly corressponding to that presently occupied by the old University building, Infirmary Street and part of the Cowgate. As a result of wars with England the royal garden fell into neglect and, later, the royal interest was transferred to Linlithgow while James III and IV developed gardens at Stirling and Falkland. It was recorded that George Campbell, Principal Gardener of the King's Great Garden fell at Flodden in 1513. In Edinburgh the gardens at Holyrood were greatly improved when it became the preferred residence. But although the royal interest in the gardens about the Castle lapsed, private gardens were established in its place. The tenants were obliged to plant trees and bushes commensurate with the size of their holding. There were severe penalties for 'stealing green wood and destroying of trees' or the damaging of orchards and the stealing of fruit.

It has been commonly believed that sixteenth- and seventeenth-century Scotland was a kind of horticultual waste land and that skilled gardeners must have been correspondingly thin on the ground. Cox (1935) provided no evidence to contradict that view, which we must now examine more closely. As noted earlier, the Earl of Crawford's inventory is also significant in the information it provides about the location and numbers of estates with orchards. Omitting the towns, Glasgow, Leith and Couper as well as the monastic ruins at Paisley and Lindores, they are, in Crawford's spelling, as follows:

| | | |
|---|---|---|
| Achans | Elie | Monimeall |
| Aitton | Gosfourd | Naughton |
| Alaways | Hamiltone | Newark |
| Ava | Hatfeild | Pinkie |
| Barnbreich | Hatton | Pitfirrine |
| Barnclugh | Inchtuir | Pitliver |
| Beill | Keneff | Powmais |
| Blaikston | Kersy | Red House |
| Bothwell Haugh | Kinnaird | Seatton |
| Cambusnethin | Kilwining | Steivenson |
| Craighall | Kirktone | Struthers |
| Culrose | Largo | Tininghame |
| Dalhousie | Leidingtone | Tulliallane |
| Deserse | Leslie | Weems |
| Dinmuir | Leuchers | Eister Weems |
| Drumond | Lundie | Wester Weems |
| Dunbuy | Maulslie | Winton |
| Dunnibirse | Milton | Yester |
| Durie | | |

It would take a great deal of research to discover just when each of these 54 orchards were established but we can infer that many were probably in existence in the latter third of the seventeenth century. Crawford's survey only applies to the south of Scotland. He did not mention the great orchard at Scone and did not report on any sites further north, especially Morayshire.

There is also evidence for the early presence of orchards and gardens in Walter Macfarlane's description of the Scottish scene. As far as is known Macfarlane was born early in the eighteenth century and died in 1767. He was an antiquary who produced a kind of reliable gazetteer of Scotland. He described the principal features and industries, delighted in historical allusions and particularly noted the castles, mansion houses and seats of the gentry. His voluminous manuscripts were edited into three volumes by Sir Arthur Mitchell. Although his descriptions of particular places cannot be precisely dated, since he was recognised an authority by 1739, they probably refer to about that time or earlier.

For the present discussion the two most relevant conclusions which emerge from his account are:

(1) There were a very large number of country houses, castles and seats occupied by the gentry in Scotland.

(2) The great majority of them were embellished with gardens, orchards, 'yeards' and often avenues, implying a spacious lay-out. A few quotations will serve as illustration.

In his reference to Skibo he noticed there is 'a fair orchard in the which there be excellent cherries'; 'The Castles and Pyles of Sutherland are Dornoch, Dunrobin, the Earle of Sutherland's special residence, a house well situated upon a Mole hard by the sea with fair Orchards, where there be pleasant Gardens planted with all kinds of fruits, herbs and flowers used in this kingdom and abundance of good saffron, Tobacco and Rosemary. The fruit here is excellent and chiefly the Pears and Cherries'; 'At Tyne the gentleman's house, whose founder died in 1690, had larges orchards'; At Dunning, Perthshire in 1723 'the mansion house called Dunscrub tis a stately old structure of considerable height, situate on a plain levell ground, decored with a pleasant garden and orchard to the South, West and North;' At 'the principle dwelling house of the Earle of Perth… there are beautiful avenues going to several airths from the front of the said dwelling house, with fine gardens producing a considerable quantity of fruit yearly;' 'In the parish of Fowlis there was the house Cultiewhey… with an orchard and closs by the westward of the house a wood. From that eastward about a mile, the house of Gorthie, belonging to Mungo Graham with many firrs, orchards and yeards thereto belonging;' 'North from said place the Castle of Killor with many parks, orchards…'; In the parish of Belly in the Enzie there was the House of Gordon Castle alias Bog of Gight 'with large gardens, orchards, plantings and parks'; At Fetteresso, the house was an old castle where the owner was reputed to have planted nearly a hundred thousand trees. Opposite his house he had planted a symmetrical array of trees, which 'with the different colours of the leaves so nicely intermixed and vareity of foliage, makes a charming show;' In Port Patrick he noted the Castle of Cardross as a good, convenient old house where there 'is a great deal of old, beautiful planting and very fruitfull orchyeards and had once pretty gardens;' In Selkirkshire, south west of Bowhill, 'there is a very fine house with orchards and planting, very plesant being ane ancient house belonging to the familie of Hardene;' 'North… to Philiphaugh a mile, there is an ancient house with orchards, pigeon house and planting;' 'South west from Hanging Shaw to Yarrow… there stands ane old toure called Dewchare Tower. It belongs to Dewar of Dewchar… with a very good mansion house and orchard;' 'Noar west from Sunderland Hall… there is a very fine house with orchards, avenues and planting very pleasent upon the skirt of a hill.' And so his account proceeds.

Although some of the mansions referred to would have been built by new recruits to the gentry, a very substantial number of the properties he describes were in the hands of long-established families, whose gardens and orchards were laid down in the seventeenth century. Many of these landowners had travelled on the Continent and would have been familiar with the gardens of France, Italy and Holland. No doubt their experience was not ignored when they set about improving their own properties. We can hardly escape the conclusion that, well before the eighteenth century dawned, there was a well established body of trained gardeners in Scotland, whose antecedents traced back to the monasteries and royal gardens.

This view receives powerful support from important archaeological evidence presented by Niall Hynd in 1984, which identified a large number of garden sites dating from the sixteenth and, especially, the seventeenth centuries. These are all associated with former dwellings of the nobility or gentry, ranging from castles or palaces to modest towers. Given the endemic warfare of those times it is not surprising that many of these old buildings and their precincts have fallen into ruin so that it calls for the skills of the archaeologist to reconstruct what was formerly present. The dating of such remains and their associated gardens rests on a variety of evience, both direct and circumstantial. When only fragments of a garden wall remain, an inset dated stone may survive. Or the likely date may have to be inferred from the style of construction and the nature of the building material. The presence of a detached sundial is very often an indicator of the former presence of a garden. Thomas Ross in 1883 published a comprehensive inventory of Scottish sundials, both attached and free-standing. He considered the latter 'among the most important class of monumental object bequeathed to this century by the seventeenth century and it is only when we come to realise how numerous they are and that many of them are fine works of artistic and scientific skill that we perceive how widespread must have been the appreciation of the sculptor's art as combined with that of the landscape gardener'. Detached sundials are classified into four groups:

(i)     Obelisk Dial
(ii)    Lectern-shaped Dial
(iii)   Facet-Headed Dial
(iv)    Horizontal Dial

A couple of examples are shown in Figures 93 and 94. Many of these sundials carried a date. Since it was conventional to site an imposing sundial in the centre of a garden we have, in such cases, a reliable dating for an early garden. When such evidence is missing, gardens may often be dated from references in estate accounts, or perhaps a surviving plan or a description by a visitor.

FIGURE 93
South Sundial at Newbattle Abbey, 1635. Thomas Ross, who made an inventory of Scottish sundials (1883), recognised them as among the most important monumental objects bequeathed by the seventeenth century. Many of them were of outstanding artistic and scientific skill. They were a regular feature of the garden landscape of that time and, although the garden may have long gone, often the sundial still stands to mark its former presence.
*Crown Copyright: Royal Commission on the Ancient and Historical Monuments of Scotland.*

FIGURE 94
Sundial at Sauchieburn House. Note the early date. Ross (1890) classified detached sundials into four categories :
(i) Obelisk
(ii) Lectern-shaped
(ii) Facet-headed and
(iv) Horizontal.
Their frequency and sophistication led him to speculate that the scientific principles of dialling may have been taught in the parish schools.
*Crown Copyright: Royal Commission on the Ancient and Historical Monuments of Scotland.*

Hynd has grouped the gardens identified in one or other of these ways into several categories, according to the nature of the evidence and/or the certainty with which a date can be assigned to a particular site. This information is very significant since it disposes of the previous belief that gardening skills were virtually absent in sixteenth- and seventeenth-century Scotland. The distribution of the sites, according to Hynd's classification, is shown in Figure 91. His lists, together with a reference date, where this can be stated wuth sufficient confidence, are as follows:

GROUP A: Gardens, other than royal gardens, which were purely of sixteenth century origin and which were enlarged and maintained in the succeeding century:

| | |
|---|---|
| Aberdour Castle | 1570–1690 |
| Craigmillar Castle | – |
| Seton Palace | – |
| Neidpath Castle | 1581 |
| Rowallan Castle | 1661 |
| Balvaird Castle | – |
| Langhaugh | – |
| Carberry Tower | 1598 |

The strategically placed Keep of Aberdour dates from the fourteenth century. In subsequent centuries the castle was enlarged and modified by the 4th Earl of Morton. A garden was well established by the late sixteenth century (Figure 95). The walled garden of the later development carries the inscribed date of 1632. Archaeological excavations during 1978 and 1980 exposed evidence for former, extensive terraced gardens, dating from the 16th century. About 1690 the 10th Earl Morton restored the gardens. We have already noted the list of shrubs supplied to him in 1691 by James Sutherland, Intendant of the Edinburgh Physic Garden. The terracing is in process of restoration (Figure 96).

At Neidpath Castle (Figure 97) it is still possible to trace the plan of a terraced garden extending down to the Tweed. Terracing appears to have been a frequent feature of Scottish gardens. According to Hynd, Craigmillar may also lay claim to an early garden, especially from the lay-out of its precinct walls, which were contructed about 1580, together with royal patronage during the sixteenth century.

GROUP B: Larger well known gardens with a known 17th century date:

| | |
|---|---|
| Edzell 1604 | Livingston 1668 |
| Winton House 1620 | Physic Garden, Edin. 1670 |
| Pinkie House 1621 | Wemyss Castle 1671 |
| Old Gala House 1629 | Pitmedden House 1675 |
| Drummond Castle 1630 | Broxmouth 1677 |
| Newbattle Abbey 1635 | Dalgety 1677 |
| Donibristle House 1639 | Leslie (Fife) 1677 |
| Coltness Castle 1654 | Scone 1677 |
| Dunrobin 1654 | Kinross House 1680 |
| Craigbook Castle 1662 | Dalkeith Palace 1690 |
| Hatton House 1664 | Culross Palace 1693 |
| Balcaskie 1665 | Melville House 1697 |
| Hamilton 1668 | Pollock House 1697 |

The garden at Edzell (Figure 92), established in 1604, is a well known example of imaginative design of continental inspiration. It has been suggested that it was not necessarily wholly original, and that Sir David

FIGURE 91
Archaeological evidence for early gardens in Scotland: distribution of sites according to the criteria used by Hynd (1983). Key to categories:

● Gardens, other than royal gardens, which were purely of sixteenth century origin but which were enlarged and maintained in the succeeding century.

▲ Lesser, well known gardens with a known seventeenth century date.

■ Little or unknown gardens with a known seventeenth century date, usually based on the survival of a dated sundial, but also from contemporary accounts, plans or a dated wall.

◆ Probable sites of seventeenth century gardens in which the dates are unknown but where evidence of terracing, the remains of a walled garden or a surviving sundial strongly indicate the presence of a seventeenth century garden.

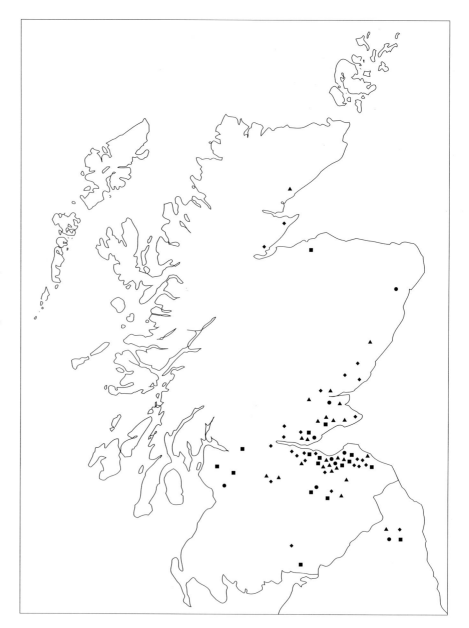

Lindsay may have benefited from the skills and materials already familiar to local craftsmen. The gardens of the Duke of Hamilton were the best of their kind. We have already noted Sir John Lauder of Fountainhall's first-hand comments. The Edinburgh Physic garden has already been considered.

GROUP C: Little known or unknown gardens with, however, a known seventeenth century date, usually based on the survival of a dated sundial, but occasionally from either contemporary accounts, plans or a date on a wall:

| | |
|---|---|
| Ravelston 1630 | Phillipstoun 1676 |
| Ormiston 1636 | North Barr 1679 |
| Peffermill 1636 | Fordell 1683 |
| Pitreavie 1644 | Niddrie 1683 |
| Northfield 1647 | Pitteadie 1686 |
| Posso 1649 | Haddington House 1688 |
| Ruchlaw 1663 | Barnton House 1690 |
| Darnaway 1668 | Traquair House 1690 |
| Ladylands 1673 | Cadder 1698 |

FIGURE 92
Edzell Castle Garden. The garden was created by Sir David Lindsay, son of the ninth Earl of Crawford. The date 1604, together with his initials and those of his wife, were inscribed above a gateway. The garden is enclosed on three sides by a wall of chequered masonry embodying the Lindsay crest. Although details of the indented walls were based on a Nurenberg design, derived from Sir David's travels in Germany, the construction of the garden probably relied on local craftsmen.

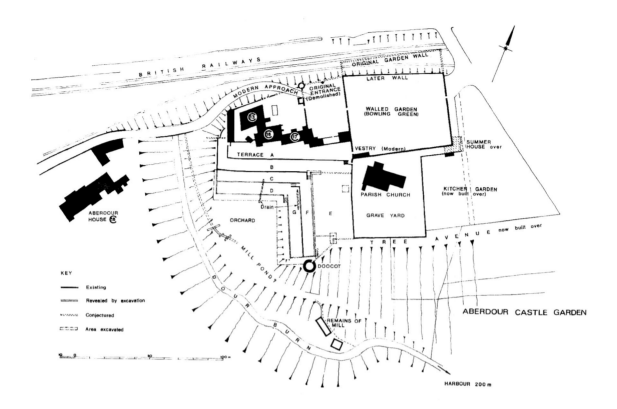

ABOVE: FIGURE 95
Aberdour Castle: plan of gardens. Excavations have revealed the former presence of extensive garden terraces, supported by stone walls, to the south of the Castle. It is believed they were established by the Fourth Earl of Morton, Regent Morton, who succeeded to the lands of Aberdour in 1548. There is also a walled garden dating probably from 1632.
*Crown Copyright: Reproduced by permission of Historic Scotland.*

RIGHT: FIGURE 96
Aberdour Castle: Current restoration of the original garden terracing.

GROUP D: Probable sites of 17th century gardens in which the dates are unknown but evidence of terracing, the remains of a walled garden or a surviving sundial strongly indicates the presence of a 17th century garden:

Balcomie
Barncluith
Barnbougle
Beil
Cadbole
Castle Campbell
Clackmannan Tower
Duntarvie
Elibank
Glamis Castle

Hangingshaw
Houston House
Inch House
Kinnel House
Lethington
Niddrie
Panmure
Pilmuir
Pitfirrane
Plora Burn

Red Castle
Spedlins Tower
Stobhall
Torwoodlee Tower
Tulliallan
Whittinghame
Whytebank
Woodhouselee
Yester

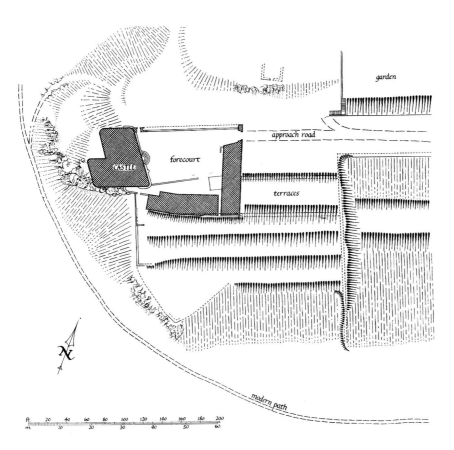

FIGURE 97
Plan of Neidpath Castle grounds. The remains of extensive garden terracing are still discernible, although the retaining walls are ruined or gone. The presence of a garden at Neidpath was noted in a record from 1581 in the Calendar of Writs preserved at Yester House, while a seventeenth century observer, Dr Alexander Pennecuik of Romano, noted the sloping Parterre in good order and also 'the three pretty Terraces, betwixt the house and water' i.e. River Tweed. It appears that terracing is a particular feature of early Scottish gardens, to be detected at other sites e.g. Plora Burn Tower, a little east of Peebles. *Copyright reserved. The Royal Commission on the Ancient and Historical Monuments of Scotland.*

Four of these sites, Hangingshaw, Elibank, Whytebank and Torwoodlee Tower, four minor castles in Selkirkshire, have the outlines of terraced gardens which are believed to date from the latter part of the sixteenth century and may have persisted to the seventeenth, hence their inclusion here. It should be noted that Barncluith, Beil, Lethington, Pitfirrane, Red Castle (House) and Yester also appear in the Earl of Crawford's list of orchards, providing independent evidence of gardens at these places in the seventeenth century. These lists are also interesting in another respect. They offer a guide to anyone interested in looking for descendants of plants which once grew in these old gardens.

GROUP E: Early 18th century, well documented formal gardens.

Crathes Castle 1701

Hamilton Palace 1708

Alloway House 1710-

Cammo House 1711-15

Taymouth Castle 1720

Castle Kennedy 1725-

Newliston House 1726

Drumlanrig 1720

Crichton House 1729

Inveraray 1730

Blair Atholl 1740

If we combine the sites mentioned in Categories A – D with the additional sites in Crawford's list, we arrive at a total of 141. How many garden sites dating from the sixteenth and seventeenth century have escaped detection is a matter of present conjecture and future enquiry. In historical terms gardens are evanescent artefacts. For each site we can infer the presence of at least one gardener, with one or more apprentices in larger establishments. If that is so we can conclude there was a substantial body of trained gardeners in seventeenth-century Scotland pursuing an ancient craft. It was these men and their immediate descendants who laid the foundations for the notable distinction of Scottish gardeners in the eighteenth century. It is fitting, therefore that we should now learn something of the working lives of these men, their wages and contracts and their fraternites, where these existed.

6

# *Gardeners' Wages and Contracts*

The historical continuity of long established gardening practice was successfully maintained in seventeenth century Scotland. Gardeners handed on, often from father to son, the unwritten rules of their craft. They held their place in the pattern of rural life in spite of the turbulence of the times. As hired men they worked for employers who ranged in affluence from earls and lords to minor lairds and country gentlemen. Some idea of where the gardeners stood in the social hierarchy can be gleaned from their contracts of employment and what they were paid. Compared with the voluminous records of the nineteenth century the information we seek for the seventeenth and early eighteenth century is not as complete as we should like. It consists chiefly of estate accounts or receipts of wages paid or contracts agreed, signed by the recipient and generally witnessed as well. They had a legalistic approach to transactions in those days.

There was considerable variation between estates in the terms of service. In the earlier period, the gardener was sometimes offered what was essentially a small holding in return for his labours. In other cases the gardener was entitled to part of the produce of the garden and might sell surplus produce, although it was not always clear whether the proceeds went to him or the estate, probably the latter. When the gardener could keep part of the produce for his own use the contracts were detailed and left no doubt as to how the yield of the garden was to be divided between him and his master. Sometimes a house was included as part of the agreement or the gardener might live in the big house. But, as time passed, the more impersonal payment of an annual wage became usual, either in Scots money or sterling. The annual wage ran from one Martinmas to the next and was invariably supplemented by an annual allowance of usually six or six and a half bolls of oatmeal, referred to as a Board Wage. A boll was the traditional Scots measure of meal, equivalent to one hundred and forty pounds. Six bolls per year works out at approximately sixteen pounds of meal per week. This must have been regarded as the average family requirement. If more was needed it could be bought from the estate girnal. Fractions of a boll were measured in firlots or pecks, of which there were four firlots to the boll and four pecks to the firlot.

Gradual increase in the nominal wage during much of the eighteenth century was probably due to inflation, but, by the end of the century, competition between estates for experienced gardeners led to an improvement in conditions. Gardeners often had assistants, commonly referred to as servants, garden labourers or even under gardeners, together with one or more apprentices or 'garden lads'. In estate accounts the gardener's and also his assistants' pay were often combined as a single entry. Where they were quoted separately we can compare the difference in their annual income; otherwise we have to infer it. In a few instances we have records of the pay of the rest of the estate staff so we can compare the status of the gardener with that of other members of the household hierarchy. Conditions of employment and pay, especially in the seventeenth century, varied so much between estates as to defy simple, tabular classification. The situation can be best appreciated from examples drawn from different estates.

## Payment by use of land

In earlier times, what we know as the garden was always referred to as the yard or, in Scots, 'yeard'. Thus, in 1565 Lady Fordell agreed with William Raa that he should look after the yard of Fordell throughout the year and plant and prune the trees. Only peas and beans were to be planted, an interesting comment. For his labours he was to have 6 bolls of meal a year together with the 'profit' of the yard, the use of two acres of ground and grass for two cows.

In 1653 the Earl of Cassilis agreed to pay his gardener 'fiftie merks' as fee from one Martinmas to the next. A merk was equivalent to two thirds of a pound so the fee worked out at thirty-three and a third pounds Scots. He was to have five bolls and two firlots of meal per year together with a house to dwell in either in the estate grounds or to be built near the byre. He was to have 'twa kyes grass' and the earl was to provide 'fodder to witt strae for feeding of them in the winter'. In another agreement with a different man, the gardener was provided with forty pounds Scots money, in two instalments, seven bolls of meal, a house and grass for two cows with winter fodder. The gardener undertook to furnish the Earl's house with kitchen herbs and salads, kale and roots. In this instance if the Earl was not 'weill served by the said gairdner he sall have libertie to dismiss him at Martinmas nixt or anie Martinmas yrafter upon three four days warning.'

On the Panmure estate in 1653 the arrangement was rather different. The gardener was paid only twenty merks with six bolls two firlots of meal per year. However, he was given the use of land equivalent to the 'half of ane cottar land', which was to be ploughed, harrowed and 'mucked' by his Lordship's horses. He was at liberty to keep a cow, like the rest of the cottars on the estate, but he had to pay a rent for the land equivalent to 'eight pounds sax shillings and eight pennyes'. His duties included looking after the garden and orchard and keeping the beds of young trees free of weeds. He was strictly forbidden to take anything out of the garden or the tree plantings without his Lordship's knowledge. This injunction was repeated. 'If I find that he or his suyse or any uther tak any uther thing out of the gardine in a covert way it shall be as so much as if they had taken all out of it that is in it'. Finally his cow was not to graze on his Lord's grass but 'to eat in the muire'. The employer does not appear over generous in this instance.

At Brechin in 1654 the Laird set down the particular conditions to be settled with his gardener which included the following:

(i) To keep a particular yard in good order, the paths to be kept clean and the floures in it 'nurrished and preserved, and that he use his best means for procuring all other floures that he can get and plant them yrin.'

(ii) All the fruit that grows in the garden to be sent to him yearly.

(iii) He should provide during the year a firlot of onions, forty cabbages, a hundred turnips, a hundred carrots and a hundred 'Hartichoks of Jerusalem'. This is an interesting entry. According to Loudon's 'Encyclopedia of Plants' Jerusalem Artichokes (*Helianthus tuberosus*) were first introduced to Britain from Brazil in 1617. It is rather surprising to find them growing in Brechin less than forty years later. In addition to these vegetables the gardener was to supply half a peck of mustard and send in some baskets of raspberries and gooseberries during the year.

(iv) He was to let his master have a few of every sort of seed of herbs that 'he wins in the garden'.

Given agreement to carry out these duties the laird would buy as much timber for him as needed to put up a house and provide three bolls of meal per year, a rather miserly allocation. He then went on to specify further duties such as taking care of the tree plantations, keeping a tally of the different sorts of tree, grafting each year some apple, pear, plum and also cherry trees, if they were available, as well as completing the planting of fruit trees on the walls.

In 1662 the Earl of Cassilis framed the agreement with his gardener rather quaintly whereby all the stone fruits, cherries, strawberries etc. were for the gardener's use except for what he, his lady and their chamberlain required. Also two timber boxfuls of both strawberries and cherries were to be sent to their son, while the early plums were to be sent to Broxmouth or disposed of as the chamberlain thought fit. The earl and his lady were free to call for what they needed when they were in Teviotdale or Ayr. A 'creill full' of gooseberries, another of cherries, and likewise of good apples and pears were reserved for one William Ancrum, while the chamberlain was to have the fruit of one or two pear trees. The gardener was to have 'the comon apples and peereis for his owin use'. A futher provision was that a horseload of best keeping apples, 'in creills made of purpose' was to be sent to Biggar fair. This record is of interest on several counts. In 1662 the orchard was well stocked with both fruit trees and soft fruit and large enough to produce surplus for sale. Although it appears that the gardener was left with the remnants of the crop, without knowing the size of the orchard, we cannot say how much that amounted to. There is no mention here of wages or other conditions of service, which were no doubt specified elsewhere.

In 1710 we meet with an agreement between Lord Banff and his gardener, which also does not refer to wages, but instead indicates a rent payable by the gardener for the use of land and produce. The gardener was to have the croft of land called 'the Gairdiners Croft' for the space of three years for which he is to pay twelve pounds after 'the separation of the crop from the ground' i.e. the harvest. The gardener is obliged to keep the croft land in good order, keep the walks in the yard clean, mow in the yard the grass, which is to belong to him and for which a scythe is provided. The grass on the east flower yard is to belong to the Lord and the gardener is obliged to mow it. The rest of the grass is to be kept 'short and tight'. The wall fruit trees are to be cared for, nails and tyes provided, barren i.e. non-fruit trees, planted in the yard as required. All the fruit in the yard, including the berries in the borders, are to belong to the master. The gardener is enjoined to 'plant strawberrie borders as he shall be advised and what foreigne seeds my Lord shall furnish. The Gairdner is to give them ground therto and Caire for them, as also what roots and flowers my Lord shal furnish, and the Gairdner is oblidged to furnish the house caile and partie small caile and roots till Martmas, and therafter to furnish the house by measure and what roots he furnishes my Lord will give him a peck of meall for each peck of roots he shall furnish'. In the event of any differences arising from this particular transaction, perhaps not unanticipated given the imprecise standardisation of weights and measures then prevailing, the matter was to be referred to the arbitration of Peter and Hary Lensaie in Banff, with a penalty of twenty pounds Scots for the defaulter. We might infer from this agreement that the gardener rented, perhaps on favourable terms, what was equivalent to a small holding on which he could raise produce for sale, provided he supplied what was agreed to the master and stuck to the barter arrangement.

A later example of the lease of land to a gardener who paid rent, is illustrated by the agreement in 1743 beween Sir Archibald Grant of Monymusk and James Bradfoot, gardener, whereby the latter took over the yard of Monymusk, and 'Grass at the burn side Extending from the Gate of the House to the Inclosures fronting it and from the River Side to the wall of the Home park, Sir Archibald haveing all free passage through it, and

Liberty to Build his piets as usuall, and that for three years from his Entry the Said James is also to have Liberty to Sheer and Cutt the grass in Hay yeard – the takeing Care of and Dressing the Hedges planted or to be planted round the same, – Sir Archibald is to remove his nurseries as soon as Conveniently Can be out of the Gairden, that James may Enjoy the Ground thereof, But James is to take Care of and Dress all Hedges already planted in the Gairden, and not to Digg any Ground therein but what hath been usually Dugg, And not to Sow Bear or Corn of any Sort therein, Except pease, nor allow Cattle of any sort to Goe into it, and is Oblidged to keep two Hives of Bees for the Said Sir Archibald, and to care for them as for his own; Also the Said James is to have the produce of what fruit trees are already planted in the Home park. he Grafting the Crab Stocks that are Sett round it… And what further Stocks the said James shall Graft on his Gairden, the Said Sir Archibald shall furnish the Stocks out of his Nurseries, and when sold, the price shall be Divided Betwixt them. the said James shall also have one Liet of Sir Arch/ds Liet piets and have sufficient accomodation in the Low parts of the House, he takeing care of the whole and Sir Archibalds furniture in it as pr Inventory, and shall have the use of the Dairy and, Brew House, and also of the killn and killn Barn'. 'Liet' or 'Leet' referred to a traditionally recognised quantity of peats for fuel. After specifying the extent of the ground the gardener could sow, measured in a total of four and a half bolls sowing, and stipulating they be kept level and dunged, the annual rent is stated as 'fifty pounds Scots for the Gairden and five pound for the Liet of piets, and at rate of ten pound for the Bolls Sowing of the Avinue Short Bank and at the rate of eight pound for the Bolls Sowing of the Avinue. Beginning the first terms payment at Martinmas Seventeen hundred and fourty four'. In addition the gardener was to have the Pigeon House, except the Dung, for which he would pay what the laird thought reasonable. A further allocation of six small walks in the avenue was specified for growing peas, turnips or potatoes, to be dug only with the spade, provided he took care of the hedges, replaced dead trees in the avenue and planted out various young trees from the nursery. We are left with the impression of meticulous accounting.

There is another agreement for the period 1770 to 1776 between the Laird of Monymusk and his gardener at Paradise, which was a separate property located between the River Don and the Hill of Benachie. Here the owner, referred to in the agreement as the Heritor, was to have one half of all the fruit, great and small, in the garden. Similarly he was to have half of all kinds of seeds gathered by the 'Undertaker' i.e the gardener in Paradise and neighbouring woods of the estate, except the berries and nuts. The gardener is to receive three bolls of meal and half the produce of the garden, the fishing on both sides of the river Don in the whole length of Paradise Wood, and also half the thinnings of the Wood. The gardener was responsible for keeping the walks, hedges and borders of the garden in decent order, while the laird's family were 'to have the pleasure of walking through the garden… none Else to Enter the Garden but as the Undertaker pleases'. The grass, borders etc. were to be limed as agreed. The laird reserved the right to punish 'such as shall ofend, Either in woods water or Garden'. And finally, a characteristic Monymusk touch, if the gardener collects meal on credit from the Heritor's girnal, he shall pay for it according to the regulations of the shire, with the interest from the day of receiving the meal until the day of payment if required.

## Payment by money and meal

We must next consider examples of payment by way of annual salary and board wages, the arrangement which eventually superseded the earlier payment by land use.

In 1643 we learn from an account rendered by James Cuthbertson, gardener to the Earl of Murray at Donibristle, that he was owed one hundred and twenty eight pounds Scots as a year's wages for him and his man. In such instances it is not clear whether the master or the gardener set the wages of the latter's assistant(s). From instances of a later period, where we know the garden labourers only got a little more than half the gardener's wage, we could guess that Cutherbertson was paid about ninety pounds Scots. Since there were twelve Scots pounds to the single English pound his wage would be equivalent to between seven and eight pounds sterling. The account also includes an entry: 'for the space of three yeirs for three suits of cloathes at 20s sterling the piece' which was equivalent in Scots money to thirty six pounds. The account includes a list of items bought for the garden such as nails, 'ane syth', 'seids three yeirs… ilk yeir', 'three scor loads of land gravell to doe the walkes of the gardeine at aughteine pennies the load', pear, apple and cherry 'Impes' i.e. scions for grafting as well as trees to 'graff' etc. as well as an item of sixty pounds 'restand to the said James of his wages since he was in Donibristle', a familiar example of the frequent tardiness with which the gentry settled their debts.

For April 11th 1681, at Hamilton, there is a discharge from Hew Wood, the Duke's gardener for the sum of two hundred and forty pounds Scots and two chalders of meal for 'him and his servants who work with him from Martinmas 1680 to Martinmas 1681'. A chalder was equivalent to sixteen bolls of meal. Assuming the usual six bolls per year we can infer that Wood had probably four men working with him at that time, although, later, the number was greater. At the same period the principal gardener at Kinross was paid sixty-two pounds Scots per year with six bolls and two firlots of meal. His three or four asistants each had forty merks per annum, i.e. twenty-six and two thirds pounds Scots or less than half the gardener's wage, together with a similar allowance of meal and a pair of bounty (free) shoes at half a crown a pair.

In 1695 the Earl of Breadalbane persuaded a gardener, who had emigrated to London, to return to Taymouth for a wage of fifteen pounds sterling a year together with 'a house to dwell in, two cows grass and six bolls and a half of meall'. These terms were good enough to suggest that, as early as 1695, the Scottish gentry were having to make an effort to tempt home experienced gardeners who had sought work in England.

In 1706 Robert Brown, gardener, acknowledged receipt from the Laird of Glenorchy's chamberlain of his own and his man's allowance for two years from March 1706 to March 1708 for five pecks of meal weekly which 'extends to Threttie two bolls two furlots meall as also payment of my own and my mans wages for these two years being yearlie for myself fourty pounds Scots money And for my man Eighteen pounds'. So in this case the gardener received a little over twice what his man got. Compared with the other accounts the pay here was pretty miserable, although the allocation of meal was a little more generous.

In 1721/2 the Earl of Breadalbane was paying his Head gardener and his four men two hundred and sixteen pounds Scots with six and a half bolls of meal each. Assuming the Head man was getting about twice the pay of his assistants, his pay would have been about seventy pounds Scots. Often, as in this case, the accounts quote the costs of a boll of meal, which varied from year to year and, in this instance, was six pounds per boll, so the total cost of thirty-two and a half bolls worked out at one hundred and ninety five pound Scots, not far short of the total wage bill. In another example, at Buchanan in 1741, the cost of meal was ten pounds per boll. The money payment of the head gardener was sixty pounds Scots, which was less than the value of his allowance of six and a half bolls of meal, valued at sixty-five pounds Scots.

In an account from another estate for 1709–10 a gardener was paid two hundred and eighty-four pounds Scots and thirty-two and a half bolls of meal for himself and four men, from which we might infer he was paid between eighty-five and ninety pounds. In 1734 the gardener to the Earl of Panmure only received an annual wage of thirty-four pounds Scots. In the same year the Earl of Breadalbane paid his gardener three pounds Sterling and six and a half bolls of meal. He also received twenty shillings for a year's snedding in the Earl's wood. His assistant received twenty pounds Scots and a similar allocation of meal. In 1738 the Earl of Cassilis paid his head gardener eight pounds Sterling with bed and board in the Earl's house, a further example of variation between estates.

George Dundas' diary for the early eighteenth century refers to employment of workmen who were general estate workers but also planted trees. Their favourable conditions of service are worth noting. In 1719 Dundas gave one of these workmen thirty-five pounds Scots per annum, a free house, grass for a cow and follower and six and a half bolls of meal. Another was hired for thirty-two pounds Scots, grass for a cow, the same quantity of meal and also permission to sow a little barley and oats on any unwanted pieces of ground.

Two comparisons of wages paid to estate staff, including the gardener, are interesting. For 1702 we have a record of wages paid to staff at Taymouth by the Earl of Breadalbane. Listed in order of declining annual income they are as follows:

|  | £ s d (Scots money) |
|---|---|
| Gardener at Taymouth | 144 00 00 |
| Cook | 70 00 00 |
| Butler | 46 16 00 |
| Groom | 40 00 00 |
| Gardener at Finlarig | 36 00 00 |
| Workman | 18 00 00 |
| Footman | 13 06 08 |
| Porter | 13 06 08 |
| Fowler | 13 06 08 |
| Under Cook | 12 06 08 |
| Herd | 7 05 06 |

In this hierarchy of social esteem the gardener at Taymouth apparently heads the list but no doubt he employed and paid for several garden labourers out of this total. Probably his effective wages were nearer what the gardener at the other property of Finlarig got but his status appears to have been about as high as that of the butler. Both cook and under cook were men. As usual the humble herd came last in the scale of pay. The meal allocation is not quoted in this list.

For 1734 we have a similar record of wages paid by the Duke of Gordon:

|  | £ s d (Sterling) |
|---|---|
| Housekeeper | 10 00 00 |
| Gardener | 9 00 00 |
| Butler | 9 00 00 |
| Farrier | 8 00 00 |
| Wheeler | 6 00 00 |
| Under butler | 4 00 00 |
| Brewer | 3 15 00 |
| Porter | 3 00 00 |
| Groom | 3 00 00 |
| Couper | 3 00 00 |
| Workman | 1 15 00 |
| Laundry maid | 1 10 00 |

Again the gardener is near the top of the list, on a par with the butler, and only exceeded by the housekeeper. Reckoning the Scots at one twelfth the value of the English pound, the Duke of Gordon's pay compares favourably with that of the Earl of Breadalbane. A generation later i.e. in 1766, the Duke was paying his gardener at the rate of twenty pounds Sterling a year, more than double the rate for 1734, but the pay of a garden labourer had risen only to a maximum of three pounds and some were paid two pounds ten shillings or less. But the gardener was a very responsible member of the Duke's staff, with twelve men to assist him. They received the usual Board Wages of two pecks of meal each per week.

To come to a later period for comparison, in 1765 David Patton, a prospective gardener for Monymusk in Aberdeenshire, set down his conditions in correspondence with Sir Archibald Grant. By that time experienced gardeners were sought after and knew their worth. His conditions included:

(ı)    Not to have to teach more than one apprentice at a time
(ıı)   A sufficient quantity of fuel to be provided
(ııı)  An adequate house, rent free, with a bedstead, two tables, three or four chairs, cupboard and press or drawers for 'holding Body cloathes'
(ıv)   One and a quarter stone of oatmeal per week
(v)    A cow or two maintained throughout the year
(vı)   The cost of transporting himself and family from Edinburgh to the intended place of residence
(vı)   Fifteen pounds Sterling wages per annum

He ended by noting that he would undertake to survey and divide land if required but would not commit himself to an agreement until he had an answer to his proposals. In the reply, presumably from the factor, Sir Archibald agreed to provide a house at the head of the garden, with an earthern floor but dry and with a thatched roof. Previously he had never provided furniture but, in view of the gardener's good character, would provide what he wanted. Again he did not normally pay for travel to the job but would allow forty shillings. As to wages, the previous gardener got six pounds and he never paid more than eight but would agree to twelve in this instance. Clearly Sir Archibald was very anxious to obtain the services of this gardener.

Although the pay and conditions of the Head Gardener and his assistants were improving, they hardly did justice to their skills. For a general comment on the wages paid to gardeners in the second half of the eighteenth century we can hardly do better than quote what William Boutcher had to say on this issue. Boutcher was a respected Edinburgh nurseryman who published a treatise on trees, which were his specialty. He was appalled at the irresponsible behaviour of some nurserymen who, with little experience or knowledge, had been attracted into what was a lucrative and expanding market. He had clear views on the qualities needed in a gardener and what they should be paid. Thus, 'I must lay it down as a principle, that some small degree of learning at least is necessary to make a good gardener; and what sensible man will bestow that on his son, to quallify him for an employment that, to all appearance will never give him more than fifteen or twenty pounds a year or what boy of spirit and genius will study a profession, from which he can only receive so poor a return. It therefore appears to me very certain, that an increase of wages to these useful men would, in a short time, have most desirable effects, and that we should then have at command twenty intelligent gardeners where we now perhaps are at a loss to find one; nor is it to be doubted the master would gain a greater proportion than the servant. A great man bestows from fifty to a hundred pounds on a French cook; to a British gardener seldom more than from twenty to forty. I despise all national reflections and esteem an honest Frenchman of any profession, but in a particular manner a French cook; yet I can by no means think him intitled to so great an advantage over the other. Everybody knows that a cook cannot furnish out a handsome tarte without the assistance of a good gardener; and perhaps there is as much judgement required in raising material of the best quality, as in dressing them well.'

## Apprentices and their role model

It was usual for the gardener to have one or more garden lads or apprentices, who were paid a pittance in return for learning their trade. At Monymusk in 1775 an account included an item of nine pounds Sterling for the yearly wages of five garden lads, while their combined victuals and lodging for the year cost thirty-nine pounds ten shillings. In addition, a letter from the gardener to the Laird noted that they were to have four pounds each during their apprenticeship and that, at its expiry, each is obliged to pay twenty shillings (i.e. one pound) if required to do so and, in the event of any misdemeanour, they have to pay that sum immediately. No doubt, apart from learning their trade, the apprentices carried out the most tedious or messy tasks the gardener was happy to avoid. It appears they were generally taught arithmetic, the elements of mensuration, how to do accounts and were instructed by the gardener in the naming of plants. With what was generally a sound basic education, their apprenticeship laid the foundations for many a successsful career. During the winter, when bad weather kept them indoors, they were set to jobs like making and repairing wooden rakes, making and mending baskets, boiling willows for white baskets and the like. They led a hard life, working a six day week, no doubt like the garden labourers who worked from six in the morning to six at night 'unless something more than ordinary should occur.' They had no time off for Christmas or Hogmanay. Only the Sabbath gave a respite together with time off to attend the sermons the day before and/or after Communion Sunday.

For comment on how gardeners and their apprentices should conduct themselves and evidence of the social standing of head gardener, we can turn to the Laird of Monymusk's Journal. For example, as winter work he recommended 'gairdners in winter might make bee sceps & elks & baskets & at least 40–50 moll traps, that they may all be set in spring to destroy that hurtful creature. Cause you keep the furrs of them they catch & also urge him (the gardener) to be reading & explaining to his apprentices books of gairdening & husbandry; this will both be good to young men and raise his own character, that he'll get money to take apprentices, & you may at leisure give them lessons of writing & arithmetick. There is pleasure to doe good by keeping them always diligent, it may make them virtuous. Give men at Mains an offer of the same, I shall pay for pens, ink & paper, for which & other purposes, secure in the cheapest way a riem of good writing paper.' Monymusk thrift was never far away.

Another reflection on the qualites and status of the estate gardener is provided by an entry in Grant of Monymusk's memorandum for 1755: 'A Gardener is wanted at Monymusk where a Good deal of new work is to goe on – and as it is a Loss to Master and Servant to be Shifting service – He must come with a purpose to settle for Life – and therefore more certain is necessary for his Qualifications besides proper knowledge he must have some proper Dignity, to be Respected and to have his Instructions regarded by those under him; and must Resolve to give them good Example in the whole of his conduct, by Sobriety honesty and Dilligence, and every article of a truly vertuous man – He will have the use of Instruments and Books – and as he must keep 2 or 3 Apprentices such as his Master shall approve of, he should be of such Character as Good ones will desire to be under him, they will have opportunitie and leisure for Instruction in writing accts and the use of Books. He must know a Litle of Surveying and Drawing, and will have some help to improve in these – and must know all articles of the Kitchen & Fruit Garden & Nurseries & how to plant and train them, and a little of the hothouse & walls & flowers & flowering shrubs – and to Study in all this his master's Interest, trusting to him to reward according to his merit'. As already noted the continuing education of apprentices in wrting, arithmetic, botany etc. was then general practice in Scotland and this was recognised by Neil (1813) as part of the reason for their finding good jobs in England.

## Complaints about pay

Sir Archibald Grant did not part readily from his money. Thus a 'Journamen Garner' named Arthur Simpson complained that although he had served for 'the space of Eight years for the first three years I have no wages – for the next two years I hade one pound ten shillings – and for the rest of the time I hade Two pound – Now as I find that is so little that it will not hold me in clothes and shoes – and as I can have four pounds several ways else I insist upon it or with a goodwill to leave the service although it be with a reluctonice'.

In 1775–6 there was a complaint from the Monymusk gardener about the wages he was getting or, rather, not getting. He pointed out in his letter that when he left the service of Lord Aboyne to work at Monymusk he had asked for the same terms, namely ten guineas as wages and four guineas for apprentice fees and 'your Honours answer was ye gave a Gardener No apprentice fees But would give money for all together. This was all that was said then.' But when he was asked by the Laird's representative, presumably the factor, what wages he wanted he said he was willing to serve for Fourteen guineas each year 'with such other necessaries as my predecessor hade'. He was under the impression this had been agreed but he was subsequently offered only ten pounds which 'would not make my Family live in any measure comfortable – neither did I agree to it at first.' He rejected any assertion that negligence in his work merited such a reduction in wages. 'Make strict Enquiry of any part of which I took in hand be Behind or wrong or neglected have I not Bound four stout lades for three years Each to work as Apprentices for their victualles only when Formerly Apprentices gott four pounds During their Apprenticeship and paid nothing. There is now six stout lades in Gardens and Nursery & not one penny Due to any But two pounds a year to one Lade – I will venture to say there is not a nobleman nor gentleman in the Country his such Like Bargons Therefor after your Honours observing this I hope ye will give orders to pay up my Wadges. My Father has twenty guineas to pay Drum (a neighbouring estate) for a new lease of his Tack just now it is my Duty to help him in such a cause'. The correspondence later became more acrimonious and the gardener complained that he had been falsely accused of applying to another place for employment. Observing that his encouragement was very small, smaller than he originally expected and not fit to support his family and also that his employer was gaining £22 per annum compared with the cost of gardeners in his predecessor's time, nevertheless he had not applied for another post. 'I positively Refuse ever making the smallest application to any person for a place or post or any Kind of Imployment from any one time I was your Servant and Earnestly begs your Honour will acquaint me the person that said to your Hon/r because these persons that said so are bitter Enemys to me who as far as I know never merited such things of them.' The correspondence ends two months later on a tragic note. On Feb 17th 1776, after giving a general account of work in the garden, the letter ends 'I hade severall more things to answer to your Hon/rs letter to me. But my son being this moment Dead I am not capable to Write more at this Time.' It was signed Will Shines or possibly Shiras; the script is ambiguous.

In spite of his reputation as a progressive landowner, the Laird of Monymusk drove a hard bargain. If this was the kind of attitude prevailing among other Scottish landowners it is no surprise that the gardeners flocked over the Border where the prospects were so much better and there was competition for their services. But the gardener's lot did improve with time. Thus in 1803 we encounter an offer by a gardener named James Walker to become gardener to Lord Melville at Dunira in Perthshire and, with proper assistance, to look after the hot house, the flower and kitchen garden and the forcing houses. But, in return, he stipulated a free house, fuel, a cow summer and winter, six and one half bolls of meal and thirty-five pounds per year, plus his carriage paid in coming from Leith to Perth by water and thence by land to Dunira and, should he find the post unsuitable, free carriage to Perth. The time had come when the professional gardener could seek employment on his own terms.

## Finding jobs

We may wonder how gardeners got news of vacant posts, especially when they had finished their apprenticeship and were moving on as journeymen. There was considerable mobility in employment, sustained primarily at first by the grape-vine of contact between gardeners in neighbouring estates and by landowners enquiring of their acquaintances of potential recruits to their staff or recommending a journeyman on the look-out for a job. However, towards the latter part of the eighteenth century this was supplemented by adverts in the newspapers and especially by the good offices of the growing numbers of well established seedsmen. London seedsmen were first in line for advice about reliable gardeners. As early as 1687 the Duke of Hamilton, on a visit to London, asked Mr London, the leading seedsman, to recommend a suitable gardener. The Duke reported to the Duchess that the seedsman had recommended a young Scotsman as honest and intelligent. Although not very experienced he thought he would be advised by Hew Wood in the 'working and overseeing of the yeards'. As to wages, he wanted twelve pounds Scots but the Duke thought he could have him for ten. Apart from the sidelight on the Duke's canny dealing, here is another instance of a young Scots gardener in London in the 1680's. In 1703, following on the death of his gardener Alex Wood, the Duke was advised by the Duchess to approach Mr. London again for a sober man and added the qualification: 'I would rather take a Scotsman than of any other nation'.

As early as 1743 the Edinburgh seedsman, David Dowie, was recommending to the laird of Buchanan, a gardener who would accept two pounds ten shillings Sterling per annum, two pecks of meal a week and a 'bed as usuall'. In 1746 correspondence between the Earl of Stair, New Liston, with Archibald Eagle, another Edinburgh seedsman, revealed that the latter was acting as go-between for a gardener who had worked at New Liston, and Sir Archibald Grant of Monymusk. The Earl of Stair confirmed the gardener's skills and reliability. The intermediary role of the nurseryman soon became the norm so that by the nineteenth century, and indeed, into the present century, the nurserymen collectively acted as the gardeners' employment bureau. In contact with the local estates and their gardeners they were well placed to know who was in need of gardening staff and where they might find suitable candidates. They brought employer and employee together to their mutual advantage, without charge to either, as part of the goodwill they established among satisfied clients. When the system was in full swing the regular way for a young man to embark on a gardening career was to apply first to a nurseryman who would assess his suitability or otherwise and, if satisfied, pass him on to a head gardener for further appraisal.

We can see this system in operation at the end of the eighteenth century in, for example, the numerous recommendations of gardeners by Dicksons of Edinburgh to Forbes of Callandar, who was establishing a large garden in the latest style and had a steady demand for staff. Thus, in March 1792 Dicksons notified Forbes that they had 'engaged John Simson for you to work as Journeyman Gardener – he has wrought for some time in our Nursery very much to our satisfaction and was strongly recommended to us by a gentleman we wish much to serve'. Again, in 1796 a letter ran: 'have engaged two good steady young men for the Gardener, one of them will be at Callandar on Monday, the other on Tuesday or Wednesday – both of them I have known for years – have every reason to believe that they will answer well'. And again, in 1798 from Dickson's: 'Have engaged a Journeyman Gardener – he is a stout and good Workman – has been working in our nursery since February. I have different Gardenrs in view which I think will answer your place.' And so it went on.

There are also numerous letters from gardeners, who had heard that there was work to be had at Callandar, and wished to impress with an account of their experience. It is noticeable how many had worked in England, sometimes stating they had done so to extend their experience of gardening. It is equally significant how many were ready to return to Scotland. Thus, one man with two to three years experience of working in England was attracted to Callandar because his wife came from that district. The gardener at Blair Drummond wrote to press the claims of his son who was 'with myself till he was man big' and then worked in a couple of Scottish gardens before moving to good gardens in the neighbourhood of London. 'I flatter he will answer Mr Forbes well.' Another had worked in Chelsea Physic Garden. Evidently the notion that emigration to England was an irreversible process is wide of the mark. Given decent pay and conditions many Scots gardeners were very happy to return home.

## Bothy life

As we have noticed, several contracts from the early eighteenth century refer to the provision of accomodation or at least 'a bed'. Such variable and perhaps rather ad hoc arrangements evolved during the eighteenth century into the standard, bothy system. Typically, the bothy was the house on the estate in which the apprentices and the unmarried journeymen lived, although it may also have been where the gardener also lived if unmarried. The bothy system became the standard arrangement and persisted in Scotland even into the present century. Life in the bothy was spartan. From 1771 we have a bothy inventory, attested by one gardener as he handed over to a successor. The list reveals the typical bothy furniture which would be familiar to any apprentice. In the gardener's words it ran as follows:

> *In the kitchen:* a Kitchen Dresser, a Plate rack, a large yetlin (cast iron) pot, a Brander (gridiron), a small frying pan, Two racks of spit (for roasting), a cran of Iron (an iron frame for supporting pots over the fire), a pair of tongs, a pair of Iron Bowls and a Crook.
> *In the high East Room*: a bed with blue Curtains ( probably a box bed), a heather bed & Bolster, Four half blankets & Coverlet, one old Box-bed, one Plane-tree square table.
> *In the Garrett:* one chaffbed & bolster, Three pairs of Blankets, one pair of coarse sheets, Two pair Do in the high East Room, Miller's Dictionary 2 vols, Four chairs, two muskats.
> *In the Parlour:* a small table, a Prespective Glass.

The reference to three beds, including a heather bed, suggests that the bothy was shared between the gardener and one or two apprentices. Miller's Dictionary of Gardening was the best text of the day and the gardeners could not have done better than rely on it. A 'Prespective Glass' may have been a magnifying glass but this is uncertain. The gardeners' working tools, from the same inventory, included the following:

> Two large rakes, Two water table Ditto, Two Dutch Hoes, Six old Ditto, Four carrot Ditto, Two Garden rules & lines, A measuring Chain, Two Dung Forks, Two Pitch Ditto, Three Wheelbarrows, Four old Ditto, A water Barrel w/t Iron hoops, Two hot-bed panes w/t four lights, Four Ditto w/t three lights, Four Ditto w/t one light, One Copper Stil-pot, two large watering pans, one small Ditto, One Bell Glas, Three...? mounted scythes, Three hatchets, Two hedge bills, One Ditto, A pair hedge Sheers, A Hand saw, Three nailing hammers, Two ladders, A large square, Three Boneing Staves, Fourteen earthen flower-pots.

In 1690, in the preceding century, an inventory of garden tools was not greatly different and was as follows:

> Six hurle Barrowes (wheel barrows), two watering pans, three pair of great sheer, one Ax & six Carrot howes (hoes), fyve new sythes, four Iron Raikes, a Ladder and a Hammer, a Turfing Iron, thre gravel harpes (sieves), Six Iron Spades and a Level, a Seed Box and two long Rules, ane Iron Reel for the Lines, a Syth pot ( filter), nyn pair of wooden Bouls, two...? sacks, a weir seive for siffing of seed.

A list of garden tools from 1745 included a rather startling entry. Sandwiched between a dung fork and three spades, was the entry of 'a man catcher'.

At Taymouth in 1795 sundries necessary for the Journeyman gardeners were as follows:

4   Pair strong Blankets each pair containing nine yards in length by one yard Broad
2   Bead Covers each 2 yards in length by 2 1/2 yards broad
18  yards of Strong sacking or as commonly called Tyking for the purpos of holding chaff for two Beads
3   yards of strong sacking to make Bolsters
1   Yetlen Poat that will hold 6 pints Scots measure
3   Wooden Plats that each will hold 1 pint Scots measure
3   horn spoons
3   wooden chists with locks on each and that will hold each chist one Boll of Meall

There were no luxuries in this bothy. The importance of the 'meall' is evident in the provision of lockable chests to secure each man's board wage.

## Garden work

Since the gardeners were not given to writing accounts of their work we have little first-hand record of how they went about it. Occasionally we have a glimpse of the daily round. We meet with reports of mowing, shearing hedges, cleaning up the wilderness, carting sand and gravel and sometimes unexpected tasks like shearing hemlock in 'the yard'. We can infer most of the garden jobs, not so different from those we know, from the lists of plants they grew and the trees they cared for. But sometimes the gardeners have left us a working list of jobs to be carried out or sometimes a copy of a schedule of tasks taken from some book of garden practice. Either way we have a picture of the eighteenth century gardener at work and sometimes learn of some procedure which has died out. To take an example, in 1725 a Saltoun gardener's list of jobs to be completed included the following:

Almonds gather their seeds
Bees straiten ye entrance
Cabbage plant y/m
Cyder make it
Collyflower plant y/m in shelter
Endive replant y/m
Gelly flowers refresh & trim them
Hemp beat out of seed water it
Peaches gather ye stones
Perry make it
Sellery continue to earth it up

Turneip how them
Beach gather Mast etc.

In this instance the gardener was responsible for some of the livestock, in addition to the bees, since his list includes 'Rams geld y/m and
Swine turn y/m to ye woods, put Boers in ye sty'.

In another list for 1742 we have the following:

Clen weids in dry else theyle overgrow ym in wett weather
Draw up Earthe of Stems of Cab & Collyflowers – best after rain
Sow Colliflower for winter plants. Soil light and rich. Shade with matts in hot weather. Water often.
plant Cab & Savoy for winter use in moist weather
purslane in same ground
Endive for blanching
Sellery transplant it into drills
Salleting of all sorts, Sow every week in a Shady situation
plant cuttings and slips of Sage Rosemary Rue Hysop Marum (Marjoram)
Methick ( Medick) and most oyr aromatick herbs
Water & shade till they take root
Beans plant for a last crop in a moist soil
Transplant lettuce into north bed
Sow…? sel (Silesia) and brown lettuce to supply ye Table in August
Collyflower break down ye Inner leaves to preserve ye…? if Sun burns ym yellow
Sow Turneep in moist ground and how yse sown in April
When cabbages begin to turn inward tye ym up it will hoden them
Kidney bean sow ym middle crop

From another note of the same period we learn that Dwarf peas should be sown in October and transplanted on the hot-bed at the end of January to provide the first crop. Hotspur peas, another early variety, should be sown at the end of October three times at fortnightly intervals to 'prevent accidents'. They should be covered with pea shaws which should be removed in 'fresh weather'. Large peas like Spanish Moratto should be sown in the middle of February in drills two and a half feet apart with one and a half inches between seeds and covered to a depth of two inches. Marrowfat and other large peas should have three feet between the rows while Rose peas should be sown with a space of eight or ten inches between seeds. The drills should run south to north.

Another laboriously written document of the same period, consisting of an inventory of garden tasks throughout the year, month by month, must have been copied from some manual The following excerpts are sufficient to indicate the kind of advice provided for the gardener. For the month of January, the work to be done in the Kitchen garden was as follows: 'If mild weather Trench Ground near walls, Poles or hedges, on warm borders. Sow early Radishes, Carrots, Spinach, Lettuce, Small Salleting. Sow Pease to succeed those in autumn. Sow Windsor or Sandwich Beans. Make hot-bed for Cucumbers & Melons as also for asparagus. Sow Cresses, Mustard, Rape, Radish, Turnip and other Small Sallet herbs. Look carefully to y/e Cauliflower plants. Those who have Cucumber, Melon plants must be very careful of them at this season, otherwise they'll all be destroyed. Keep ye Beds to an Equal temper for heat. Give them air, that ye Steam may pass of but this must be done with great caution. If mild weather you may transplant Cabbage plants of Sugar loaf kind and you may sow the ground with Spinach before the plants are planted. Transplant Carrots, Parsnips, Leeks and Cabbages for seed. You may now destroy snails and other vermin.' There follows a remarkable summary of the kitchen garden produce available in January, which includes Cabbages, Savoys, Parsnips, Turnips, Carrots, Potatoes, Leek, Onions, Garlic, Shallots, Beets, Borecole, etc. as well as Celery, Endive, Lettuce; and, upon moderate hot-beds, all sorts of young 'sallet herbs' as Cresses, Turnip, Radish, Rape, Mustard, Coriander, Mint, Skirrets, Broccoli, Spinach and Cardoons, as well as Asparagus on hot-beds made in November. If this truly reflects the array of fresh produce the gardener could supply in the depths of winter we can only salute him and marvel at the expertise at his command. At the end of January hot-beds were to be made of dung for the sowing of the choicest flower seed. Towards the end of February it was timely to transplant Canterbury Bells, French Honeysuckle, Daisies, Rose Campions, Foxgloves, Pinks, Sweet William, Perennial Catchfly, Campanulas, Thrift, Scarlet Lychnis, Columbine, Starwort and Golden Rod into the borders of the pleasure garden. In frost Ranunculus, Anemones and Tulips were to be covered with mats. The following month was the time to plant slips of Tarragon, Penny Royal, Camomile, Baum, Savoy, Sage, Rosemary, Hyssop and most of the aromatic plants as well as Silesia, Cos and Imperial lettuce and also Endive. And so it went on, including tasks to be completed in the orchard and greenhouse. Two items are worth noting in this excerpt. Firstly, how early in the season many seeds were planted out compared with what we would consider safe. Secondly, there was frequent reference to 'sallet' or 'salleting' which were general names for the young leaves of quite a large number of different species, as noted earlier.

There are occasional references to vermin, especially moles, which were viewed with hostility. Estate workers supplemented their earnings by catching them. Thus at Gordon Castle, 1775, we have the entry:

|  | L | s | d |
|---|---|---|---|
| To the workman for Catching of |  |  |  |
| 46 Moles – at 1 ½ d per mole | – | 5 | 9 |

and for 1778:

|                                                                          | L | s | d |
|--------------------------------------------------------------------------|---|----|---|
| To Alexander Smith and James Paterson for catching 84 moles at 1 1/2 d per mole | – | 10 | 6 |

## Contacts between Estates

Gardeners in neighbouring estates were in regular contact and often bought plants from one another or exchanged them. For example from the Ravelston records of Sir John Foulis, 1681, we have the following entries, set down with the usual arbitrary disposition of capital letters and unconstrained spelling:

'to Rot. rorie gardiner to pay allane lindsay for 20 cherrie imps at 1 2s p. piece; to Rot. rorie, gardiner, to buy from Jamie louristone 1000 bowcaill (cabbage) plants; to 7 imps from ye gardiner in ye Surgeons yard, viz. a black pippin, a pear dangerous, 2 honie pears, a bon criteon, a swaneg, a bona magna plum; to malcolme to give ye gardiner in ratho for artichock slips; to James orr yesterday to get slips of clove and curnaon gilliflower out of Cambo; for 2 drap colliflower from mrs Shaw over against ye stinking styll; to davie ye garner to goe to gogar and corstorphin to get Solomons seall for lady raith; to davie to get whyt raspberrie bushes from craigcruick gardiner; to James steinsone, gardiner at Heriots work etc...'

Between the years 1715–1719 George Dundas' diary refers to sundry dealings with gardeners of other estates. In 1715 he bought a cartload of box from the gardener at Alva. In 1717 he obtained beech from Hopetoun and also got from the Hopetoun gardener two beds of holly which were growing at Duddingston. In the same year he bought yews from the gardener at Newliston and in 1719 obtained horse chestnuts from the same source. In the same year he exchanged a bed of holly for two pecks of holly berries with the gardener at Duddingston. In addition there are a number of references to gifts of oak trees, elm, ash, plane, thorns, roses etc. to neighbouring landowners. No doubt their respective gardeners were closely involved in these gifts and exchanges. From such evidence we can infer that the gardeners of a district were in regular contact with one another and often had surplus plants for sale or exchange. They comprised a sort of informal association with similar backgrounds who shared a common devotion to their trade. Some of their contemporaries had gone further to set up organised societies which are described in the next chapter.

# 7

# *The Gardeners' Fraternities*

The natural solidarity which existed between gardeners engaged in similar tasks and duties found more tangible expression in the Gardeners' Fraternities, Incorporations or Societies, as they were variously called. By the early eighteenth century these were well established in Glasgow, Aberdeen, Haddington, Falkirk and probably also Banff. In Glasgow the Incorporation can be traced back to the beginning of the seventeenth century and, in East Lothian, to the 1670's. The significance of these associations seems to have been overlooked in earlier discussions of the history of Scottish gardening. They offer further, documented evidence of the historical continuity of the gardening tradition in Scotland and the public recognition of the gardener's status as skilled craftsman.

These associations were in part trade guilds, designed to secure the rights, privileges and integrity of 'gardenry', and in part friendly societies, designed to assist members or their families who had fallen on evil times, due to sickness or misfortune. As time passed the latter aspect assumed greater importance. Indeed, there was a proliferation of so-called Gardeners' Friendly Societies in the nineteenth century in which the link with gardening was non-existent and membership had no relation to gardening skills. With these we are not concerned. Only the original societies merit recognition in the present context.

Such societies were not confined to this country. According to Loudon (1826), they had long been established in mainland Europe, especially in Germany, where the further back their history went the more they partook of freemasonry, with secret signs and guild exclusiveness. It appears that the tradition of such societies was stronger in Scotland than England, evidence of the often closer affinity of Scottish institutions with those of mainland Europe.

The organisation of these societies conformed to a standard pattern. They were very democratic, with a periodically elected Deacon and various elected officials, none more important than the two or more Box Masters who held the keys to the Box, which held the monies, bonds, securities and important papers belonging to the society. It was their Bank from which was drawn the funds to assist members in need or even support loans, if the

Deacon was agreable. The best way to appreciate the aspirations and role of the societies in their early years, is to look at some of their rules and ordinances and how they interacted with the Town Councils which accorded them legal status. The record for Glasgow is particularly complete so we can take it as an example for comparison with what we know of the others.

## The Incorporation of the Gardeners of Glasgow

A record book survives of what came to be known as the Incorporation of the Gardeners of Glasgow, with the following intimation inscribed on its first page:

> *This buik belangis to the Gairneris of Glasgow; begun be Johne Blair, Notar, thair clerk, the xviij of November 1626; delyverit to me be Johne Govane, Elder, their Deikin.*
>
> L. Blair, Notar

But the record goes back further than that. According to the official account of the Incorporation, published in 1903, some time after 1605, a number of practising gardeners successfully petitioned the Provost, Magistrates and Council of the Royal Burgh of Glasgow for a charter which incorporated them and gave them the same kind of rights and privileges enjoyed by other tradesmen, such as those enjoyed by hammermen or fleshers. This was probably between 1613 and 1620. However the original charter was lost, probably in 1646, when there was an outbreak of the plague, which infected the Deacon who was sent to the 'foull muir' to be cleansed. The charter may have gone with him and was lost. The Incorporation did not apply for a new charter but carried on as before until 1690 when a further petition was submitted to the authorities who endorsed the recommendations. The preamble refers to the 'Gardeners of the said good toune' having 'neer thes hundrete years bygaine bein incorporat as ane of the trades of the burgh, and were formerlie in use to elect their oune Deacon, and did enjoy alse many and alse free priviledges as many of the rest of the crafts enjoyed or possesst frae the time of their first erection in a craft till the year of God 1646.' Since the need for an association or society would not have arisen until the numbers of craftsmen were such that they were perceived by both themselves and their community as a distinct group, we can assume there was a recognisable craft of gardener at work in Glasgow before the beginning of the seventeenth century.

Among the rules and privileges which went with the Incorporation there are several particulalrly worth noting e.g. 'that non be allowed to set up or exerce a freeman's trade till he be first burgess and freeman and beis found a qualified tradisman by the deacon and such masters as shall be appointed by him, and able and fitt to serve the king's leidges: that each freeman at his entrie shall pay the soumes following for their freedom and upset, viz;

Apprentice of freeman's son 10 merks Scots
Apprentice of an unfreeman's son 8
Outten tounsmen and apprentices 40 merks
Quarterly accounts for freeman 3s (shillngs)
And that no unfreeman have libertie to present geir to the mercat
above the value of four shillings scots bot in fair and mercat dayes
under the like paine'

From time to time further statutes were enacted by the Magistrates and
Council and several are of particular interest. Thus, on May 16, 1671 it was
'statut and ordained that all persons who bring fruit to be sold within this
burgh to those who retaile the same thereuntir or who buy fruit in great
quantity to be sold over again with the visitor of the gardeners' guess, whilk
is sealed with the Dean of Guild's mark and seale, and pay the ordnarie dues
therfor, conform to old use and wont and that under such paine as it shall
please the magistrates to inflict upon them'. The Incorporation, through the
tacksmen of petty custom, held a set of standard fruit measures which could
be used by the public to check the accuracy of the measures used by the
dealers. The 'guess' or 'gess' was the standard wooden measure used by
sellers and buyers of fruit to guarantee fair dealing and any lapses were
dealt with seriously. This in 1701 we learn that Andrew Somervell and John
Reid were fined 3 pounds Scots each for having made and used 'gessis' not
authorised by the trade. The said gessis were to be broken in pieces in the
Deacon's house. On May 4th 1727 the Council considered a petition from
the gardeners 'that the sale of fruit and onions having been formerly used
to be by heaped peck measure was afterwards appointed to be by a measure
equal wt the timber commonly called guesses, for which the Corporation
of Gardeners have two pennies p. guess for support of their poor; and that
a custom has crept in of selling fruit and onions by heaped guesses to the
diminishing of the poor's fund and creating of debats and strife: that therefore for preventing of such practises it is their opinion that the Council
should appoint that fruit and onions for the future be sold by the guess
measure by the wood and not heaped and for that two covers for the
guesses be made and no other measures to be used with respect to fruit and
onions…'

On November 15th 1626 it was 'Statute that every ane of their calling sall
pay to the craft and box, sextein penneys Scottis money for ilk boll fruit,
oynzeouns, or other stuff that it sall happin frieman to have growand mett
or unmett, and every landward or unfrieman sall pay two schillingis for ilk
boll or efferand to the quantitie of their stuff, and it es also ordenit that
quha sall borrow the ges beis not brocht hare within half ane hour eftir
they have done they sall tyne their pand silvir by their mettage silvir.'

These rules guaranteed the benefits to the Incorporation which were
derived from the sale of produce at the expense of those who were not
members, especially men from outside the burgh. On Jan 4th 1751, an Act

of 1663 was rescinded to the effect that a freeman of the trade could sell his herbs and plants at his own house and at his stand in the common market but not elsewhere and must not annoy the inhabitants by having his goods hawked through the streets by his servants. Anyone breaking this law was to be fined three shillings sterling 'toties quoties' to the collector of fines for the use of the poor. Also the fine for 'crying people from buying at one anothers' stands and undervalueing their neighbours Goods shall be restricted to one shilling sterling to be paid as above and that Masters shall be liable for their wives and servants'.

A further source of revenue to the Box came from the centralised buying of seed from Holland and England. All such seeds, according to an ordinance of 1731, were to be bought by the Deacon and Collector and sold by them to the members of the trade at a small profit which was to be used for the benefit of indigent members thereof. To prevent 'confusion' in dividing the seeds, the barrels and containers were to be opened in the presence of the Deacon and Masters and the members of the trade were called to receive their share according to the 'Call Role of the Trade' which was presumably a record of seniority. Furthermore the Deacon and Masters had the discretion to order what they thought fit for sale to strangers and gentlemen for 'common or ordinar profit'.

In November 1719 it was enacted that no person could be entered Freeman of the Trade and allowed to engage in business until he first 'make ane essay at the sight and appointment of and which shall be approven by two sworn Essay Masters to be named by the Deacon'. This was an important feature of the Glasgow Incorporation of that time since it guaranteed a generally recognised standard of competence in kitchen gardening and probably also the handling of fruit trees. In 1750, in place of the essay two shillings and sixpence could be paid for the relief of the poor.

In May, 1705, a meeting was convened by the Deacon to consider the current practice whereby apprentices had to complete five years training and two years further work 'for meat and fee', before they could be admitted to the Incorporation as freemen. It was noted that the contribution to the Box would be increased, and therefore the poor beneficiaries would be better off, if men were allowed into the Incorporation, after their five years apprenticeship, for twenty four pounds Scots. The proposal was agreed so that after apprenticeship a man could join within the succeeding two years provided he paid the above sum and his master had agreed to release him. If no one wished to employ him a man who had served his time could nevertheless be admitted to the trade.

From the earliest times the Incorporation was concerned to maintain the quality of the produce on sale to the 'leidges'. Thus in 1676 there was a meeting of the officers and most of the members of the Incorporation in the 'trades hospitall' to consider the 'severall inormities committed by severalls of the trade at leist some persones who inhances the libertie of tradesmen and freemen of the Incorporatione by sewung and settiin of bow kaill plants and selling the samen as soufficient bow kail plants to the leidges which are unsufficient in themselves to the great prejudice of the leidges and affront to the said trade. Therefore they all unanimouslie and with on consent have statute and ordained that in all tyme comeing ther sall be three of their number elected yearlie by consent of the majaor partie of the said trade for sightin and visiting of all plants aither growing in yairds or selling in mercat to the effect the leidges may not be deceaved or the said Incorporatione affronted theranent.'

The officers of the Incorporation increased in number as time passed. The earliest Deacon was assisted by two Masters, appointed by the Deacon, and two by the members. This was increased in 1689 to three and in 1674 to four from each side. The officers had a busy time looking after the funds, entering the fees from new members, collecting quarterly accounts and impost dues, 'guess money' and generally looking after the affairs of the market. In addition they had to ensure that members wore hats at meetings, collect fines for swearing or, having been notified, non-attendance at a member's burial which incurred a fine of ten shillings and also 'meikill to the baillies'.

Friction between members was not unknown. One of the pleas in the original petition to the Council was to have the latter's authority in dealing with not only 'outten and unfreemen' but also members of the Incorporation who are 'contumacious and disobedient' to all statutes made by the Deacons and the Masters of the Craft. In spite of the rules there was scope for intrigue in the competition for the posts of Deacon and Box Masters. From 1728 there is the account of an extraordinary case brought by members of the Incorporation against one John Wilson, gardener, who was accused at some time during 1726 of having cut and taken away several 'burdens' of grass and rye belonging to James Stark, Baillie of Kilsyth, and his spouse. The baillie's and Wilson's yards were adjacent and without an intervening fence. Wilson was willing to concede, in the interests of having an end to the matter, that he might have inadvertently gathered a little of the baillie's grass. The latter was unconcerned and on good terms with Wilson. When the case came to Court the defence for Wilson alleged that in recent years there had been sundry parties and factions in the choice of the Deacon and Masters. Wilson happened to be in the minority party. The opposition, having failed to induce him to change sides, decided to have him expelled and had trumped up the charge about theft of the baillie's grass. They had even offered to drop the case if Wilson would change sides, or, at least, absent himself from the election, which would evidently be pretty close. The chief interest of this incident lies in the implied importance of the Deacon and Masters, either in social standing or other benefits and advantages attached to these posts.

On a lighter note, for many years it was the custom for the outgoing Deacon, on the night of the election of a new Deacon, to treat the Masters and other members of the Incorporation to a supper at his own house.

However by 1764 this had become increasingly inconvenient and it was decreed that from August 9th onward the outgoing Deacon should arrange a supper at a public house in the town for as many members as he thought fit and also that he should contribute 10 shillings sterling towards the costs, the rest being met by the members present. To make sure this annual event was observed it was further enacted that any Deacon 'transgressing this act should forfeit 30s sterling to the poor of the Incorporation'.

The Box (Figure 98), which was central to the activities of the Incorporation, was adorned in a manner suited to its status. On the front of the Box there was an iron plate with the Arms of the Incorporation, the blazons of which were 'azure, for a Mount in base the Tree of Paradise environed with a serpent between Adam and Eve, all proper; above to the dexter the sun in his glory, to the sinister the moon decrescent: on a chief vert. having in the nether part therof a fillet argent, a dibble and a garden line crossways surmounted by a rake and a spade saltireways between two escutcheons argent, the dexter charged with a pair of measures open, the sinister with a hoe-iron, above each escutceon a cherub displayed. Motto: Gardening the first of arts'.

Finally, it is of particular interest that in 1705 the Incorporation purchased a 'great yard or orchard and a stone wal surrounding… which was of old a manor place with a yard or orchard belonging to the Minor Brethren or Franciscans lying within the city of Glasgow'. So here we have proof of a former old monastic garden being brought back into use by the monks' secular successors.

It is evident from this brief survey of the Glasgow Incorporation that, from early times, it catered for a substantial body of organised gardeners in

FIGURE 98
The Box of the Incorporation of Gardeners of Glasgow. The administration of the Gardeners' Fraternities revolved around the Box. Often handsomely embellished, as in the illustrated example, and with access in the hands of generally two Box Masters, it was both bank and respository of important documents. Membership dues, various levies and fines for misdemeanours were paid into the Box for the support of widows and orphans as well as gardeners who were in financial difficulties. The Box of the Glasgow Incorporation is an important relic of an ancient craft society. *Photograph by permission of the Incorporation of Gardeners of Glasgow.*

Glasgow who had all served their five years apprenticeship and who enjoyed a status and recognition comparable with that of any of the other craft associations. The Glasgow Incorporation still exists and is entitled to be proud of its ancient lineage.

## The Edinburgh Gardeners

The situation in Edinburgh was different. We can infer on various grounds there must have been a substantial number of gardeners at work in and about the city duriung the seventeenth century. The feu charters reveal the existence of a number of market gardeners with yards in Dalry and nearby, but, surprisingly enough, they were not organised during the seventeenth century like their Glasgow counterparts. Apparently, it was not until 1722 that any formal association was established but that was very different in nature and intention from what prevailed in Glasgow or Aberdeen. 'The Society and Association of Gardeners in the Shire of Midlothian' was founded in 1722. Rather incongruously the members of this society were mostly well-to-do businessmen, who owned property in Fountainbridge, then an upmarket district, and who thought investment in gardening a profitable enterprise. On Sept. 25th 1722 the Society rented 4 and 3/4 acres and 30 falls of the land of Dalry. The area lay to the north east and included what later was known as Romilly Place as well as the ground on which Gardner's Crescent is built. It appears that immediately after taking over this land they erected a house known as Gardener's Hall. The lands of Dalry had long been recognised as ideally suited for market gardening, evident in the many feu contracts issued to nurserymen, as already noted. In 1729 James Bain of Bainfield was Deacon. Charles Duncan, Treasurer, was an Edinburgh goldsmith while the ordinary members included a brewer, an apothecary and John Weir who was gardener at Heriot's Wark. In 1722 the Society set in tack to John Smith, the lower story of Gardener's Hall and the adjacent yard for 21 years. However Smith fell into arrears and there were legal wrangles which need not detain us. The Hall was finally sold in 1731 by public roup and the whole horticultural enterprise seems to have fizzled out. Its relevance to our story rests in the oblique evidence it offers that market gardening was flourishing in Edinburgh, in the early eighteenth century, to such an extent that a group of local entrepreneurs, who were no gardeners, thought they could make money out of it. There is not enough evidence to discover just why they failed.

Quite separate from this undertaking we have a few references from the Council minutes which suggest a thriving body of market gardeners like those in Glasgow. Thus, in 1772 there was a report from Bailie McDowal's Committee anent a dispute involving the rent for the Gardeners' stalls in the Green Market. It was agreed that the rent should be reduced as follows: For the expense and loss they may sustain by delay of payment of the Tack duty Ten pounds – a deduction of two pence per week for thirteen stands to be set at four pence in place of six pence. In an earlier preamble there was reference to three classes of stand. On Feb 13, 1788, the Council noted the inconvenience caused by the selling of potatoes, greens and other garden stuff in the streets of the City and in the entries to Closes and therefore banned the practice and confined sale of such produce to the Green Market.

The gardeners in Edinburgh had to wait until 1782 for the establishment of an association exclusively devoted to their interests. This was called The Friendly Society or Caledonian Gardeners' Lodge of Edinburgh. In the preamble to the Articles of the society it was noted 'Wheras a great number of Gardeners have resorted to and settled in Edinburgh and its vicinity and seeing that although many of them are at present in easy circumstances, yet in case of a reverse of fortune, there is no fund for their support under diseases or sickness it was resolved by a number of them in the year 1782 to form themselves in a Society under the names or designation of etc...'

The principal conditions of membership were as follows 'Every person desirous of being a member must be above age 16 and not above age of 40 years, but a non-operative shall in no case be admissible if his age exceeds 32 years. He must be of a fair unblemished character in perfect health at the time, he must be recommended by at least 2 members who have known him full two years prior to his application for admission and he must produce certificate of age and state of health if required, and if any member object to his admission his application shall lie over until the next quarter day when the Society shall consider the objection and the candidate shall be received or rejected as a majority of votes shall decide, only one of any other prefer-ence than an operative gardener shall be admitted and the following rates of entry money shall be exacted... etc.' The terms of this association reflect the changed role of the trade association. The entrepreneurial success of the Edinburgh gardeners had eroded the traditional aspects of a craft guild, but the need for mutual support in times of stress was still recognised. Also, in spite of the name 'Friendly Society' membership was restricted essentially to working gardeners.

The Caledonian Lodge flourished for many years with a large member-ship. We have proof of that in the diary of Thomas Blaikie, a Corstorphine gardener, who, in his late twenties, moved to France where he won a respectable place in French garden history, designing 'jardins anglais' for the nobility and hob-knobbing with royalty. In 1822 Blaikie on one of his periodical visits to his relatives in Edinburgh, wrote home to his wife in Paris as follows: 'I went to see Mr Macdonald and the fine Palaces and gardens at Dalkeith. But there was a great procession and the Lodge of free gardners and a great dinner of about 160, so that I was obliged to join my brethren and the Whisky flowed in Plenty and many capital toasts were drunk'.

## The Aberdeen Societies

In Aberdeen there were two societies, one in Aberdeen city and the other in Old Aberdeen, which we deal with first. The Gardeners' Society was established by Act of Council at Old Aberdeen on May 11th 1754. Its rules and regulations were consolidated in 1794. This society was purely a friendly society; 'The sole design and intention of the fraternity is to raise a fund for relieving the necessities of such of the members as may be reduced to poor circumstances'. The conduct of The Gardener Fraternity of Old Aberdeen was well defined, was confined to residents of Old Aberdeen and followed the usual pattern with the Box lodged with the Treasurer and the keys of it with the Box masters. From the records of entries dating from 1754 to 1793, the year before the rules were formally consolidated, we learn that virtually all the trades were represented among its members, although the largest number of entrants over this period, 37 in all and just under a quarter of the total, were gardeners. Next came farmers with 20 entrants, 14 millers, 11 shoemakers, 9 weavers, 9 wrights, 6 masons, 5 tailors together with smaller numbers of a great variety of occupations, including that of perfumier and riddle maker. This evidence certainly suggests that gardeners made up a significant proportion of the skilled working population in Old Aberdeen.

In Aberdeen city the gardeners presented a petition to the Town Council in 1716 for an act of council to endorse their setting up of a society in which members would pay a levy which would be used to assist indigent members, pay for their burial etc. in the same fashion as the masons, horsehirers and other trades. It was proposed that 'every person in time comeing which should sett up to be a Gardener in this place might pay into their box the sum of Three pounds Scots money att their Entry'. There was also a quarterly levy of three shillings Scots. This proposal was accepted and endorsed by the Provost, Baillies and Council. The society became known as the Gardener Fraternity of the Burgh of Aberdeen.

We encounter the familiar drive to exclude outsiders. Thus in 1730 the Council supported the Fraternity in their complaint that several people annually 'cam in and about the Toun noways incorporate in the said Community and did daily exerce the said Gardener trade and did sell and dispone all Gardner roots... to the petitioners great hurt and prejudice who pays taxation yearly'. The interlopers paid no tax and were regarded with hostility. Among the rules laid down by the Council, following this petition, we can note:

(i) Every entrant pay to the dean of Guild ten pounds Scots money and twenty merks Scots to the Gardners' Box for the use of their poor with the quarterly penny viz three shillings Scots per quarter.

(ii) When any Gardener orders into the Fraternity they pay only 5 pounds to Dean of Guild and ten merks to the Box with quarterly penny and other dues.

(iii) When any Gentleman or Burger or other goodman shall come into the Fraternity, not being a handycraft man to pay nothing to the Dean of Guild but only their free compliment to the Box and quarterly penny and other dues.

(iv) That the said Master, Box Master and Keymasters be impowered to examine the qualiification and ability of every Entrant Gardner with respect to his knowledge in Gardnery and stock of money and, if they be found insufficient, not to be admitted to the said community. Providing the Magistrat: shall approve of the Reason for rejecting such.

(v) That none who are not incorporat with the said Fraternity have liberty to go through the Toun with their roots and herbs or expose them to sell at their own house or to sett up or sell any such goods at the Cross as the Gardeners are in use to deal in except the Mercat Days viz Wednesday and Friday of each week… any person whatsomever shall have liberty to sell all manner of Roots and herbs upon either of the said Mercat days, or upon the ground where they grow any other day of the week… reserving liberty to any of the Inhabitants to employ what Gardner they please for dressing of their yeard whither they be incorporat or not'… etc. The 'said gardners' were also prohibited from importing seed or exporting any of their products, presumably to ensure that such transactions were under the control of the Fraternity and hence, Council, to ensure that the approviate levies were collected.

Particularly important to note in these rules are:

(i) The emphasis on professional competence and financial security, as conditions of entry to the Fraternity.
(ii) The indication that people interested in gardening other than professionals could join.
(iii) The evidence that the townsfolk employed gardeners to look after their gardens.
(iv) That the Baillies and Council, while supporting the gardeners' Fraternity and awarding them certain exclusive rights in the sale of produce, did not prevent other non incorporated gardeners from earning a living, subject to the restrictions noted above.

From time to time some problem encountered by the gardeners appears in the Council minutes. Thus in 1706 we meet the recurring concern of the Fraternity: 'Extranears prohibited from selling herbs, roots and other in the town, except on the public market day'. In 1718 there was an act of Council 'for protecting their Roots herbs and green crops'. In 1729 the gardeners complained that the herbs and roots they grew were being destroyed and eaten by horses, sheep 'and other bestial' belonging to persons living in the Town. The Council was sympathetic and ruled: 'all persons herd their horses, sheep, swynne and goats, the winter as weel as the summer and house or inclose them in the night under the paine of halfe ane merk'. This rule was to be intimated 'throw the Town and Suburbs therof by the Drum twice in the year and oftner if found needful.'

## The East Lothian Fraternity

The last well documented gardeners' society we shall consider is the The Ancient Fraternity of Free Gardeners of East Lothian, centred in Haddington. Minute books from its inception are preserved in the Scottish Record Office. The first bears the inscription 'this Book belongeth to the Fraternity of Gardeners in east Lothian, and comprehends all done by Ym from ye 16th day of August 1676', so we are dealing with another ancient association. Among the fifteen rules were the following:

(i) That none of the said Fraternity presume to admit any Brethern without the presence of the President or Chairman, or one of the Joint Masters, and if there is a Quorum, ye Clerk always being present, who shall be oblidged to take a Minute of the Quorum, their Names, day, place and Brethern then admitted, under Twenty pounds of penalty toties quoties. 'Toties quoties' was a favourite legalistic qualification defined by O.E.D.: 'as often as something happens or occasion demands'.

(ii) That none of the said Fraternity presume to curse or swear under the penaltie of Two shillings, Scots, toties quoties, for each oath to be given in ye Box for the use of the poor.

(iii) At the admission of any of the Fraternity, Gentlemen to pay one half Crown, a Gardener ane Merk, with ane Annual annuity.

(iv) That none professing to be handie labouring and working Gardeners be admitted until they be first tryed, examined, and approved by a sufficient Quorum of the Fraternity appointed for the effect, that Noblemen, Gentlemen, and others may be suffiiciently served with well qualified gardiners, under the penalty of Twentie pounds toties quoties.

(v) That none of the said Fraternity shall presume to back byte, or speak evil of any of the admitted Brethren to their Masters, nor supplant or take their Yeards over their heads, without the Gardiners leave first had and obtained therewith, under the pain of Fourtie pounds, and half to be payed to the Box, and the other half to the party grieved.

(vi) That if it please God to remove any of the Fraternity, and he leave a Widow and Children, That none of the said Brethren shall enter into the Service without satisfying the Relict for her Husbands loss on the

Ground and Propertie belonging to him and there, at the sight of any four of the Fraternity concerned for that effect, under the pain of One hundred Merks, and atone, paying the relict for the Goods on the Ground.

(vii) That all Gardiners of the Fraternity upon their Travells for procuring further science, be intertained by the Brethren unto whom they come, till they have shown them their labour, Procedure and Skill – if it were for two or threes days time, without any cost, under the penalty of Ten pounds toties quoties.

(viii) That every one of the Brethren admitted shall give his best counsell to his Brother for Levelling, Contryving, Planting and Dressing of ground, they being always required so to do, if they have not more urgent affairs of their own impeding them, under the pain of Five Pounds, to be given to the Box.

(ix) That all and every one of the Fraternity shall attend the Yearly meeting being advertised, or any other Meeting that the fraternity shall appoint, except he show a relevant excuse, or advertise any of the masters therof, under the penaltie of Fourtie shillings, to be paid into the Box.

(x) That if any of the Fraternity betwixt Meetings, finds out or learns any art concerning Plants, for furthering their fruits, he shall publicly and openly reveal the same at the yearly meeting in presence of the whole fraternity then present, at least to those who require the same, and worthy and deserving therof, under the penaltie of twenty pounds toties quoties.

(xi) That none of the fraternity shall presume to take it upon himself, to accept and receive a Prentice under four years with ane Prentice fie as may be agreed upon by the parties, and that the Indentore be seen by the Clerk of Fraternity and Booked, under the penaltie of Twentie pounds toties quoties.

(xii) That all money by Fyns, Entries, Collections or otherwise gathered, to be employed for the use of the distressed Widows, Orphans, and the poor of the Fraternity, and that, by order of the President or one of the Masters, with a quorum of the fraternity giveth order, is to be subscribed by them for the Treasurer, his warrant.

(xiii) That when any Gardiner removes from one Yeard, he shall not transplant, nor take away furth, of any Trees, Bushes, herbs or any other growth of the Ground, that was planted in the samen, on the Masters charges and expense, without his special licence had, and obtained therto, under the penaltie of Ten pounds toties quoties.

(xiv) In respect there is frequently a thin Meeting, wherby those present are putt to extraordinary charges, that these absent are not only exeemed of, but have the advantage of waiting on the business, Therfor its enacted that whoever of the fraternity is absent at any of the Meetings shall pay three shillings Scots every Quarter day and which is the Quarter count is to be putt in the Box and that in place of all former penaltys, and which is to be enacted with all vigor, and no excuse to be admitted, except when any of the fraternity are called off upon the Kings Service.

A further rule was added in 1759 to deal with the many who entered into the Fraternity 'upon no other design than selfish views, which when they have obtained, desert the Meetings'. It was also enacted that all above 36 years are excluded, except those who are children of the Members, or those 'who has been members are to received in to the said fraternity'. All absent one year and who had not paid their quarterly account, and the other public levies would forfeit any right to assistance from the Box.

The Fraternity must have had considerable standing in their community. They had their own seat in the parish church. In 1776 it was repaired and painted 'a neat green colour' with a group of flowers on the middle panel. When a member of the fraternity died the seat was covered with a black cloth. The Annual General Meeting was well attended. In 1803 there were as many as 93 present, an unprecedented high turn-out. After the meeting the members would march to some inn for a dinner. In 1772 it was noted 'For the General Meeting, resolved to have a decent dinner of Beef and Greens. Bro. Nisbet is empowered to provide for fifty persons, not exceeding 50lbs weight, 5 pints of Rum for punch, Sugar and Lemons in proportion, with glasses and bottles, to cost 1/- per head.' The meeting was advertised by employing the Town piper to lead the Procession. He was followed by a traditional figure known as 'Jock in the Green'. In 1775 there is the record that Bro. Nisbet, who evidently was a man of authority, was deputed to make a bower of flowers to be carried in the procession on June 13th. This floral decoration, to which all members were to contribute, consisted of a 'Headgear or Diadem of Flowers' representing a bower in the garden of Eden. The procession and the attendant Jock in the Green were discontinued at the beginning of the nineteenth century.

The important conclusion, which can be compared with what took place in Glasgow and Aberdeen, is the proof that a substantial number of gardeners were at work in East Lothian throughout the eighteenth and, at least, the latter part of the seventeenth century. They enjoyed an esprit de corps as men who had served a similar apprenticeship, who periodically met together for amusement and jollification and who were recognised by their communities as craftsmen of a distinct trade. How well the members of the Fraternity lived up to the high ideals spelt out in their constiution we cannot say. But we can hardly fail to be impressed by the professionalism of their approach, their desire to preserve the highest standards of behaviour in their work and their intention to foster and disseminate among themselves anything of value in the care of plants. The Fraternity was in existence until the time of the First World War after which it was wound up.

In Falkirk the Society of Gardeners was founded in 1725 and came either then or later into possession of a garden in Falkirk. No doubt they were organised like the other gardeners' fraternities but, so far, further historical evidence has not come to light. According to Loudon there was also a gardeners' society in Banff.

We can only guess at the proportion of all the gardeners in Scotland who were members of a fraternity or incorporation, whose records refer so often to 'landward or outen men' i.e. gardeners living outside the burgh who were potential competitors. In total the latter may have equalled or exceeded the fraternity men; we just do not know. But together they made up the foundations which sustained the eighteenth-century burgeoning of Scottish horticultural enterprise, which took so many of them and their successors to positions of responsibility on English estates.

# 8

# *The Achievements of Scots Gardeners in the Eighteenth Century*

The eighteenth century witnessed a remarkable Scottish contribution to British gardening and practical horticulture. Scots gardeners were already emigrating to England in the latter part of the seventeenth century, several instances have been already noted. During the next century the flow south was so great that estates in Scotland were hard put to it to recruit staff. Thus, in 1732, John Drummond acting on behalf of the Earl of Morton, sent him a letter from London: 'I am to see some young men of our country who have been some years here with gardners and if I can find one fit for your Lordship's purpose that's well recommended and will accept your price I shall send him down, £15 is the lowest that any good man will accept of'. He added an expression of concern that his niece will keep the Earl's kitchen garden well stocked 'which I could never bring her mother too for want of a gardner'.

On Sept. 8th, 1787, a Mr Steuart Moncrieff replied to a letter from the Duke of Fife in the following terms: 'My Dear Lord, As soon as I had the honour of your Lordship's letter I consulted my gardener, and desired to know from him, whether he had at present any of his Lads he could recommend or if he knew of any att dalkeith or Lord Abercorn's that he thought proper for your Lordship and he told me that he had none himself, and added that one in three years he with difficulty could find one fit for an experienced Gardener and those always went to England. I am extremely sorry that I coyuld not give a more satisfactory answer to your Lordship etc…'. Evidently the drive to emigrate was irresistable, although one suspects that if the Scottish gentry had been prepared to dig a little deeper into their pockets they would have been in less difficulty.

The Scottish gardeners almost monopolised for a time the management of the gardens of the English nobility and gentry, while their compatriots took over the London seeds and nursery trade. Although already quoted by Hadfield, no other first-hand comment describes the scene better than that of Dr Andrew Carlisle, Minister of Inveresk, who went on a tour of

English estates in 1758. Early in his tour he visited the estate of Bulstrode in England and 'discovered the truth of what I had often heard that most of the head gardeners of English noblemen were Scotch for on observing to this man (the Bulstrode gardener) that his pease seemed late on the 4th of May, not being fully in bloom, and that I was certain there were sundry places I Knew in Scotland where they were further advanced, he answered he was bred in a place that perhaps I did not know which answered this description. This was Newhails, in my own parish of Inveresk. This man, whose name I have forgot, if it was not Robertson, was not only gardener but land-steward, and had charge of the whole park and the estate around it:- such advantage was there in having been taught writing, arithmetic and mensuration of land, the rudiments of which were taught in many of the schools in Scotland. This man gave us a note to the gardener at Blenheim, who he told us, was our countryman, and would furnish us with notes to the head gardeners all the way down'.

It appears that their reputation was such that English landowners wanted to employ them. For example, in 1754, a Mr. Thomas Barret of Belhouse wrote to his friend Sir Hugh Dalrymple at North Berwick for assistance in finding a good gardener from Scotland. He was offering eighteen pounds a year plus food and lodging. He considered these terms by no means bad ones and what a reliable man deserves. He was looking for a man 'who understands not only every thing relating to the Kitchen Garden but also the raising of Pines (pineapples) and all sorts of melons: especially the latter; as likewise the management of nurseries and raising all sorts of shrubs and forest trees as well as Evergreens as those that shed their leaf. I could wish likewise that the man was middle aged neither very young nor very old: since I have found the inconvenience of those two Extremes'. He ended with the comment that he did not want a fine gentleman who would walk about and give orders but wanted one who would work with his men himself, and for the right person he would be willing to increase the annual wage by fifty shillings although he thought eighteen pounds was really enough. Apart from the information about wages this letter summarises what was expected of a head gardener – quite a lot for eighteen pounds a year.

Before long there were so many Scots gardeners in England that, in the popular mind, a Head Gardener was assumed to be a Scotsman. Hence George Elliot's comment that a gardener is Scottish as a French teacher is Parisian. The distinguished Dutch entomologist and pupil of Linnaeus, John Christian Fabricius, who was a regular visitor to England from 1767 to 1791, noted that James Lee, the leading nurseryman of the time 'is a Scot like almost all the seedsmen and gardeners around London. The Scots have established a near monopoly in this occupation to the virtual exclusion of the English, and businesses are handed from one Scot to another'. Not surprisingly this provoked resentment among English gardeners so much so that Stephen Switzer tried to reactivate an old law which would curtail their influence. However, the initiative fizzled out and the Scottish take-over continued. As Neil Hynd has remarked the situation was reminiscent of the predominance of Scottish engineers in the nineteenth century, although the gardeners had a longer run.

The foundations laid in the eighteenth century ensured a disproportionate Scottish contribution for a long time. For example, even in 1872 there was an editorial in The Gardeners' Chronicle for April 6th which began 'Scotch gardenrs and gardening have long enjoyed a well sustained reputation. Various reasons have been assigned for this, such as their teeming numbers, climatal difficulties, and the genius and education of the people. As to the first, the Scotch have been called a nation of gardeners; they are, as it were, to the manner born. It has been facetiously added that they strike gardeners in Scotland like Gooseberry bushes, and that, moreover, most of them find good, warm, roomy quarters in the south'. The article goes on to debate the merits of Scots versus English gardeners. Even as late as April 3rd 1920, again in The Gardeners' Chronicle, there was a letter from an English gardener relating how he and a Scots gardener with the same number of years experience and references were interviewed for the same job of head gardener by a lady who had advertised the post. To quote: 'The lady read my reference first, then asked for my friend's. The moment she saw his name, and before reading one reference, she exclaimed 'You are Scotch. I am sure you will suit me'. The author has it from a distinguished English gardener with a long career in Scotlnd, that he remembers his father, also a gardener, grumbling about all these 'damned Scots' who multiplied in the profession. So there is no doubt we are dealing with a social phenomenon of historical interest which merits closer scrutiny, especially as to how it came about.

Although the emigration had started before then, there is no doubt that the poor economic conditions in early eighteenth century Scotland provided a spur to emigration, which took many young men to the plantations. The Darien Scheme had been a national disaster while the Act of Union in 1707 brought unemployment in its wake. Centrally imposed taxes and regulations ruined much of the native industry which was undercut by English products. To many a needy Scot the likelihood of a better paid job in England was more than attractive. As for the gardeners, prospects were opening up with the burgeoning of English estates and the desire of landowners, often recently affluent, to improve their grounds and gardens. For the Scottish gardeners the door of opportunity swung open and they fairly swarmed through it. It was a tradition in Scotland for a son to follow in his father's footsteps so those who had emigrated to England would see that their sons found jobs as gardeners and, no doubt, they encouraged other relatives to follow their example. With native cohesion they preferred to do business and keep in contact with fellow Scots, helping thereby to consolidate their position.

Among the various contributory factors we can identify the significant influence of Philip Miller, who was in charge of the Chelsea Physic Garden for many years. He was the son of a Scottish nurseryman who had set up a successful business at Deptford in London. He gave his son the best education he could afford. This certainly paid off since Miller came to dominate British horticulture in the eighteenth century. He published extensively, including his massive Dictionary of Gardening, which ran through many editions and was, in its time, the gardener's Bible. He corresponded with the leading botanists of the day, including Linnaeus, and was generally regarded as the horticultural authority. He also trained a great number of apprentices in the Chelsea Garden and, so it appears, would only accept Scots. He was regularly consulted by the English gentry and nobility looking for head gardeners, so Miller's Scottish gardeners went to the top jobs.

There has been no shortage of other explanations. As we have seen, Dr. Carlyle thought the success of Scots gardeners was due to the sound education provided by rural schools, although this cut little ice with Cox in his History of Scottish Gardening (1935). Patrick Neill, a Secretary of the Royal Caledonian Horticultural Society at its formation, addressed the problem at length in his book 'On Scottish Gardens and Orchards', published in 1813, at the instance of the Board of Agriculture. After noting yet again that most of the head gardeners on the English estates were Scots, he advanced several explanations. First among these was education and his belief that the parochial system of schools was spread more widely in Scotland than in most other countries of Europe. Ordinary labourers had a sound grasp of the three R's and practical geometry, so necessary in understanding how to lay out symmetrical garden designs. He noted that master gardeners of former times spent part of the evening instructing their apprentices in arithmetic, drawing plans, botany or, at least, the naming of plants and that the practice had lingered on until the beginning of the nineteenth century. Beyond that he was straining to find additional explanations, such as the sharpening of gardeners' wits by converse with their employers – hardly convincing – or their frequent role as 'skilly men' versed in herbal remedies, the variable climate which offered a stimulating challenge and a stretching of the mind to advantage and, finally, the native, dogged temperament, familiarity with labour and ability 'to undergo great fatigue subsisting on a fare which would not be thought homely but scanty by their brethren in England'.

Of these suggestions the most relevant appears to be the emphasis on education. T.C Smout in his recent 'History of the Scottish People', notes that in 1696 a statute was enacted which decreed that a school must be established in every parish in the kingdom and that the salary of the teacher should be met by a tax on the local heritors and tenants, with powers to see that it was enforced. However far practice may have fallen short of intention, Smout concludes that almost everyone in rural towns and villages could read and write by the mid-eighteenth century and that this achievement was not parallelled in England nor in other countries, except for Prussia, parts of Switzerland and a few Puritan areas of America. Gardeners' accounts and the like from that time certainly provide evidence of a sound basic education.

In this context it has been suggested by Oldham that an important contributory factor in the Scottish take-over derived from the English Poor Law, whereby parishes restricted support to those in need to those born in the parish, thereby curtailing scope for employment outwith parish boundaries in England, whereas Scots were not handicapped in this way and could move at will. There does not appear to be any independent evidence to support this view. The obligation of parishes to support only those belonging to the parish was also in force in Scotland, as specified in the Act of 1579, restated in 1625 and nominally in force until 1845.

Taking all these factors into account, the essential problem still remains. How was it that so many Scots gardeners moved so quickly and so confidently to positions of responsibility in England? Education was indeed important but they did not teach gardening know-how in the village school. Where did all this practical skill come from? The gardeners did not suddenly materialise from thin air. Indeed not, they were already on the ground, at work on many estates in the Lowlands of Scotland during at least the second half of the seventeenth century and probably earlier. We have already been driven to that conclusion by the compelling archeological evidence of early gardens, the Earl of Crawford's inventory of fruit and orchards, together with the information revealed in the records of the Gardeners' Fraternities, which only admitted experienced men, who had generally served several years' apprenticeship. The Glasgow Fraternity dates from the early seventeenth century, so we can push the earliest evidence for gardeners producing produce for sale, back into a period not so long after the dissolution of the monasteries and abbeys, which had hitherto been the major influence in the establishment of orchards and kitchen gardens and the training of lay gardeners.

A case has been made for the continuity of the European tradition of gardening since the establishment of the monastic institutions in Scotland. The men caring for the orchards and gardens of the seventeenth century were the inheritors of that tradition. When times were hard at home, while in England there was an apparently limitless demand for gardeners, is it surprising that so many headed south? No doubt the more enterprising and adventurous men were the first to go. Once established they would have sent word home to relatives and friends and would have been well placed to advise them about job opportunities. It was a synergistic process of gathering momentum which led to the pervasive Scottish influence. But for it to take place with such effect there had to be a long established core of trained men at work on their home ground.

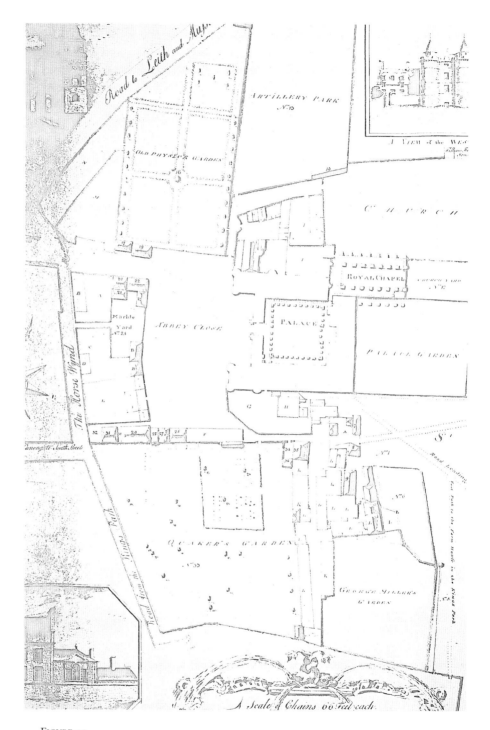

FIGURE 99
Plan of the gardens at Holyrood House, showing the location of the Physic Garden, the Quaker Garden of William Miller and also the garden of George Miller who later left to serve as gardener at Kinneil.

9

# *Quakers, Nurserymen,*
# *Botanists and Authors*

The Scottish influence on the eighteenth century gardening scene was not confined to the throng of Head Gardeners working on English estates. There were also men who, although they generally started their careers as gardeners, became successful in a wider context, either as innovative nurserymen in London, collectors of foreign plants, botanists or authors of widely read books on plants and gardens. Their careers contributed significantly to the pervasive Scottish influence discussed in the last chapter. They made an important contribution to horticulture and no historical account would be complete without recognising their contribution. As the demand for their services grew the numbers of seedsmen and nurserymen increased. Their history belongs to a different enquiry and we shall only note those who turn up in the records for our period.

## *Quakers*

We consider first what might be termed 'The Quaker Connection'. During the seventeenth and eighteenth centuries a remarkably large number of the leading gardeners were Quakers. This religious sect, which was greatly harrassed and regarded almost as much a threat to the establishment as the papists, was but a small band in Scotland, reckoned only in hundreds. Yet the number of Quaker gardeners was quite disproportionate to the number of Quakers in the general population. In Scotland we have to start with Hew (or Hugh) Wood who, for some twenty-five years, was gardener to the Duke and Duchess of Hamilton. The town of Hamilton was one of the places where the Quakers established a foothold in Scotland. Apart from being a gardener Wood was very active in promoting his religious beliefs in pamphlets, including one which deplored the vanity of periwigs and the unlawfulness of making them from women's hair. On more than one occasion he was roughed up by a Presbyterian mob. Hew Wood died in 1701 and was buried in his garden. His elder son, James Wood, began his career at Stonehill, married the daughter of another Quaker gardener at Kelso and later moved to serve the Duke of Queensferry at Drumlanrig.

The younger son, Alexander succeeded his father at Hamilton. Both sons were Quakers.

We get to know Hew Wood from his letters to David Crawford, the Duke of Hamilton's Chamberlain, in which Wood reports on the work he and his men have carried out and often ends on a pious note. A few examples illustate his simple earnestness. A report on work carried out read as follows: 'thine I have dated 25th feb 93: and in answer thereto, shew my Master that We stand in need of a considerable number of those elms at Paisley to help our north avenue in the little park for many of the elms planted there are but insuffiicient but I think it is late in the year now to transplant them. And for Horse Chesnuts except it be in the mid-walk kitching-garden that runs east and west to plant them betwixt the cherry tries on both sides... As for the thorn hedges we began as I was ordered at the east gate in the Kitching-garden and came westward with the holey-hedge and if this present storm had not hindered we had by this gotten the lenth of both gravell walks planted, for I have already gott ten hundred thorns. The aller (alder) trees are planted: the saughs ( willows) on both sides burn are cutt... this last week since the storm began we have taken in the dung to the garden, the workmen is all employed with the kairts at Netherstoun, separating the stones from the earth and helping to raise the earth and fill the kairts and with spaids cast the earth to the hollow-places. I shall (if god permitt) give accompt by the next how soon it may be done ... being so much hindered by the pruning of the holly-hedges. I hope not to forget the straw-berrys, when tyme of planting them comes. This all I mind at present, farewell faith thy friend. Hew Wood'.

In his latter days Wood's religious preoccupation became more pronounced and he would end his letters in the following vein: 'This being all at present that I have to acquaint my Master with but wisheth you all to doe well and be well, and that will make you lay doune your head in peace, both upon your bed here, every night: and in your beds where the Living in this world seldom or never sooth for any more. And that all of you my kind friends may land at last in the heaven of Blissidness is the earnest desire of thy friend Hew Wood.' It is probably letters of that nature which prompted Crawford to remark that 'Hew Wood is now quite dozed'.

In his hey-day Hew Wood was pre-eminent among estate gardeners since he ran the best endowed gardens in the country. Throughout much of this time he had about six men working under him. We know that James Reid, author of the first book on gardening in Scotland, worked for a year at Hamilton. There were probably others who worked with him and later did well elsewhere. Hew Wood was also something of a nurseryman, as we know from Reid's reference to what he could supply and the account, noted earlier, of pear trees which he sent to Sir William Bruce in 1674.

John Reid (1655–1723) was the son and grandson of the gardeners at Niddry Castle, Kirkliston, where he was born and where his grandfather was at work in the late sixteenth century. At first he opted for a career as vintner but when his employer died in 1673 he returned to Niddry and bent his mind to learning 'garden'ry'. At the age of nineteen he went to work with Hew Wood and became a Quaker, quite likely under Wood's influence. After the year was up he moved to Drummond, in Perthshire, and later to Lawers where he married Margaret Miller, who was also a Quaker. In 1680 he moved to Shank in East Lothian, which was in the hands of Sir George Mackenzie, 'the Bloody Mackenzie' of the Covenanters. He stayed there until he emigrated in 1683 to Woodbridge, New Jersey, where he prospered, becoming Surveyor -General of the province and owner of an estate he called 'Hortensia,' which ran to three thousand seven hundred acres. In later life he abandoned the Quaker faith for that of the Church of England.

Reid left his mark on history as the author of the first book on gardening in Scotland. Published in 1683, the full title read:

> 'THE SCOTS GARD'NER in two parts, The First of Contriving and Planting Gardens, Orchards, Avenues, Groves: With new and profitable wayes of Levelling; and how to Measure and Divide land. The Second of the Propagation & Improvement of Forrest, and Fruit-trees, Kitchen-Hearbes, Roots and Fruits: with some Physick Hearbes, Shrubs and Flowers. Appendix shewing how to use the Fruits of the Garden: Whereunto is annexed The Gard'ners Kalendar. Published for the Climate of Scotland. By John Reid Gard'ner.'

The contents are accurately summarised in the title page. The first part gives detailed instructions on how to construct the elaborate geometrical patterns of flower beds which were then in fashion. The second part deals with practical gardening with plenty of sound advice, based on his own experience. It was rounded off with a calendar of tasks throughout the year. Reid's book was successful and used as a practical guide for many years. It was reprinted in 1721 and two edited editions appeared in 1756 and 1766. It was eventually superseded by Justice's 'Gardeners Director'. His book needs to be set in context. In the seventeenth century the chief gardening books were the French 'Maison Rustique', Thomas Tusser's 'Five Hundred Points of Good Husbandrie,' John Rea's 'Flora sue de Florum Cultura', published in 1655 and John Evelyn's translation of 'Le Jardinier Francais' by Nicolas de Bonnfons, which appeared in 1658. It has been noted (Hope 1987) that there are overtones of this work in Reid's book, not surprising since Reid was well read and could hardly fail to be influenced by what others had written before him.

To return to the Quakers, in 1680 a gardener friend of Hew Wood, William Miller (1655–1743) was married in Hew Wood's house to Margaret Cassie, a kinswoman of the Quaker Barclays of Urie, Aberdeenshire. It is little short of remarkable how often the name Miller turns up among apparently unrelated gardeners of that time. Miller went to work at New Park, Glasgow. Nine years later he walked with his family and his goods on two pack donkeys, to take up the important post of hereditary kitchen gardener at the Abbey of Holyroodhouse, probably due to the influence of Hew Wood and under the patronage of the Duke of Hamilton, who had been appointed by the Crown as hereditary keeper of Holyroodhouse. This William Miller, was also active in the Quaker cause and came to be known as 'The Patriarch'. Two of his sons became gardeners. The eldest, George, took over a piece of ground at Holyrood and ran it as a nursery garden. Later he left to become gardener at Kinneil, which was a Hamilton estate. His second son, also called William (1684–1757), went into partnership with his father and, together, they built up a thriving business, which regularly supplied seeds, trees, shrubs etc to estates all over Scotland. He maintained the Quaker tradition and later was to be known as 'The Auld Quaker'. Like many of the Quakers, and gardeners generally, he was a Jacobite and among his customers was Prince Charlie of the '45, to whom he supplied five hundred spades for trenching.

The map of Holyrood House and precincts on page 192, (Figure 99) shows the location of 'The Quaker Garden' i.e. William Miller's garden and also that of George Miller. The former garden contained an impressive collection of plants. A list of 1741, preserved in the Saltoun papers, includes some 120 different herbaceous plants and shrubs together with a long list of apple, pear, plum and cherry trees, as well as peaches, nectarines, hazelnuts, vines etc. The second William Miller was succeeded by a third (1722–1799), who by now had become very prosperous, with lands at Craigentinny, earning him the title of 'The King of the Quakers'. For the best part of a century the Quaker Millers played a most influential role in the Scottish nursery and seed business. There are few Scottish estates of that period whose records do not reveal accounts from one or other William Miller at the Abbey.

Yet another, unrelated Quaker Miller (Raistrick, 1968), was Philip Miller (1691–1771), who as already noted, was the son of a Scottish nurseryman, settled in London. At first he worked in his father's garden but later set up as a florist in Pimlico, London. He had acquired sufficient reputation as a gardener for Sir Hans Sloane to recommend him as Curator of the Apothecaries Garden in Chelsea. He took up this appointment in 1722 and remained there for the rest of his life. Under his direction the Chelsea Physic Garden became famous. Miller had a scientific bent as well as being a skilled plantsman. He developed methods of germinating seeds of tropical plants, studied insect pollination, designed hothouses etc. His lasting memorial was 'The Gardener's Dictionary' which went through many editions and was recognised as the standard work on horticulture for much of the eighteenth century. At first he refused to accept the Linnaean binomial system but was ultimately persuaded of its utility and adopted it in the 1768 edition of his book. Philip Miller certainly played an important part in enabling Scottish gardeners to get good jobs on English estates. He had the ear of the gentry who applied to him for advice on gardeners, so his apprentices – he only took on Scots – had excellent prospects. Among those who achieved distinction were James Lee, William Aiton and William Forsyth, to mention the most familiar.

The Quaker influence in horticulture was not confined to Scotland. In England Peter Collinson (1694–1768), a successful haberdasher established a famous garden, well known for its collection of American plants. It was Collinson who was largely responsible for supporting and encouraging John Bartram (1699–1777), an American Quaker, to collect native American plants and despatch them to Britain, on commission. Another Quaker, Dr. John Fothergill, used the proceeds from his flourishing practice to create what has been referred to as the finest garden of its time in England. He is generally regarded as the first to cultivate alpine plants. It was he, in collaboration with Dr. William Pitcairn, a Scottish physician and gardener, who sent Thomas Blaikie to Switzerland to collect mountain plants.

The remarkable association between horticulture and those who followed the Quaker faith raises the question whether it was just an historical accident or whether there were other influences at work. In Scotland, Hew Wood was both a leading Quaker and Head Gardener of the most important gardens in the country. He may well have played a significant role in establishing at Holyrood his friend and fellow Quaker, the first William Miller and hence the three generation dynasty of Millers. He very likey converted John Reid to the faith and there may have been other gardeners we do not yet know about. As far as the Duke and Duchess of Hamilton were concerned, Hew Wood's ability as a gardener was all that mattered. They were powerful enough to disregard the popular clamour against Quakers. So, for Wood and his sons and the Millers, historical accident seems to have been responsible. But it is difficult to resist the inference that the more general association with gardening reflected the Quakers' pious regard for the natural world as a manifestation of God's handiwork, as well as their attraction to quiet, contemplative pursuits like gardening.

## Seedsmen and nurserymen trading in Scotland

The first of the Scottish seedsman that we know much about was Henry Fergus(s)on, who ran his thriving business 'A little above of Black Friars Wynd', in Edinburgh during the second half of the seventeenth century. He regularly supplied the Hamilton estate from 1660 onwards with vegetable and flower seeds. His first historically significant broadsheet advertising his seeds (Figure 77) has already been noted. In a later catalogue just under one hundred sorts of 'Flowers and other choice plants' were listed together with a comprehensive choice of vegetables, including a dozen different kinds of pea and seventeen different physical herbs. He also sold Queen of Hungary's water, a distillation of rosemary infused in spirits of wine, to be applied after bathing and popular with the upper classes, including the Duke of Hamilton. In later versions of his broadsheet he advertised the 'Catalogue of Plants in the Physical Garden of Edinburgh', which presumably was Sutherland's 'Hortus'.

Arthur Clephane was a contemporary of Ferguson. A younger son of the Laird of Carlogie, Fife, he first pursued a career as a ship's captain which he abandoned to set up as a general merchant in Edinburgh in 1706. He particularly dealt with seeds, both agriculural and for the garden. For the next twenty years he sold them to all classes of society, generally on a modest scale, within a radius of fifty to sixty miles about Edinburgh. According to Donnelly, who researched his life, Clephane obtained his seeds from two London seedsmen and also from Holland. In the latter case he dealt either directly with merchants in Amsterdam and Rotterdam, or relied on ships' captains to purchase goods on his behalf. He distributed his orders by local carriers, including those for Haddington, Dunblane, Newcastle and Kinross.

Clephane had a hard time. He was up against serious competition from William Miller and complained about it to his suppliers. Also, he was plagued by frequent failure of his clients to settle their debts and had to resort to the law to recover his dues. He was not alone in that respect. Time and again estate records reveal seedsmen's accounts long overdue for payment, often by several years. No doubt the unfortunate merchant was torn between desire to have his cash and fear of falling out of favour with an influential customer. Clephane finally ran out of credit in 1730 and was imprisoned in the Tolboth in Edinburgh for failing to pay eight shillings sterling, so complete was his bankruptcy. There is no record of his trading after that time.

The three generations of the Quaker William Millers have already been noted. They must have dominated the seedsman business in Edinburgh for a long time, during which they accumulated great wealth. Like other seedsmen and nurserymen, the Millers imported seeds and stock from London and Holland. For example, a typical advertisement in the *Edinburgh Evening Courrant*, for Jan 18–22, 1722 was as follows: 'There is just come from Abroad, varieties of the *very* best new garden seeds, with several Sorts of Fruit Trees, Dutch Allers (alders); and gardners Tools to be sold by William Miller, Gardner, at the Abbey of Edinburgh: as also of his own propagating, several Sorts of Fruit Trees, Forrest Trees, and Evergreens, and Thorns for Hedges, with different Sorts of Linnen Cloath; all sold at the very lowest Prices.'

Another name which turns up in the estate accounts of the 1730's was that of Archibald Eagle. He had several apprentices who later did well. In 1723 he became official seedsman to the Honourable the Society of Improvers in the Knowledge of Agriculture in Scotland. This association included about three hundred members, drawn from the top brass of society – the nobility, gentry, professional classes and the occasional tradesman, like Eagle and the nurseryman William Boutcher. The members met from time to time for discussion and exchange of information. In 1743 the Transactions of the Society were published.

The best known of Eagle's apprentices was Patrick Drummond, who was apprenticed in 1735, and later went into business at the Lawnmarket, opposite to the Head of Libberton's Wynd, Edinburgh. He carried on a flourishing business until he died in 1760, the same year which saw the death of Eagle. In both cases their respective businesses were carried on by their widows. Patrick Drummond was commended by James Justice in his 'Scots Gardeners Director', 1754 and some copies of this work included Drummond's catalogue. This was very comprehensive and included seven sorts of onion, ten sorts of cabbage and no less than twenty-two varieties of pea. The number and variety of flowers do not show a great advance on Ferguson's list and amount to about a hundred, although various 'roots' like ranunculus, anemones, irises, tuberoses etc were also included. The catalogue also featured a long list of gardener's tools, including scythes for short or long grass, scythes for broom, willow or whins, 'roonds' i.e. bindings for tying up wall trees, traps for rats, mice and moles, glasses for holding water or bird seed, all sorts of seed for birds (presumably cage birds) and an assorted variety of stationery. The later catalogue, issued by his widow, included the following intriguing item : 'The true Scots Specifick Anodyne Necklace, so well known for its extraordinary Efficiency, in assisting and keeping Children easy and free of Pain while Teething continues to be sold at the above shop, and no where else, for 2s. Sterling each, for ready Money only, with printed Directions.'

We have already noted that William Boutcher was a member of the Society of Improvers. He was the son of a landscape gardener and surveyor, also called William. Boutcher was an expert on trees and specialised in selling thorns, larch, beech, hornbeam, oaks, silver fir etc. to the many estates which were planting on a large scale. Boutcher wrote 'A Treatise on Forest Trees', which was published by private subscription in 1775. Early on we encountered his sceptical approach to catalogues which promised more than they could provide. He also railed against incompetent nurserymen who overcrowded their tree seedlings, which they then sold at a knock-down price. Apart, perhaps, from a modicum of resentment at being under-cut, it does seem that he had a real case against what we should term 'cowboys', who invaded a rapidly expanding market in the hopes of quick returns, with little regard to the accepted practices of arboriculture.

Another name which often turns up quite often is that of David Dowie who supplied the Duke of Atholl with larix (larch) trees. In Glasgow John McAslan set up a nursery in 1717 which developed into the business of Austin & McAslan when his son-in-law became a partner. This firm had great success and survived until recent times. In the late eighteenth and the nineteenth centuries their name was linked with the development of the Scots Rose which gave rise to a great many varieties.

James Gordon was another nurseryman who merits notice. He was based in Fountainbridge, Edinburgh, where he ran a successful business. In 1758 he published a catalogue of Shrubs and Flowers, but is chiefly remembered for his book entitled: 'The Planters, Florists, and Gardeners Pocket Dictionary; being also a Practical Collection from the Most approved Authors in the English Language, Relating to the above Three parts of Gardening, Founded on Experience, worthy of Notice, and adapted to the Climate of Scotland'. The dedication is to The Operative Gardeners in Scotland whereby 'he humbly submits the following sheets to his Brethren, whose countenance and protection will sufficiently recompense him for the trouble and expense he has been at in compiling it…' After some flowery expressions of hope that his work will please he ends 'Meantime, it gives me peculiar pleasure to declare, that I am extremely happy in being accounted one of your number: – that I ever loved the employment, and always cultivated the acquaintance of those eminent in it; – which still is the sincere desire of, Gentlemen, Your very humble Servant, And affectionate Brother, James Gordon.' Although the Caledonian Gardeners Lodge of Edinburgh was not established until 1782, the tone of this preamble reflects the corporate solidarity among working gardeners which inspired it.

Gordon's book lived up to its title and intentions. It is an excellent, succinct, alphabetically arranged account of varieties of vegetable, flowers, shrubs fruit trees etc, with advice on management, in short, a first-class little reference book.

The Dickson family founded another dynasty whose members, extending over five generations, were still trading in recent times. It started with Robert Dickson who established a nursery in Teviotdale at Hassendeanburn in 1728/9. He sold the usual run of vegetables and, as noted earlier, was among the first to grow and sell potatoes on a regular basis. Trees, both fruit and forest trees, appeared early in his accounts and steadily increased in the numbers sold. He became a major supplier to estates all over Scotland, exporting to England and Ireland and taking an active part in establishing plantations. Near the end of his life he was asked to estimate how many trees he had planted. He went through his books and concluded he had sold forest trees sufficient to plant thirty-eight thousand Scots acres, equivalent to forty-seven thousand seven hundred and seventy English acres. Robert Dickson was succeeded at Hassendeanburn by his son Archibald; there was also a branch at Hawick. Another son, James, set up a business in Perth. Later he took a partner and the firm traded as Dickson & Turnbull. A third son, Walter, established a nursery in Leith and this developed into the Edinburgh firm of Dickson & Co. He later joined forces with yet another, although unrelated James Dickson, and they traded as Dicksons & Co. Apart for some minor name changes along the way this firm survived well into the present century.

Although none of them were as important or as well known as the foregoing seedsmen and nurserymen, there were plenty of others doing business in the early eighteenth century. Robert McClellan, was supplying the Earl of Cassilis with a full range of vegetable seeds as well as flowers in the 1730's, Ben Darling of Aberdeen was selling flower seeds to Monymusk in 1722, Andrew Bruce of Stirling was dealing with the Laird of Rossie, Fife, in 1726 etc. Advertisements in the contemporary press reveal others like Samuel Robertson, gardener at Kelso and James Tait, gardener at Tyninghame, both of whom advertised produce for sale in the *Edinburgh Evening Courant*, 1722. Later in the eighteenth century there were many more with profitable businesses like Robert Anderson, John Richmond, Peter Lawson etc. but they belong to a later period which falls outwith our present enquiry.

## A diversity of horticulturalists

We next consider, in rough chronological order, other Scotsmen who made a significant contribution to horticulture in the eighteenth century – as nurserymen in London, garden designers in France, plant collectors, authors or botanic garden curators. Often they were trained as gardeners and frequently their interest in botany was inseparable from their interest in horticulture. Although all born in the eighteenth, in several instances their careers extended into the following century and therefore fall outwith the period to which the record of garden flora applies. Although there is virtue in confining a survey of garden flora to a particular interval of time, such a restriction is a good deal less compelling with respect to the men whose lives overlapped that period or followed soon after. They had their origins in the same social traditions and circumstances shared by Scottish gardeners of the eighteenth century. They were part of the Scottish influence in horticulture discussed in the last chapter and it would be too arbitrary to exclude them. We acknowledge our debt to Hadfield, Harling and Highton's 'British Gardeners', and other sources for sundry biographical details.

We have to start with Robert Morison (1620–1683) who was a native of Aberdeen, graduating M.A. with distinction from the University at the age of eighteen. He is the earliest of the men we have singled out for attention. He took part in the Civil War on the King's side, was seriously wounded at the Battle of the Brig o' Dee, and, like many another Jacobite, fled to France. He continued studies at the University of Angers and graduated Doctor of Medicine. From that time on he devoted himself to the study of Botany. In Paris he studied under Vespian Robin, Botanist to the King. On Vespian's recommendation he took charge of the royal gardens at Blois where he remained for ten years. Soon after the Restoration Charles II summoned him to London to be King's Physician and appointed him Professor of Botany, with a stipend and so he became the first holder of the Chair of Botany at Oxford University. By 1669 he had completed and published his Praeludia Botanica. At Oxford he worked on his ambitious

'Historia Plantarum Universalis Oxonensis', of which the first volume appeared in 1680, dealing with a third of the sections into which he classified herbaceous plants. He did not live to complete the work. On a visit to London in 1683 he was knocked down by a coach in the Strand and died the following day. The rest of the Historia was entrusted to Jacob Bobart the Younger who, at last, in 1699 completed the volume which covered the rest of the herbaceous plants.

Morison's chief interest was in plant classification but his approach was based on the earlier work of Cesalpino, who was not given the credit to which he was entitled. Although no doubt a competent gardener Morison was not in the first flight of botanists, but, as Linnaeus remarked, he deserved recognition for rescuing plant classification from the low esteem and ignorance into which it had fallen. His countrymen certainly respected him. James Sutherland claimed to have arranged the plants in the Physic Garden according to Morison's principles of classification while James Justice acknowledged his authority.

James Sutherland (1639–1719) was probably a native of Edinburgh, although that is uncertain. He attracted the attention of Robert Sibbald, the Edinburgh physician and botanist, who, along with Andrew Balfour, laid the foundations of the Edinburgh Botanic Garden, as noted earlier. According to Sibbald, Sutherland had attained 'by his own industry a great knowledge of plants and medals'. He was appointed intendant of the garden at Holyrood that Sibbald and Blafour had created. As the enterprise evolved Sutherland remained in charge and became, in effect, the first Curator of what was to develop into the Edinburgh Botanic Garden. In 1683 he published 'Hortus Medicus Edinburgensis', which was a catalogue of the plants in the Physic Garden, of which the frontispiece is shown in Figure 100. This is a scholarly work, with an index of more than 2000 entries, in which plants are listed under their Latin and English names. He completed this work within eight years of taking charge of the garden. In 1695 a Chair of Botany was created for him and in 1710 he became Regius Professor of Botany, having been appointed King's Botanist in 1699. Sutherland arranged his plants systematically, according to the precepts of Dr. Morison. In his last years Sutherland seems to have lost interest in the garden and pursued his other interest in medals.

James Justice (1698–1763) was born in Midlothian, the son of a merchant who imported bulbs from Holland. This trade stimulated his early interest in plants. Justice trained as a lawyer and became a Principal Clerk to the Court of Session. But his real interest lay in horticulture for which he developed 'an unbridled passion' and on which he lavished his wealth to the point of bankruptcy, which landed him in the Tolbooth from which he was rescued by the intervention of Lord Milton, one of his numerous aristocratic friends. He made two visits to Holland to study horticultural practice in the country which, quite early, had attained European supremacy in the arts of raising plants for both profit and pleasure. He

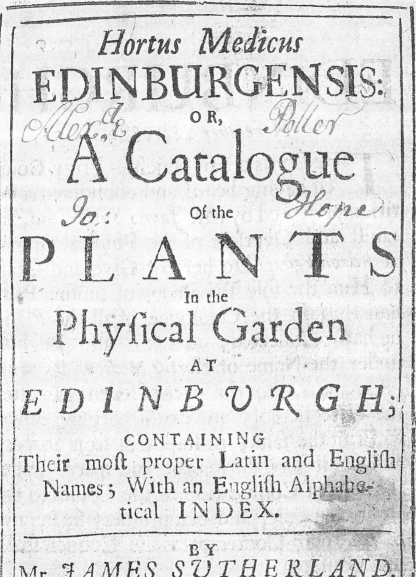

FIGURE 100
The title page of James
Sutherland's *Hortus
Medicus Edinburgensis*,
1683. This catalogue of
plants in the Physic
Garden at Holyrood,
including both the
English names and the
Latin descriptions, and
with some 2000 items
in the index, is the first
catalogue of a plant
collection in Scotland.

achieved sufficient recognition as a gardening expert to be elected to the Royal Society of London, although he was later struck off because he failed to pay the annual subscription. His major contribution was the publication of 'The Scots Gardener's Director' (1754). This was a detailed, practical manual, covering all aspects of gardening, especially with regard to the Scottish climate, including even the heating arrangements for the culture of pineapples, which were first grown in Scotland by Justice. He included lists of varieties of vegetables and herbaceous plants and also a section in which he brought some degree of order to the bewildering array of names of bulbs in the Dutch catalogues, especially that of Voorhelm, who named a hyacinth after him i.e. Mynheer Justice. In his account of garden flowers it is a pity he confined his attention to what was mentioned in Voorhelm's catalogue, which used many names difficult to identify, rather than prepare his own account. James Justice could hardly be regarded as modest. He dismissed the work of his predecessor, James Reid, as worthless and boldly asserted his claim to be the leading authority. But there was some basis in his assertion for his was a very practical guide to gardening which won acclaim. In addition to the 'Director' he also published in 1743 'Directions for propagating Hyacinths' in the Transactions of the Society of Improvers of Agriculture in Scotland. In 1759 he published 'The British Gardener's Calendar chiefly adapted to the Climate of North Britain'. In this he covered the necessary work, month by month, in the Kitchen, Fruit and Pleasure garden as well as in the Nursery, Greenhouse and Stove together with a Dissertation on Forest trees, a catalogue of seeds, roots etc, in all a comprehensive treatment. In 1764 and 1765 there appeared revised editions of his earlier work: 'The British Gardener's Director' and 'The British Gardener's New Director'. At his death his plant collection, advertised for sale in the Caledonian Mercury, included the finest Auriculas, Ranunculus, Anemones, Hyacinths, Tulips, Double Polyanthus, Narcissus, Jacobea and Guernsey Lilies, Tuberoses etc. They were bought by Drummond & Co.

James Gordon (1708-10–1780), the precise date of his birth is uncertain, was not related to James Gordon, the Edinburgh nurseryman. Nothing seems to be known of his origins, apart from the statement, in the correspondence of one of William Forsyth's descendants, that he was from Aberdeen or Aberdeenshire. Before setting up his nursery business in London at Mile End, he worked for private employers, including the eighth Earl Petre, who had an immense establishment and arboretum at Thornden Hall in Essex. We know from Scottish estate records that Gordon supplied many of them with seeds and plants. He was an outstanding plantsman who succeeded in growing many species which had defeated others. One of Linnaeus' correspondents, John Ellis, a merchant with a passion for botany, wrote of him thus: 'He has more knowledge in vegetation than all the gardeners and writers on gardening in England put together, but he is too modest to publish anything. If you send him anything rare, he will make you a proper return.' He introduced the Gingko tree about 1754 and propagated extensively from the original specimen. He introduced the Camellia and had particular success with Azaleas, Rhodendrons and Kalmias. Gordon comes across as a very modest man who seems almost diffident about his horticultural success.

James Lee (1715–1795) was born in Selkirkshire. Nothing is known about his early life except that he was well educated, with a knowledge of Latin, so he may have attended the grammar school in Selkirk. We first hear of him in 1732 when, at the age of seventeen, he set off to walk to London, armed with his Andrea Ferrara sword; travel was hazardous then. At Lichfield he contracted smallpox. After recovering he apparently went to work at the garden at Whitton, belonging to his compatriot, Archibald Campbell, the 3rd. Duke of Argyll. There is also evidence that he spent some time with Philip Miller at Chelsea. However, in 1745 he went into partnership with Lewis Kennedy to establish The Vineyard at Hammersmith. This developed into the premier nursery in Britain, and indeed in Europe. An immense number of exotic plants from America, Australia and elsewhere were introduced, totalling some one hundred and forty species between 1753 and 1795, including *Fuchsia coccinea* which was a great success. Lee, who was highly respected among horticulturalists and botanists, was well known for his generosity in giving away plants to botanists. Many apprentices passed through the Vineyard nursery and since Lee was often asked to advise on gardens and gardeners by the gentry, his apprentices, like those of Philip Miller, had good prospects.

In 1760 he published 'An Introduction to Botany', which was, in large part, a translation of Linnaeus' 'Philosophiae Botanica,' whose system of classification was thus brought to a wide audience. Lee had help in the preparation of this work, probably from an importer of bulbs and roots, Samuel Gray, who, wished to remain anonymous. Lee's 'Introduction to Botany' was very successful and added considerably to his reputation as an authority on all things horticultural. Lee's daughter Ann (1753–790) was a talented painter of plants and insects, who had studied under Sydney Parkinson, who was employed by Sir Joseph Banks to accompany Captain Cook in his voyage on the *Endeavour*. Ann Lee assisted her father in preparing illustrations which he used in correspondence with Linnaeus and others. When James Lee died in 1795 he was succeeded by his son, also James.

John Hope (1725–1786) was born in Edinburgh and educated at Dalkeith School. He studied medicine in Edinburgh and, as so often the case for Scots, in various continental schools. During his time abroad he studied Botany under Bernard de Jussieu (1699–1777), who was Professor of Botany and Demonstrator at the Royal Gardens in Paris, where he developed a modified form of the Linnaean system of classification. When Hope returned to Edinburgh he was elected to the Royal College of Physicians. Botany was his spare time passion and in 1761 he was appointed first Professor of Botany and Materia Medica in the University of Edinburgh and also King's Botanist and Superintendant of the Botanic Garden. During Hope's term of office he supervised the transfer of the Botanic Garden to Leith and secured a permanent Crown endowment for the Garden. Hope arranged the plants systematically in the new garden, established conservatories, a pond for aquatics etc. He carried out experiments on plant physiology and he and his students travelled widely in Scotland, collecting and studying the native flora.

John Abercrombie (1726–1806) was born at Prestonpans, East Lothian, and educated at the local grammar school. He was the son of a gardener and at first worked in his father's market garden. After some kind of disagreement he migrated to England and worked for a time in the Royal Gardens at Kew, before going into the nursery business on his own at Hackney. In 1767 he published a book entitled 'Every Man his own Gardner', not under his own name but of that of Thomas Mawe, gardener to the Duke of Leeds in Yorkshire. This book was very successful and ran to many editions. Only by the twenty-third edition did Abercrombie's name appear as a joint author, although, in fact, it was all his own work. Why Abercrombie was so bashful in this respect remains a mystery. The book was a comprehensive guide to horticultural practice, extending to some seven hundred pages of small print. Abercrombie published other works on every aspect of gardening, including 'The Universal Gardener and Botanist ' (1778) and, three years later, 'The Gardener's Pocket Journal', so he earns his place as an early contributor to the innumerable books on gardening aimed at the general public.

William Aiton (1731–1793) was born at Hamilton, Lanarkshire. He trained as a gardener in Scotland before coming to London in 1754 to work with Philip Miller at Chelsea. In 1759, the Earl of Bute, who, of course, was also a Scot, employed Aiton to manage Dowager Princess Augusta's garden at Kew and also, at a later date, the adjacent Richmond Garden, where he was provided with a house. So William Aiton became the first curator of Kew which flourished under his regime. In 1789 he published his 'Hortus Kewensis', which was a catalogue of more than five thousand plants growing at Kew. This was extended by his son, also William, who succeeded him at Kew, to include more than eleven thousand species. His other son became royal gardener at Windsor.

Willliam Forsyth (1737–1804) was a native of Old Meldrum, Aberdeenshire. He went to work in the Apothecaries Garden under Philip Miller, whom he succeeded when Miller retired. He is credited with creating what may have been the first rock garden in the country, using forty tons of old stone from the Tower of London, Icelandic lava contributed by Sir Joseph Banks plus other stones. Before following Miller he worked at Syon House for the Duke of Northumberland and later became George III's gardener at Kensington. He established a considerable reputation, almost on a par with that of Lee. In 1802 he published a comprehensive 'Treatise on Fruit Trees', listing all the varieties he could find word of. However in his latter years, he made rather a fool of himself by promoting a 'plaister' reputed to cure ailing trees. He even engineered a government grant in return for revealing its nature. However the remedy was later shown by Richard Knight to be of no value, hardly surprising since cow dung and lime were principal components.

James Dickson (c 1738–1822) was born in Traquair, Peeblesshire. As usual we are ignorant of his early life, beyond the fact that he worked in the Earl of Traquair's garden. When quite young he moved to London to work in the nursery of Jeffrey & Co and then in other garden jobs until he set up business as nurseryman and seedsman in Covent Garden in 1772. Dickson was on friendly terms with James Lee and Sir Joseph Banks through whom he was appointed gardener to the British Museum. He is remembered for his pioneering studies of mosses, with the assistance of a Pole, John Zeir. He toured Scotland where he studied the flora of Ben Lawers, in the company of Mungo Park. He was one of the founders of the Horticultural Society which later became the Royal Horticultural Society. The genus of tree ferns, Dicksonia, was named after him.

Francis Masson (1741–1806) was yet another man from the North East. A native of Aberdeen, he came to work at Kew, under William Aiton. At the age of thirty he became the first of a long line of plant collectors sent out from Kew. Sir Joseph Banks canvassed the King in favour of a plant collecting trip to the Cape of Good Hope, which was agreed. Masson was appointed and in 1772 set sail to spend two and a half years in the Cape, during which he undertook three expeditions into the interior, accompanied on the first by a Dutchman called Oldenburg and, on the second and possibly also the third, by Dr. Thunberg, a distinguished Swedish botanist. Masson's account of his travels and finds was published on his return. In 1776 he again set off to visit Madeira, the Canaries and thence to the West Indies. From the Canaries he sent plant specimens to the younger Linnaeus. The war prevented him from collecting in the West Indies. When the French attacked Granada, he was forced to become a soldier and was taken prisoner. In 1780 he lost all his collection and much of his clothes and papers in a hurricane at St Lucia. In 1783 he left for Portugal and Spain where he collected many plants, returning in 1785. Two years later, he was back in the Cape for a long and successful stay. His last trip took him to North America in 1796, in the course of which he was captured by French pirates, who put him on another ship bound for Baltimore, from which he later transferred to another vessel bound for New York, which he eventually reached after many hardships due to shortage of food and water. Such were the hazards of travel in those days. In America he visited Niagara, Lake Ontario and Fort Erie. In 1806 he died in Montreal.

It is a tragedy that all Masson's extensive correspondence with William Aiton was destroyed by Aiton's brother at his death. Masson's discoveries of new species were impressive. He added more than four hundred species to the Kew collection and greatly augmented Banks' herbarium. He collected about half the species of Cape Pelargoniums and many of the bulbous species. He also introduced the ancestor of the familiar 'cineraria' (*Senecio cruenta*). Masson was a good artist who produced competent paintings and drawings of the plants he collected and which he described lucidly in both English and Latin. Throughout a life of frequent hardship and danger he never wavered in his interest in plants and natural history. At the news of his death James Lee's son wrote to Sir James Edward Smith to make the point: 'He was very hardly dealt with by, in being exposed to the bitter cold of Canada in the decline of life, after twenty-five years services in a hot climate, and all for a pittance. He has done much for botany and science, and deserves to have some lasting memorial given of his extreme modesty, good temper, generosity, and usefulness. We hope when opportunity serves you will be his champion.' After all these years we can echo those sentiments.

John Fraser (1750–1811) was born in Inverness and went to London in his late teens to set himself up as a linen draper. However he got to know William Forsyth who played a large part in persuading him to go to Newfoundland as a plant collector. We can hardly fail to notice how the Scots in London encouraged and supported one another; they must have been a formidable combination. Fraser's first trip was sufficiently successful to persuade him to become a professional collector. He made a number of further trips to North America and then, in 1795, he set up a nursery at Sloane Square to propagate and sell his American finds. He was no businessman and the enterprise foundered. However he took on the job of completing the 'Flora Carolensis' which had been started by another botanist who had died. It is also of some curiosity that in 1796 he went to Russia, where Catherine the Great purchased all the plants he had brought with him.

Thomas Blaikie (1750–1838) was a very different sort of person, who achieved success as a garden designer in France. He was born in Edinburgh, son of a gardener with a modest property at Corstorphine. Nothing is known about his early life. We are left to guess where he served his apprenticeship; probably it was in Edinburgh. By the age of twenty-five he was in touch with many leading gardeners and botanists of his time and again we may wonder how this came about. Fortunately from this time onwards he kept a diary, which was edited and published by Francis Birrell in 1931 under the title *The Diary of a Scotch Gardener at the French Court at the End of the Eighteenth Century*.

Blaikie can be regarded as the first professional collector of alpine plants. In 1775, he was commissioned by Dr. John Fothergill and his friend Dr. William Pitcairn to undertake a journey to Switzerland where he was to collect mountain plants. This he did with enthusiasm and no small success since he collected several hundred species of alpines. He met some famous people like de Saussure and Voltaire. He was very athletic and had a poor opinion of the stamina of most of the Swiss who accompanied him on trips in the mountains, including the subsequent conquerer of Mont Blanc, Gabriel Pacard, who he thought tired easily.

After his return from Switzerland Sir Joseph Banks had in mind to send him to collect in the East Indies but the American War of Independence ruled that out. Instead James Lee, the leading nurseryman in London, who knew him well, arranged for him to enter the service of the Comte du Lauragais, a charming but feckless aristocrat. Blaikie spent the rest of his life in France and became so assimilated that he passed as French, unlike his wife, who, we can infer, remained attached to her Edinburgh ways. Blaikie moved regularly in aristocratic circles, and was friendly with members of the royal family, including Marie Antoinette. He became well known as a garden designer. In collaboration with a French architect he laid out the garden known as Bagatelle, for the Comte d'Artois. The garden at Morceau, belonging to the Duc d'Orléans, was one of several he designed for the nobility. The Revolution ruined him. He was employed by the Revolutionary Directory to plant potatoes in the Tuileries but was never paid for his labours.

In spite of his assimilation to the French way of life Blaikie retained his links with the little estate at Corstorphine, which was managed by relatives. In 1825 he referred to taking part in what was probably the annual celebration of the Caledonian Gardeners' Lodge of Edinburgh. Blaikie leaves the impression of a lively and enterprising man who was equally at ease with both peasant and nobleman.

William Malcolm (dates unknown) was a native of Kemnay, Aberdeenshire, the son of a farmer and originally intended for medicine. However, his father died prematurely and he had to step into his shoes and look after the farm until he could hand over to his next oldest brother. About 1745 he took ship to London to look around and see what opportunites might turn up. He chanced to visit James Lee's Vineyard nursery which impressed him. On enquiring about the possibility of an apprenticeship Lee signed him up right away for three years and he started work at once. Later he set up a successful nursery business at Kennington, London, where he introduced *Paeonia tenuiflora* in 1765. He is included here because of the first-hand information we have, in his correspondence, of a young Scotsman in London quickly finding a career in horticulture.

John Veitch (1752–1839), a native of Jedburgh, went, at an early age, to work in a garden in London. Not long after, he moved to Killarton in Devon, where he worked as land steward for Sir Thomas Acland. By 1808, with Acland's assistance, he had set up a nursery near Killarton and never looked back thereafter. He laid the foundations for a five generation dynasty of nurserymen and horticulturists, who developed and managed the leading horticultural business of Veitch & Co. In its heyday, the largest enterprise of its kind anywhere, it was famous for its plant collectors who were sent to all parts of the world.

George Don (1764–1814) was born in the parish of Menmuir, Forfarshire, the son of a small farmer. After leaving school he went as apprentice gardener to Dupplin House, near Perth and took up his life-time pastime of plant hunting in the Highlands. After later apprenticeship to a clockmaker in Dunblane and some years spent in England, he returned to Scotland, working first as a clockmaker in Glasgow. As we learn from J. Grant Roger's account of his life, he continued his plant hunting, finding alpine plants new to Scotland and becoming acquainted with Robert Brown, later known as an eminent botanist, and another botanist, John Mackay, who had trained as a gardener at the premises of Dickson & Co in Leith. In 1797 Don acquired an acre of ground known as Doohillock in Forfar in an attempt to sustain his family by growing vegetables. In 1802 after the premature death of James Mackay, who had been Principal Gardener at the Royal Botanic Garden, Don was reluctantly persuaded to succeed him. During his time there he attended most of the medical classes with the intention of becoming a physician. But it was not to be. Four years later he resigned and returned to Forfar, practising as nurseryman and country surgeon, when he was not botanising in the Highlands. He died in 1814 leaving his wife and five surviving sons penniless. His friends rallied round and contributed to a fund which rescued them from destitution. Of the five sons three became gardeners and the other two botanists of repute.

Don had an unrestrained zeal to discover and grow new plants. He discovered many of the rarest alpines growing in Scotland. Some of his discoveries have turned out to be errors of identification, but others, long doubted, have been confirmed, such as the rediscovery of *Homogyne alpina* in Clova in 1951. His 1813 catalogue of plants for sale listed 2000 species. His friend, Patrick Neil, confirmed that his garden was crammed with an admittedly disordered assemblage of an immense number of species. For example he grew more than a hundred different grasses and more than sixty kinds of sedge. His devotion to botany was wholly unconstrained.

Finally, although he belongs to a somewhat later era we can hardly pass by John Claudius Loudon (1783–1843) since he belongs to the same tradition of Scottish gardeners. He was born at Cambuslang, the son of a Lanarkshire farmer. From an early age he displayed a remarkable talent for learning which was the key to his subsequent success. He started off as apprentice to Robert Dickson of Hassendeanburn, founder of the Dickson dynasty of nurserymen, but broke this off to seek his fortune as a free-lance journalist in England. He published articles on the layout of public squares, hothouses, plantations and country residences and, at the age of twenty-three, was elected to the Linnaean Society. He contracted rheumatic fever, which led to the shortening of one arm and immense suffering in later life. He rented a farm and persuaded his father to join him. This was a success and he took over a larger farm, which did well enough for him to sell it and use the proceeds to pay for travels through Northern Europe. When he returned he found that his investments had failed and he was in dire straits. Undeterred, he proceeded to start work on his 'Encyclopedia of Gardening' which was published in 1822. This is an immense work of twelve hundred pages of the small type favoured by printers of that period. Every aspect of gardening was covered, including the history and style of gardening in different countries, a bibliography of works on gardening in different languages, long lists of cultivars, comprehensive technical information etc. For anyone interested in the history of gardening Loudon's Encyclopedia is an indispensable source of accurate information which has been quoted on innumerable occasions, often without acknowledgement. It went through many editions and became the standard horticultural manual for much of the nineteenth century.

Loudon went on to found 'The Gardenr's Magazine', to which he regularly contributed. He edited the 'Encyclopedia of Plants' in which the comprehensive text was provided by John Lindley of the Horticultural Society. He produced the impressive eight volume work: 'Arboretum et Fruticetum Britannicum or The Trees and Shrubs of Britain, Native and Foreign'. All these works displayed meticulous scholarship. He was greatly assisted by his wife Jane, who was an accomplished writer and horticulturist in her own right. Together they dominated the horticultural scene and wrote for a very wide audience.

We can hardly fail to feel something like awe at Loudon's immense productivity and his unswerving devotion to his work. As a result of the ministrations of an incompetent masseur his damaged arm was broken and he had to have it amputated, without anaesthetics. His wife recounts how, on the day of the operation, Loudon entertained the surgeons to lunch and then led them upstairs for the operation. After the amputation and the binding of his wound he was on the point of calmly going downstairs to continue his work and only the entreaties of the doctors persuaded him to rest in bed.

The lives and achievements of the men we have been considering, complemented those of the Scottish working gardeners. The relations between them were often close, sometimes established during apprenticeship, but nurtured by the shared sentiments, aspirations and attitudes dictated by their national origin. As we have seen, many circumstances came together to engineer the eighteenth-century burgeoning of Scottish horticultural enterprise and talent. Ultimately, it was rooted in the continuity of the European tradition of management of orchards and kitchen gardens, fostered and developed by the Scottish monastic institutions and handed on to their secular successors.

# Bibliography

**Published References** The number(s) in brackets after each entry refer(s) to the Chapter(s) to which the reference applies.

1. Amherst, A.M.T. (1895) *A History of Gardening in England* (3)
2. Bailey, L.H. (1949) *Manual of Cultivated Plants* (3)
3. Bean, W.J. (1936) *Trees and Shrubs Hardy in the British Isles* (3)
4. Birrell, F. (1931) *The Diary of a Scotch Gardener at the French Court at the End of the Eighteenth Century* (10)
5. *Boutcher, W.* (1775) *A Treatise on Forest Trees* (1,7)
6. Britten, J. (1884) 'Frances Masson'. *Jour. Bot* XXII: 114–123 (10)
7. ——— (1920–2) Some Early Cape Botanists and Collectors; *Jour. Linn. Soc.*, XLV: 22–51 (10)
8. Britten, J. and Holland, R. (1886) *Dictionary of English Plant-Names* (3)
9. Brown, P.H. (1891) *Early Travellers in Scotland* (1)
10. Bunyard, E.A. (1920, 1925) *A Handbook of Hardy Fruits more commonly Grown in Great Britain* (4)
11. Carlyle, Dr. Alexander, *The Autobiography of, 1722–1770* (1860) (9)
12. Coats, A.M. (1992) *Garden Shrubs and their Histories* (3)
13. Coulton, G.G. (1933) *Scottish Abbeys and Social Life* (4)
14. Cox, E.H.M. (1935) *A History of Gardening in Scotland* (4,9)
15 Crawford, D. (Ed.) (1900) *Journals of Sir John Lauder of Fountainhall, 1665–1676*, Scot. Hist. Soc. Vol. 36 (3,4)
16. Dennistoun, J. (Ed.) (1842) *The Coltness Collection*. Maitland Club, publ. No. 58 (4)
17. Dilworth, M. (1995) *Scottish Monasteries in the late Middle Ages* (1)
18. Donnelly, T. (1970) 'Arthur Clephane, Edinburgh Merchant and Seedsman 1706–30', *The Agricultural History Review*. XVIII Part II : 151–160 (10)
19. Duncan, A. (1814) 'Observations on the propagation by cuttings of the Original, the Mother, the Oslen or the Bur-Knot Apple Tree', *Memoirs of the Caledonian Horticultural Society* (1): 237–241 (4)
20. *Edinburgh Evening Courant*. From 1722 onwards many advertisements for Edinburgh houses for sale with gardens and/or orchards, for fruit trees and plants by nurserymen both in and outwith Edinburgh and also for medicinal herbal preparations (5,6)
21. Fletcher, H. and Brown, W.H. (1970) *The Royal Botanic Garden, Edinburgh* (5, 10)
22. *Foulis, Sir John of Ravelston, 1671–1707* (1894), Scot. Hist. Soc. Vol. XVI (2,4)
23. Forsyth, W. (1802) *A Treatise on Fruit Trees* (4)
24. *Gardeners' Chronicle*, April 6, 1872, 401–2 (9)
25. *Gardeners' Chronicle*, April 3, 1920, 172 (9)
26. Gerard, J. (1597) *The Herbal or General History of Plants* (3)
27. Gibson, J. (1768) *The Fruit Gardener* (4)
28. Gordon, J. (1774) *The Planters, Florists and Gardeners Pocket Dictionary* (3,4)
29. Gorer, R. (1970) *The Development of Garden Flowers* (3)

30. Graham, J.E. (1924) *The History of the Poor Law in Scotland previous to 1845. From The Poor Law Magazine* (1917–1918) (9)

31. Gray, W.F. (1925) *An Edinburgh Miscellany* (5)

32. Grieve, M. (1976) *A Modern Herbal* (5)

33. Guthrie, D. (1961) 'The Surgeon-Apothecaries and the Physical Gardens of old Edinburgh', *Journal of the Royal College of Surgeons of Edinburgh*, 6 Oct. 1960–July 1961 (5)

34. Hamilton, H. (1959) 'Economic Growth in Scotland 1720–1770', *Jour. Pol. Econ.*, 6: 85–93 (9)

35. Hamilton, H. (1945) *Selections from the Monymusk Papers 1713–1735*, Scot. Hist. Soc. 3rd. Series Vol. 39 ( 2,3,7)

36. Hamilton, H. (1946) *Life and Labour on an Aberdeenshire Estate, 1735–1750. Being selections from the Monymusk Papers.* Third Spalding Club (2,3,7)

37. Harvey, J. (1972) *Early Gardening Catalogues* (2,3)

38. Harvey, J. (1981) *Mediaeval Gardens* (1,2,5)

39. Harvey, J. (1993) *Restoring Period Gardens* (3)

40. Harvey, J. (1978) 'Gillyflower and Carnation', *Garden History*, 6 (1): 46–57 (3)

41. Hynd, N.R. (1984) 'Towards a Study of Gardening in Scotland from the sixteenth to the eighteenth centuries', *Studies in Scottish Antiquity* (Ed. D.J. Breeze) (6)

42. Innes, C. (Ed.) (1859) *The Book of the Thanes of Cawdor.* Spalding Club, publ. No. 30 (2,3)

43. Justice, J. (1754) *The Scots Gardener's Directory* (2,3)

44 Lauder, Sir John of Fountainhall (1928) 'Historical Notes of Scottish Affairs, 1661–1688', *The Book of the Old Edinburgh Club*, Vol. XVI: 79–167 (2,3)

45. Leith, A.W. (Ed.) (1839) Editor, *Ferrerii Historia Abbatum de Kinloss.* Bannatyne Club (1,4)

46. Loudon, J.C. (1826) *An Encyclopedia of Gardening* (2,3,4,9)

47. Loudon, J.C. (Ed.) (1836) *An Encyclopedia of Plants* (2,3,4,5)

48. Macfarlane, W. *Geographical Collections Relating to Scotland.* Edited by A. Mitchell (1906–8) Scot. Hist. Soc. Vol V, 51–3 (6)

49. Machray and Gorrie (1814) *An account of the orchards in the Carse of Gowrie. Memoirs of the Royal Caledonian Horticultural Society*, (1): 317–332 (4)

50. Mackechnie, A. (1988) 'James Smith: Small Country Houses'. In *Aspects of Scottish Classicism and its Formal Setting*, Ed. J. Fraser, and D. Jones (6)

51. Macphail, A.M. (1881) *History of the Religious House of Pluscarden* (4)

52. Malcolm, C.A. (1925) 'The Gardens of the Castle'. *The Book of the Old Edinburgh Club*, XIV: 101–120 (6)

53. Marwick, W.H. (1948) *A Short History of the Friends in Scotland* (10)

54. Marshall, R. (1970) The House of Hamilton in its Anglo-Scottish Setting in the Seventeenth Century. Ph.D. Thesis, Univ. of Edinburgh (2,3)

55. Meyvaert, P. (1986) 'The Mediaeval Monastic Garden'. In *Mediaeval Gardens*, Dumbarton Oaks Research Library and Collection (1)

56. Miller, P. (1768 Edition) *The Gardener's Dictionary* (3)

57. Minay, P. (1991) 'Eighteenth and early Nineteenth Century Edinburgh Seedsmen and Nurserymen', *Book of the Old Edinburgh Club*, New Series, 1: 7–26 (10)

58. Minay, P. (1976) 'James Justice (1698–1763). Eighteenth Century Scots Horticulturist and Botanist', *Garden Hist.* (2) : 41–62. (10)

59. Morison, R. (1680–1699) *Plantarum Historiae Universalis Oxoniensis* (10)

60. Neill P. (1812) *On Scottish Gardens and Orchards* (2,4,9)

61. Oldham, S.A.J. (1994) 'Scotland, the Home of Good Gardeners'. Procceedings of a Conference on Horticulture in Education and Conservation, Sept. 1992 (9)

62. Oliver, F.W. (Ed.) (1913) *Makers of British Botany* (10)

63 Parkinson, J. (1629) *Paradisi in Sole Paradisus Terrestris* (2,3)

64. Plant, M. (1952) *The Domestic Life of Scotland in the Eighteenth Century* (2,3)

65. Prior, R.C.A. (1879) *Popular Names of British Plants* (3,5)

66. Raistick, A. (1968) *Quakers in Science and Industry* (10)

67. RCAHMS (Royal Commission on the Ancient and Historical Monuments of Scotland) Inventories: *Peeblesshire* ( 1967); *Selkirkshire* ( 1957), *Stirlingshire* (1963) (6)

68. Reid, J. (1683) *The Scots Gard'ner.* Reprinted 1988, Introduction by A. Hope (2,3,5)

69. Roach, F.A.(1985) *Cultivated Fruits of Britain, Their Origin and History* (4)

70. Robertson, F.W. (1997) 'Thomas Blaikie, Alpine Plant Collector', *Journal of the Scottish Rock Garden Club,* XXV (2) No.99: 121–134 ( 10)

71. Robertson, F.W. (1997) 'Working Conditions of Scottish Gardeners between the Wars', *Review of Scottish Culture,* 10 (7): 67–85

72. Robertson, F.W. (1998) 'The Garden of Cullen House in 1760' (*Garden Hist.* 26 (2): 136–152 (2,3,4)

73. Robinson, M. (1985) *The Concise Scots Dictionary* (2,3)

74. Robinson, W. (1889) *The English Flower Garden* (3)

75. Roger, C. (Ed.) (1848) *Rental Book of the Cistercian Abbey of Coupar-Angus. With the Breviary of the Register,* Grampian Club. publ. No. 18 (4)

76. Rogers, J.G. (1986) 'George Don, 1764–1814', The *Scottish Naturalist,* 1986: 97–108 (10)

77. Rose, H. (1848) *A Genealogical Deduction of the Family of Rose of Kilravock,* Spalding Club, No. 18 (2,3)

78. Ross, T. (1890) 'Ancient Sundials of Scotland'. *Proceedings of the Society of Antiquaries of Scotland,* XXIV: 16 –273 (6)

79. Somerville, T. (1861) *My Own Life and Times* ( 2)

80. Sibbald, R. (1684) *Scotia Illustrata* (3,5)

81. Smith, J. (1935) 'Dalry House: Its Lands and Owners'. *The Book of the Old Edinburgh Club,* Vol XX: 26–30 (8)

82. Smith, M.W.G. (1971) *National Apple Register of the United Kingdom* (4)

83. *Statistical Account of Scotland* (1979), Ed. D.J. Withrington and I. Grant. Vol 3: 455 (10)

84. Shepherd, R.E. (1954) *History of the Rose* (3)

85. Stace, C (1991) *New Flora of the British Isles* (3,5)

86. Stuart, D. and Sutherland, J. (1992) *Plants from the Past* (1, 2)

87. Sutherland, J. (1683) *Hortus Medicus Edinburgensis* (2,3,5)

88. Tait, A.A. *The Landscape Garden in Scotland: 1735–1835* (1)

89. Turner, W. (1548) *The Names of Herbes* (3)

90. Vilmorin-Andrieux, M M. (1977, English Edition) *The Vegetable Garden* (2)

91. Walker, J. (1808) *An Economical History of the Hebrides and Highlands of Scotland* Vol 2 (10)
92. Wilson, E.J. (1961) *James Lee and the Vineyard Nursery, Hammersmith* (1)


## Unpublished Records in the National Register of Archives (Scotland)

GD 16 Airlie Muniments (2)
GD 18 Clerk of Penicuik (4,5)
GD 24 Abercairney Muniments (2,3,4)
GD 25 Ailsa Muniments (3,4,7)
GD 29 Kinross House Papers (4)
GD 30 Shairp of Houston Muniments (2)
GD 35 Dundas of Ochertyre Papers (7)
GD 44 Gordon Castle Muniments (2, 3,7)
GD 45 Dalhousie Muniments (2,3,4,7)
GD 110 Hamilton-Dalrymple of North Berwick Muniments (2,3)
GD 112 Breadalbane Muniments (2,3,5,7)
GD 124 Mar and Kellie Muniments (2,3,5,7)
GD 135 Rose of Kilravock Muniments (2,7)
GD 150 Morton Papers (2,3,7)
GD 164 Rosslyn Muniments (7)
GD 170 Campbell of Barcaldine Muniments (2,4)
GD 171 Forbes of Callander Papers (7)
GD 190 Smythe of Methven Papers ( 2)
GD 220 Montrose Estate Papers (2,7)
GD 224 Buccleuch Muniments (7)
GD 248 Seafield Muniments (7)
GD 331 Dick Cunyngham of Prestonfield Muniments (2)
GD 345 Grant of Monymusk (2,3,4,7)
GD 406 Hamilton Muniments (7)
GD 421 George Heriot's Trust (3)
GD 427 Gillanders of Highfield (2)

*NRA(S) Collections*
NRA(S) 332, 396 Hamilton Papers (2,3,7)
NRA(S) 888. Hopetoun Papers (2,3,7)
NRA(S) 776 Mansfield Papers (4)
NRA(S) 217 Moray Muniments (5,7)
NRA(S) 1100 Roxburghe Papers (4,5,7,)

*National Library of Scotland*
ACC. 860 2. Forsyth correspondence (10)
Adv.MS.80.6.13. Dundas of Dundas (7)
MS 1514. Delvine (7)
MS 3554. Dickson of Hassendeanburn (2,10)
MS 6153. Sir John Foulis of Ravelston (2,4)
MS 10885 Graham of Airth (2)

MS 13299. Lochgelly (2,3)
MS 14641, f.130. Henry Ferguson (2,3,10)
Saltoun Papers. A long series from No. 16662 to No. 17889 (2,3,5,7)
MS 13563 Tweeddale Papers (2,3)

*University of Aberdeen, Dept. of Special Collections and Archives*
AUL MS 3175. Duff House (Montcoffer) Papers (2,4,9)

*University of St. Andrews Library*
Cheape of Rossie Papers – Items 4,5 and 6 (2,3,5)

*Gardeners' Fraternities and Associations* (8)
GD 420. 1–15. National Register of Archives (Scotland) The Ancient Fraternity of
      Free Gardeners of East Lothian
Martine, C. (Ed. W.H. Brown) n.d. 'The Ancient Fraternity of Free Gardeners of
      East Lothian', East Lothian Antiquarian and Naturalists' Society
Acts of Council, City of Aberdeen, 1706, 1709, 1716 (CR 59, p.87). These relate to
      the Gardener Fraternity of Aberdeen
Constitution rules and regulations of the Gardener Fraternity of Old Aberdeen.
      SBL 1794 C 6, University of Aberdeen, Dept. of Special Collections and
      Archives
History of the Incorporation of the Gardeners of Glasgow. 1903. Mitchell Library,
      Archives Dept. Glasgow
Articles of the Friendly Society or Caledonian Gardeners' Lodge of Edinburgh.
      Instituted A.D. 1782. National Register of Archives (Scotland)
Munro, A.Mc.D. (1899) *Records of Old Aberdeen*

# Index